T0215578

Beginning Azure IoT Edge Computing

Extending the Cloud to the Intelligent Edge

David Jensen

Apress®

Beginning Azure IoT Edge Computing: Extending the Cloud to the Intelligent Edge

David Jensen
Powder Springs, GA, USA

ISBN-13 (pbk): 978-1-4842-4535-4
https://doi.org/10.1007/978-1-4842-4536-1

ISBN-13 (electronic): 978-1-4842-4536-1

Managing Director, Apress Media LLC: Welmoed Spahr
Acquisitions Editor: Joan Murray
Development Editor: Laura Berendson
Coordinating Editor: Jill Balzano

Cover designed by eStudioCalamar

Cover image designed by Freepik (www.freepik.com)

Distributed to the book trade worldwide by Springer Science+Business Media New York, 233 Spring Street, 6th Floor, New York, NY 10013. Phone 1-800-SPRINGER, fax (201) 348-4505, e-mail orders-ny@springer-sbm.com, or visit www.springeronline.com. Apress Media, LLC is a California LLC and the sole member (owner) is Springer Science + Business Media Finance Inc (SSBM Finance Inc). SSBM Finance Inc is a **Delaware** corporation.

For information on translations, please e-mail rights@apress.com, or visit http://www.apress.com/rights-permissions.

Apress titles may be purchased in bulk for academic, corporate, or promotional use. eBook versions and licenses are also available for most titles. For more information, reference our Print and eBook Bulk Sales web page at http://www.apress.com/bulk-sales.

Any source code or other supplementary material referenced by the author in this book is available to readers on GitHub via the book's product page, located at www.apress.com/9781484245354. For more detailed information, please visit http://www.apress.com/source-code.

Printed on acid-free paper

This book is the result of my wife, Tara, supporting me in yet another big idea that lacked much detail at the time. She loves me and supports me in ways that would fill volumes more than the technical content you're about to read. She is truly my favorite person on the planet. Thanks, babe, for bearing with me and believing in me for the past several months.

— *David Jensen*

Table of Contents

About the Author

David Jensen is an IoT and Cloud architect with over 20 years of experience. He has spent over six years designing, building, and deploying IoT solutions based on the Microsoft Azure Cloud platform, dating back to before there were any publicly available IoT services on Azure. He is passionate about building software solutions that interact with the real world and is fascinated by the devices that surround us and how we can leverage them to instrument our environment to build connected ecosystems.

About the Technical Reviewer

Amol Ajgaonkar is the Chief Architect for IoT at Insight Digital Innovation, with more than 15 years of experience successfully implementing technology for business outcomes. He is focused on architecting and implementing IoT solutions using Azure for manufacturing, agriculture, retail, and other industry segments. Amol is a frequent speaker at technology conferences, most recently presenting on IoT-based solutions to increase operational efficiencies in the field and creating safe public spaces.

Acknowledgments

I would like to thank Amol Ajgaonkar for his technical expertise in reviewing this book and Mike Shir and David Pheasant for their support in the early days of wrestling with these technologies.

Jared Shoemaker, Jeff Dodge, Brandon Elliot, and David Lewerke have all supported me, encouraged me, and cheered me on at one time or another during this process. Working with people like you has made work fun again. Thank you!

One last HUGE thank you to the team at Apress for their patience with me and guidance on this journey.

Introduction

If you have been paying attention to advances in technology over the past 7–8 years, you have no doubt heard the term *cloud. Cloud* has come to mean any processing or data collection that happens somewhere other than on my machine, which gives way to terms like "private cloud," "public cloud," "self-service cloud," "managed cloud," blah, blah, blah.... With such a broad definition comes a plethora of misunderstandings, misrepresentations, and misguided advice.

To complicate matters more, even if you have navigated through the pitfalls of *cloud* overuse, there are architectural patterns that are easier to design and implement in the cloud-aware world in which we live, but those, too, have been overrun with vague definitions and meaning. You've no doubt heard of the Internet of Things (IoT) and Big Data.

And, lastly, one of the latest victims of vague-term disorder is *Intelligent Edge.* You have most likely heard that term or you wouldn't be reading this book. If this term has lost its significance for you, then read on.

To level set, let me clarify the meaning of *cloud* for the purposes of this book. In this book, *cloud* refers to a public, managed platform that uses a consumption-based cost model (pay only for what you use) and supports public-facing endpoints as well as endpoints that are provisioned to only be available within a private network, even though they are hosted on a public platform. This description of *cloud* also includes a self-service management portal for developers to create, remove, and otherwise manage the resources and services running on the platform.

Shortly after this type of *cloud* emerged on the horizon, one of the architectural patterns mentioned above, Internet of Things (IoT), also began to gain popularity and a significant amount of attention. Over the past few years, it has been one of the most intriguing technologies and patterns that has come about.

The canonical example of the IoT pattern involves using an electronic device to instrument and monitor a physical, real-world device. Once instrumented, the electronic device transmits measurements from the physical device for collection and analysis in some back-end data store. The building blocks of this pattern have existed for a few decades, but they have not been as affordable and, consequently, widespread as they are now, leading to the massive increase in interest it has generated.

As more and more companies bought into the idea that they could quickly and cheaply implement their own instance of an IoT architecture and the cloud was gaining momentum in other areas, the idea of "push everything to the cloud" became the mantra of the most "edgy" or "disruptive" companies. If you wanted to be known for pushing the envelope and really innovating, then you had better be pushing all your data to the cloud... along with the other thousands of companies that were doing the same thing, sometimes without considering whether it was the right approach.

As more and more companies architect solutions that involve the cloud in some way, there are more and more examples of when that "cloud or bust" mentality breaks down. Not every problem can tolerate the bandwidth and latency required to push everything to the cloud. Not every company can access a public-facing endpoint from their devices.

So, here we are, a decade after the cloud came on the scene, and we are learning that maybe we don't need to push everything to the cloud. Maybe we need to consider when to push data to the cloud and when to process the data where it originates. Enter *The Intelligent Edge.*

The "edge" in the intelligent edge refers to the proximity to where the data originates. Intelligent edge computing then indicates that some intelligence has been pushed out from the cloud to a point as close to the data origination as possible. There are examples of this all around us.

Think about cars that automatically apply the brakes for you if they sense an object in front of the car. Or the alerts that sound if you attempt to change lanes while another vehicle is in your blind spot. Those decisions must be kept as close to the edge (data origination) as possible. When deciding whether to stop the car or not, milliseconds of latency could potentially be a life-or-death situation.

Having the option to apply intelligence to data as it originates gives options to developers and architects as they architect cloud-enabled solutions. No longer must all data be sent to the cloud to perform analysis on it. Analysis can now happen on the edge, and based on that analysis, a subset of the raw data streams can be sent to the cloud. This saves bandwidth, time, money, and storage.

The Azure IoT Edge platform enables some of the advanced services, once only available on the Azure platform, to be run on a custom Windows or Linux machine. Azure IoT Edge is a little over two years old and is continually being updated with more advanced analytics. Currently, there are Azure IoT Edge modules for Stream Analytics, Machine Learning, image detection, and custom code in either C#, Python, Java, or Node.

It's an exciting time to be a developer or architect working with the intelligent edge concepts, tools, and solutions. But, it can also be overwhelming. As I have built IoT Edge solutions, I have spent a lot of time trolling forums and message boards just hoping someone else was having the same issue/error I was having that day. Because when you're working on cutting-edge solutions, the documentation is lacking which makes troubleshooting much more difficult when you hit an error that you don't understand. So, you resort to others in your position who might have hit the same issue as you (and took the time to post about it on a forum).

So, my hope for this book is that it will help answer lots of questions for you and help you on your journey to become the IoT Edge master in your organization. This book contains most of what I've learned over the past year or so as I have been working in this space. I wish I had had this book a year ago. I could have saved myself a lot of time and pain. I hope you find it useful. Let's get started!

CHAPTER 1

Do I Need an Intelligent Edge?

Businesses today are faced with an unparalleled number of choices and technology decisions as they try to intelligently evolve their systems. There are decisions about if, how, and when they should virtualize their datacenter, or if they should just continue to leverage the investment in their current physical assets. If they virtualize, should they use their own data center or a cloud provider, or a hybrid of both? If they decide to leverage a cloud platform, which of the hundreds of available service options should they use? How do these services fit together? What is the most cost-efficient option? The decision points and options can be very overwhelming. Cloud platforms have created a culture where the question is not "Is that possible?" but rather "Is that the most efficient way to do that?" In this environment, where so many tools and advanced capabilities are a click away, being innovative is not about having the capabilities but about correctly applying the capabilities to most accurately match the business need. It can be quite confusing if the right decision factors are not identified. Busyness does not equal productivity. In technical terms, having a fault-tolerant, highly available, cost-optimized, cloud-native architecture is still the wrong architecture if it does not correctly meet the needs of the business.

In this chapter, we will discuss the aspects of edge computing that need to be considered when you are determining whether it satisfies the needs of your business and discuss a few real-world scenarios to examine an architecture that properly includes an intelligent edge.

© David Jensen 2019
D. Jensen, *Beginning Azure IoT Edge Computing*, https://doi.org/10.1007/978-1-4842-4536-1_1

Edge Computing

Much like the technology options mentioned earlier, edge computing can be inaccurately identified as the solution when the needs of the business are poorly defined, or the benefits of the intelligent edge pattern are poorly understood. Edge computing must be correctly applied to reap the benefits. In fact, it may even be more susceptible to causing additional problems when it is misapplied. In order to avoid this pitfall, edge computing must be correctly defined and understood. So, what is edge computing? The term *edge* is a relative term. It is helpful (but not complete) to think of it as "not centralized" computing. The centralized computing model equates to computing in one (central) location, whether that is in the cloud or in your own datacenter. So, one aspect of edge computing is that it is much different than the centralized approach where all data is pushed to a single ingest or storage endpoint. Edge computing is very decentralized.

But, what nuance about the word "edge" makes this an accurate description? "Edge" implies that something is located as close as possible next to a reference point. Think about the two worlds we operate in – one world is our physical world and the second is the digital world. The physical world is the natural world we live in that contains everything we can observe with our five senses. The digital world is a world in which we are merely visitors. We can't touch, feel, or smell data or digital signals. And for the longest time, the digital world was kept very separated from our physical world. It lived in a far-off land known as the *Data Center*. Then it moved, seemingly, even farther away to a further-off land known as the *Cloud*.

However, now, the digital world is moving closer. It's becoming very integrated into our physical world – so integrated in fact that the lines between the two worlds are becoming blurred. The things in our physical world have become the gateway through which we encounter the digital world. We used to go to specified locations to access the digital world. But now, we encounter the digital world continuously. This border of hybrid things that are part physical and part digital is the edge that is referred to in the term *edge computing* or *intelligent edge*.

In a sense, the edge has existed as long as both worlds have existed, but it was previously just very isolated and did not affect us most of the time. Now, the edge is growing and with it, our awareness of it. Figure 1-1 illustrates an intelligent edge, which has several data origination points, each coupled with some computing (intelligence).

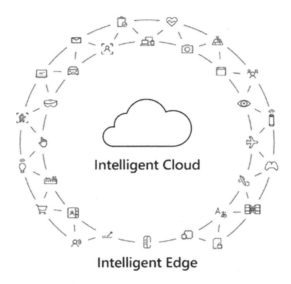

Figure 1-1. *Edge computing (Image from Microsoft News Center, Build 2017)*

If you have been in the IoT space for any length of time, you may have heard the term *field gateway*. Intelligent Edge computing is an evolutionary step forward from a field gateway. It addresses many of the same concerns and eases some of the management and maintenance difficulties that had been associated with the previous generations of field gateways. Additionally, it enables some scenarios and functionality that were difficult to implement up until now. Table 1-1 shows a comparison between the typical field gateway implementation and an intelligent edge implementation leveraging a platform like Azure IoT Edge.

Table 1-1. *Comparison of Field Gateway to Intelligent Edge implementation*

	Field Gateway	**Azure IoT Edge**
Target Business Scenarios	• Protocol Translation • Enable Internet connectivity for non-Internet devices • Occasionally connected devices • Event aggregation or filtering	• Protocol Translation • Enable Internet connectivity for non-Internet devices • Occasionally connected devices • Event aggregation or filtering • Improve business decisions with more advanced intelligence running on the edge
Message Processing Updates	• Refactor custom code and redeploy (or possibly physically deploy where connectivity is poor)	• Adjust message workflow through configuration and reusable containers
Deployment Management	• Custom monitoring and management of the deployment process	• Platform supported reporting and monitoring
Monitoring	• Custom monitoring or third party monitoring solution not integrated into the platform	• Integrated monitoring support

Edge Computing Adoption

Now that we have conceptually established what edge computing is and that it may not be a fit for every architecture, one of the next points of discussion is: how do I know if edge computing is the right option for my company? Another way of asking that is: what factors should I be considering regarding the edge computing pattern and in my organization when making this decision? In the next few sections, we will look at some of the requirements for edge computing that might be countercultural for your organization. No doubt, some of these requirements can be challenging for an organization to embrace and cause internal teams (like networking or security) to object or resist. For an edge computing solution (really, any solution) to be implemented successfully, it must be supported internally. If you are the trailblazer tasked with researching edge computing for your organization, the next sections will help you understand what concerns to address when discussing edge computing with your organization's decision-makers who may not be ready (yet) to make the necessary changes to their practices and policies.

Security

Security is probably the most common objection whenever a change in computing patterns begins to emerge. Rightfully so. If any new approach is going to endure, it must be secure. The IoT pattern and the related security risks have been scrutinized over the past several years and have been discussed at length. So, I will not repeat that discussion here, but I would like to list some of the most common concerns relating to the IoT Edge pattern to establish a baseline understanding of the objections.

Direct Access

Direct access to the device is one of the most commonly stated concerns about any IoT solution. The concern stems from the fact IoT devices are not deployed to a secure location like a data center. Rather, they are deployed to unsecured, remote locations that are susceptible to various forms of tampering. Tampering can include but is not limited to:

- **Device manipulation:** Someone holds a lighter up to a heat sensor to set off an alarm

- **Device firmware hacking:** Someone connects to the device and accesses the firmware to modify the code or replace the code altogether

- **Device secret hacking:** Someone gains access to security secrets like access tokens, certificates, device identity keys and more

Once the security layer of restricted physical access is removed, other security mechanisms must be leveraged that address the additional security risks introduced.

Untrusted Execution

Another common security concern is the inability to trust the code that is running on the device. It's the same issue as the device firmware hacking concern listed above. Essentially, the problem statement is: how can I guarantee that the code I provisioned to a device is the same code that is running now? How do I know that someone has not modified the code and injected their own logic and circumvented my logic? The Security chapter discusses the countermeasures Azure IoT Edge has put in place to defend against this category of attacks.

Message Replays

A third security concern related to IoT and IoT Edge deployments involves replaying messages. Message replaying is when a third party captures data from a device message transmission and uses that information, in whole or in part, to generate additional messages that are not valid and do not originate on the device. An example of this is a burglar who sniffs network traffic for home automation systems and captures messages to unlock a door or disarm a security system so that they could replay them when you're not home. The only reason this is not more common is the effort home security and home automation vendors have invested to protect their communication.

Direct Access to the Internet

A fourth, but certainly not final, security concern with IoT and IoT Edge deployments is the fact that many IoT architecture designs require the IoT/Edge device to connect directly with a public internet endpoint. This can be problematic for companies that have segmented their network through subnets and firewalls such that the device network has no direct connection to the public internet. In these cases, a discussion is required with the IT and security teams to help them understand how these devices can communicate securely with a public internet endpoint. You may face strenuous objections within your organization, but the fact remains that this problem has been identified and solved (refer to the chapter titled "Security" for a more in-depth look into this topic). You must keep in mind, organizations that evolve are organizations that succeed. If new opportunities are eliminated simply because they are new or different, then it is only a matter of time until your organization is obsolete.

Network Bandwidth

IoT solutions frequently involve low-bandwidth devices and networks. If you measure your device or network throughput in Kbit/sec instead of Mbit/sec or Gbit/sec, this is you. Previously, the main concern was pushing out an updated firmware image which can be anywhere from 1 to 15 MB and in rare cases, even more. With IoT edge, there is significantly more processing power and intelligence being used at the edge, which does not come without its own set of issues. One of the main issues is the size of the code that must be provisioned to an edge device. The binaries can range in size from 40 MB up to 2 GB. It is simply not realistic to push updates that size over a low bandwidth connection. If you are in this situation, you will need a plan on how to design for device provisioning.

Maintenance

Maintaining edge devices varies greatly from maintaining a canonical IoT device. Edge devices have an OS. Most IoT devices do not. Most IoT devices are either built on bare metal or have some onboard firmware. Most IoT devices are not running a version of Windows or full-blown Linux. This is different for IoT Edge devices because IoT edge devices are usually more powerful than an embedded device and are running either a full installation of Linux or a version of Windows.

This makes a difference when considering the long-term maintenance of the device. Is that OS treated the same as other OSes in the organization and is it patched and updated just a regularly? Or is it treated as a higher-powered embedded device? In which case, the updates to the underlying OS are not handled through the normal desktop OS patching mechanisms. Should the device be joined to the domain or treated as a peripheral? These are some of the unique concerns that must be discussed and accounted for when designing IoT edge solutions vs. IoT solutions.

Recognizing Your Organizational Mindset

What I listed in the previous section is just the tip of the iceberg when it comes to issues that must be discussed and designed around related to IoT edge computing. You might have been asking "what about this?" and "he completely forgot to mention that!" That's okay. The point of the previous section was not to create an exhaustive list of every issue you might encounter when designing and deploying IoT edge solutions. The goal is just to get you thinking about what some of the hurdles and roadblocks might be specific to your organization. Because even though, as we will see later in this book, Azure IoT Edge solutions are extremely cool and very powerful, they are not a silver bullet. If you're only focused on the benefits of these solutions and not the difficulty they might pose for your specific organization with your specific set of requirements and needs, then you won't properly prepare for the change that's coming and it will likely catch you off guard.

Given all that and because intelligent edge computing solutions are fairly new, your organization must have the right mentality when considering this type of approach. Even with a platform as solid and secure as Azure IoT Edge, when implemented poorly or partially, it will likely not meet your expectations.

What is the right organizational mentality? Curiosity, adaptability, open minded, investigative. These are some of the best examples of the right mentality for your organization. These characteristics promote investigating new technologies to determine if they will fit into the existing solution landscape within the organization. On the other hand, preferring process over discovery or making every attempt to minimize change and risk will severely limit the organization's ability to gain helpful information in a test or pilot phase that can assist the production-ready solution and architecture.

If you or your organization is not willing to give a second thought to the way you derive and collect data, you will not gain the competitive advantages you could with an intelligent edge solution. If you immediately eliminate an intelligent edge solution because it poses different security risks than you're accustomed to solving, then you will miss out on the competitive advantages. If you assume the strain on the low bandwidth segments of your network will be too great and you consequently eliminate an intelligent edge solution before researching alternative approaches, you will miss out on the competitive advantages. The point to realize is that you cannot expect to integrate an intelligent edge solution without evaluating other systems. Because intelligent edge solutions are a new paradigm for many organizations, the integration points must be reconsidered for the best results. If your goal is to minimize the effect on other systems, you will end up evaluating the effectiveness of a partially or poorly integrated solution and that will not give you an accurate understanding of the benefits and power of an intelligent edge solution for your specific organization.

Business Cases

If your organization has the right mentality and is open to intelligent edge computing, examining real-world business cases can help to illustrate how the benefits of intelligent edge solutions are realized. In the following sections, I will walk through four different real-world business scenarios and point out the benefits that an intelligent edge solution provides along the way.

Industrial Automation

Industrial automation involves process controls used in the process of manufacturing, materials processing, such as chemicals or raw materials, and the enforcement of related quality or safety thresholds. Because industrial processes are based on very repetitive tasks, precisely automating the process can provide accurate feedback on quality thresholds, defect detection, and general system anomaly detection which leads to a more economical, consistent and safe solution.

As automation capabilities have evolved, the scenarios that can be managed by automation systems have become increasingly advanced. More and more knowledge and decision making that was previously only possible by a human brain, due to the complex nature and the variety of the inputs, is being extracted and codified in monitoring and control solutions based on AI.

Industrial automation has come to be known as the fourth industrial revolution, or Industry 4.0. The revolutionary aspect of this wave of industrial advancement is made possible by the technological advancement in sensors, devices, and machines that allow more tasks to be handled through automation. The capabilities of intelligent edge computing match perfectly with the capabilities required by the demands of industrial automation.

An example of how intelligent edge computing fits well with industrial automation and advances the capabilities can be seen in a typical SCADA[1] system. Figure 1-2 shows a very simplified version of a SCADA system.

---

[1]Supervisory Control and Data Acquisition, in its simplest form, is an architectural style that involves supervisory computers that ingest sensor information and respond with sending the appropriate control signal.

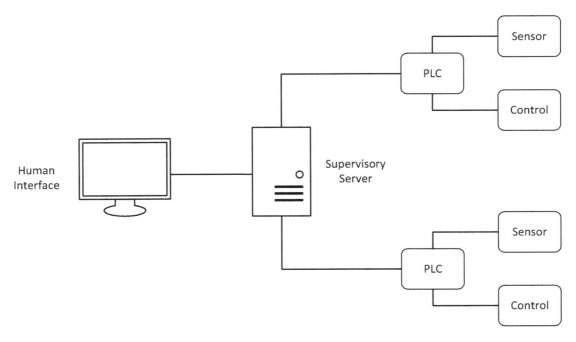

Figure 1-2. *SCADA architecture*

In this simple architecture, the supervisory server communicates with the PLCs and reads the current values from the various sensors. If a sensor reading is out of range or appears to be an anomaly, the server will typically send a control signal to the controller associated with the sensor that generated the anomalous reading. This ingest-interpret-respond pattern is a great match for an intelligent edge solution. Figure 1-3 shows how this same simple architecture would look with an intelligent edge implementation.

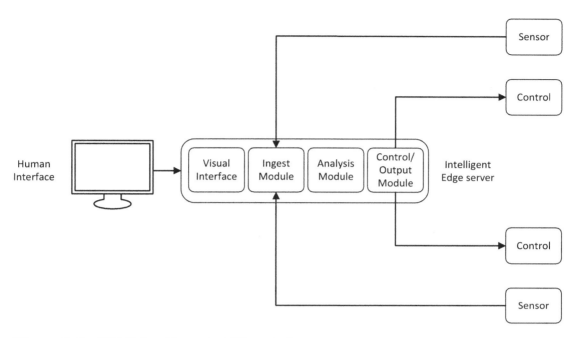

Figure 1-3. *SCADA with an intelligent edge*

Figure 1-3 shows how the implementation of an intelligent edge solution does not drastically alter the architecture. It simply rearranges where the ingest and control logic happens as well as (optionally) providing a visualization of the current process state. It is optional on the edge device because many times there is a separate network machine that provides a human-readable display.

One of the main benefits of using an intelligent edge solution comes from the use of a chain of independent modules that can be rearranged, independently updated and managed, and even harness the power of third party modules from a module marketplace. This flexibility allows the intelligent edge to evolve and advance much quicker than the typical SCADA implementation, which is usually a very fixed and closed system that does not change quickly.

Enhanced Analytics

A second use case where an intelligent edge solution can provide value is in the use of advanced analytics like Machine Learning (ML) algorithms or other Artificial Intelligence (AI) systems. Prior to intelligent edge computing, most advanced processing workloads, like those required by ML/AI solutions, were handled in a

11

cloud environment. That architecture performed adequately for most cases, but there are instances where the latency of a round trip to the cloud and back was too great, not to mention possible inconsistencies in network throughput for larger workloads. Intelligent edge computing allows these advanced scenarios to be performed very close to the origination of the data, which produces a very tight feedback loop yielding some powerful yet performant solutions.

Imagine your company has invested time and money to develop some intellectual property in the form of custom machine learning algorithms. Currently, those algorithms are being applied to large data sets that exist in your data center or in the cloud. These data sets represent accumulated telemetry from machines deployed in a factory or field. The algorithms are used to detect any anomalies and then generate an alert if one is found. This is a very common approach and falls under the "big data" pattern of solutions. This architecture can be seen in Figure 1-4.

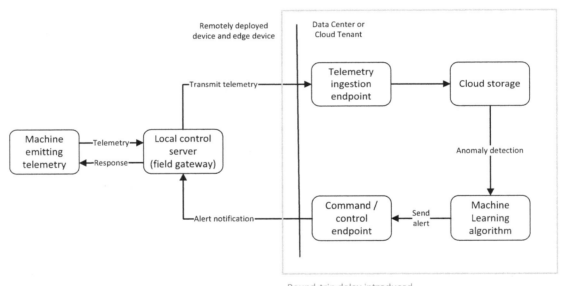

Figure 1-4. Cloud-based algorithm pattern

One of the biggest drawbacks from this pattern is the introduction of (potentially significant) delays from the time the telemetry is emitted from the data originator to the time a response based on the algorithm can be returned. In some cases, an almost immediate response is needed.

Think about a scenario where the telemetry is generated by sensors on a car and there are on-board computers running algorithms continually determining if the brakes should be applied to avoid hitting an object or person in front of the vehicle or if a lane change warning should be displayed to avoid hitting another vehicle in a blind spot. Both scenarios must occur in milliseconds. There is no tolerance for the time it takes to send data to the cloud, analyze the data, generate the alert, and transmit that alert back to the car. The tight feedback loop described in this car telemetry example, which is an intelligent edge solution, has become increasingly commonplace and organizations need a platform to deliver solutions that provide the advanced processing logic. Figure 1-5 shows an intelligent edge version for the architecture shown in Figure 1-4.

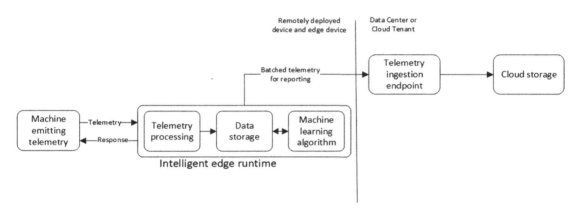

Figure 1-5. *Intelligent edge-based algorithm pattern*

In Figure 1-5, the telemetry is processed, stored and analyzed all in the intelligent edge runtime. In a background (and most likely asynchronous) process, the telemetry is sent to the cloud ingestion endpoint for reporting purposes, but the real-time decision logic and feedback loop is all on the edge.

Occasionally Offline

A third use case that benefits from an intelligent edge solution is devices that are occasionally offline. Occasionally offline devices are not always offline because there is no network/internet connection. Sometimes, battery-powered devices intentionally shut down or go into a low power mode in which the device turns off the Wi-Fi or cell radio to save battery life. It later wakes up on a certain schedule, transmits the data, and returns to the low-power state. But the most common scenario for devices being offline is when there is no active network or internet connection. This could be due to mobile solutions that go through a network dead spot or some temporary interference with the network connectivity. In these cases, the data that needs to be collected can be stored on the edge device and then transmitted to the cloud when the network connectivity returns. This removes the burden of monitoring connectivity from the device and allows the edge device to manage that functionality. Figure 1-6 shows an example of this scenario.

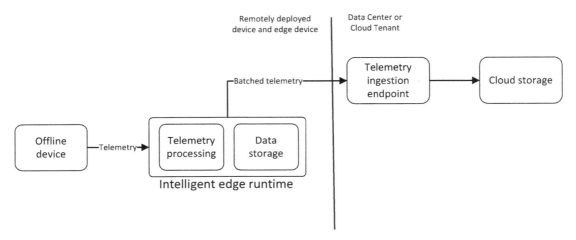

Figure 1-6. *Occasionally offline devices*

In Figure 1-6, the offline device is connected to the edge device either through a LAN connection or through a direct connection like a serial cable. In this case, the IoT device does not need to concern itself with connecting to the internet. As long as it can connect to the edge device, it can forget about the delivery of the messages to the cloud or data center endpoint. In this scenario, the edge device manages the entire process of verifying the internet connection, storing the messages in the event of lost connection and the delivery of the messages when the connection is restored.

Protocol Translation

One final use case that needs to be mentioned is protocol translation. Protocol translation is needed when devices use a protocol that is not a preferred internet-based protocol or is a proprietary protocol. In these cases, the edge device can parse the data from the downstream device(s), transform it into a format that can be sent over the internet to the telemetry ingestion point. Figure 1-7 shows an example of this.

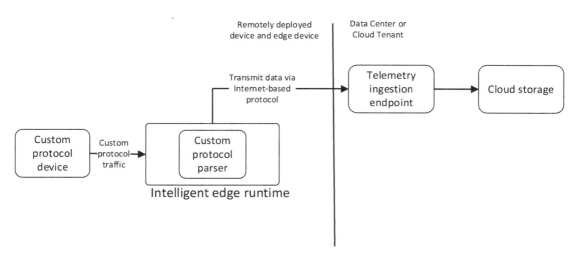

Figure 1-7. *Custom protocol translation*

One of the biggest benefits of this use case is the ability to collect data from devices that previously had no way to transmit data over the internet and connect them with the cloud suite of services. This provides modern visibility into legacy devices that may have otherwise been ignored or eliminated from consideration in advanced analytic scenarios.

Summary

In this chapter, we looked at the emergence of edge computing, some of the challenges that edge computing might create for your organization, as well as some of the use cases where edge computing really shines. In the entire edge computing evaluation approach, you must create and maintain the right organizational mentality, which is one of openness to change and a desire to understand how your company can benefit from an edge solution when it is rightly understood and applied correctly and specifically to the needs of your organization. In the next chapter, we will review some of the core concepts of the Azure IoT Edge platform.

CHAPTER 2

Azure IoT Edge Core Concepts

The Azure IoT Edge platform is an extension of the Azure IoT suite of services and, consequently, leverages the same Azure platform services. There are some differences between a canonical IoT solution and an IoT Edge solution in the IoT Hub service and I will highlight those differences where appropriate. To begin your journey toward using and benefiting from the Azure IoT Edge computing platform, you must understand the basic concepts of Azure IoT, Azure IoT Edge, and some of the related technologies. Azure IoT Edge makes use of some existing technologies, like containers, and therefore requires at least a basic understanding of those as well. If you are new to building Azure IoT solutions, this chapter will help you understand the basics of IoT in Azure and catch you up on the changes that have been added to support the IoT Edge platform.

Azure IoT Hub

Azure IoT Hub is the primary service in Azure for IoT and IoT Edge solutions. It supports not only device-originated messages destined for the cloud like telemetry, but also cloud-originated messages destined for the device, like command and control messages. When building and designing IoT solutions, ingesting messages into the cloud is simple when compared to sending messages from the cloud to the device. The device-originated messages are at a far higher scale, but scaling services up to handle millions of messages is a known pattern that's been solved. Sending messages from the cloud to the

17

© David Jensen 2019
D. Jensen, *Beginning Azure IoT Edge Computing*, https://doi.org/10.1007/978-1-4842-4536-1_2

device, even though the scale is typically only a fraction of the ingest side, creates a lot of concerns and raises questions like:

- How do we verify the identity of (trust) the service sending messages to the device?

- How do we send messages to the device if the device is offline?

- If the device is never offline, should it continually listen for incoming messages from the cloud?

- How do we keep hackers from overwhelming our devices with falsified messages?

- How do we send configuration updates to the device? Are they handled differently than a command that needs to run on the device? If so, how do we do that?

The Azure IoT Hub service helps solve many of these issues. It provides a secure way for devices to communicate with the cloud as well as a secure way for the cloud to send messages to the device. Furthermore, it provides a set of REST APIs that allow users to manage, maintain, and monitor devices. These APIs can be consumed to power custom monitoring or operations dashboards. It also easily manages device-specific security keys. Once the device credentials have been verified and device messages start flowing into the IoT Hub instance, messages can be routed to other Azure services including BLOB, Table and Data Lake storage, Service Bus Queues and Topics, Event Hub, and Stream Analytics.

All of this functionality is the same whether the device is a typical IoT device or an IoT Edge device. But there are some areas where there are differences for IoT Edge devices. For starters, you can see in Figure 2-1 that the IoT Hub settings blade in the Azure portal has separate sub-blades for IoT devices vs. IoT Edge devices.

EXPLORERS

📄 Query explorer

▣ IoT devices

AUTOMATIC DEVICE MANAGEMENT

IoT Edge

IoT device configuration

MESSAGING

📋 File upload

⊝ Endpoints

〵 Routes

Figure 2-1. *IoT devices vs. IoT Edge devices in IoT Hub settings blade*

All of the IoT Edge specific functionality in the Azure portal is contained in the IoT Edge device management blade. Figure 2-2 shows a simple version of that management blade. The features and functionality shown in this blade are specific to IoT Edge devices.

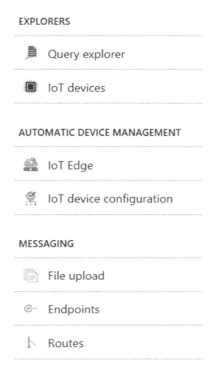

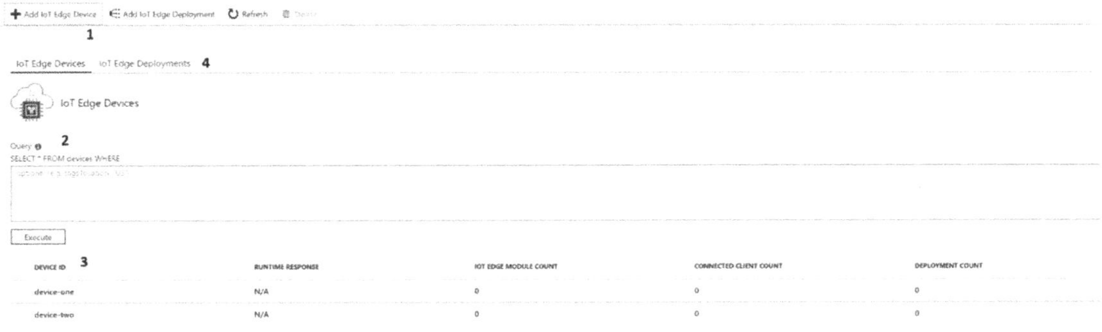

Figure 2-2. *Azure IoT Edge device management blade*

Let's review a few of the tasks you can perform in this blade.

1. **Add IoT Edge device:** This option creates a virtual device in the IoT Hub and creates the associated device security keys and device identity needed to configure and secure the device.

2. **Query device twins:** This allows device administrators to filter a large list of devices to view a summary of a subset of devices.

3. **Edge device list:** This area lists the current devices, based on the selection criteria in the query window. If no query is specified, this area lists all the edge devices in the IoT Hub.

4. **Edge deployment management:** This area of the edge device management blade is for creating and managing edge device deployments. Deployments are used to manage versions of code that are targeted for a certain subset of devices. They are discussed in more depth later in this chapter.

If you were to select a device from the list and click on it, you would see the device management blade, as shown in Figure 2-3.

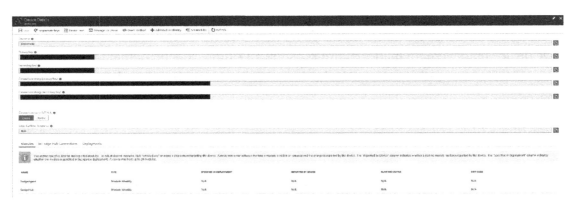

Figure 2-3. *Device management blade*

Across the top bar, there are several actions that are available for a device, including regenerating the device's access keys if they have been compromised, or sending a device a message. Arguably, the most significant action that can be performed in this blade is the ability to assign the modules for a device. The modules (described later in this chapter) contain the actual logic for the device. So, in effect, when you set and configure the modules for a device, you are assigning that device to a specific role. If the device is a refrigerator, then there will be logic to monitor and adjust temperature, send alerts when the temperature exceeds certain thresholds, and possibly monitor the state of the door – whether it is open or closed. All of these pieces of logic are generic when considered in isolation, but when combined in a specific grouping and configured for a certain role, then that unique configuration of logic defines the role that device should carry out. Figure 2-4 shows the Set Modules blade.

Figure 2-4. *Module management blade*

In the module management blade, there are two sections. The top section is where any credentials needed to access a container registry can be entered. These will be added to the configuration information, called a *twin,* for the related module. More than one container registry can be configured, since you may be using modules from multiple registries. Note that not all container registries require credentials. There are some publicly available registries that can be accessed with no credentials. Microsoft provides several containers for use in Edge development like that.

In addition to collecting registry credentials, this blade allows users to add modules for this device. If you click the "Add" option in the Deployment Modules section, you will be presented with a screen to collect the configuration for that module. Figure 2-5 shows what that blade looks like and following that, is a brief overview of the fields and what they mean.

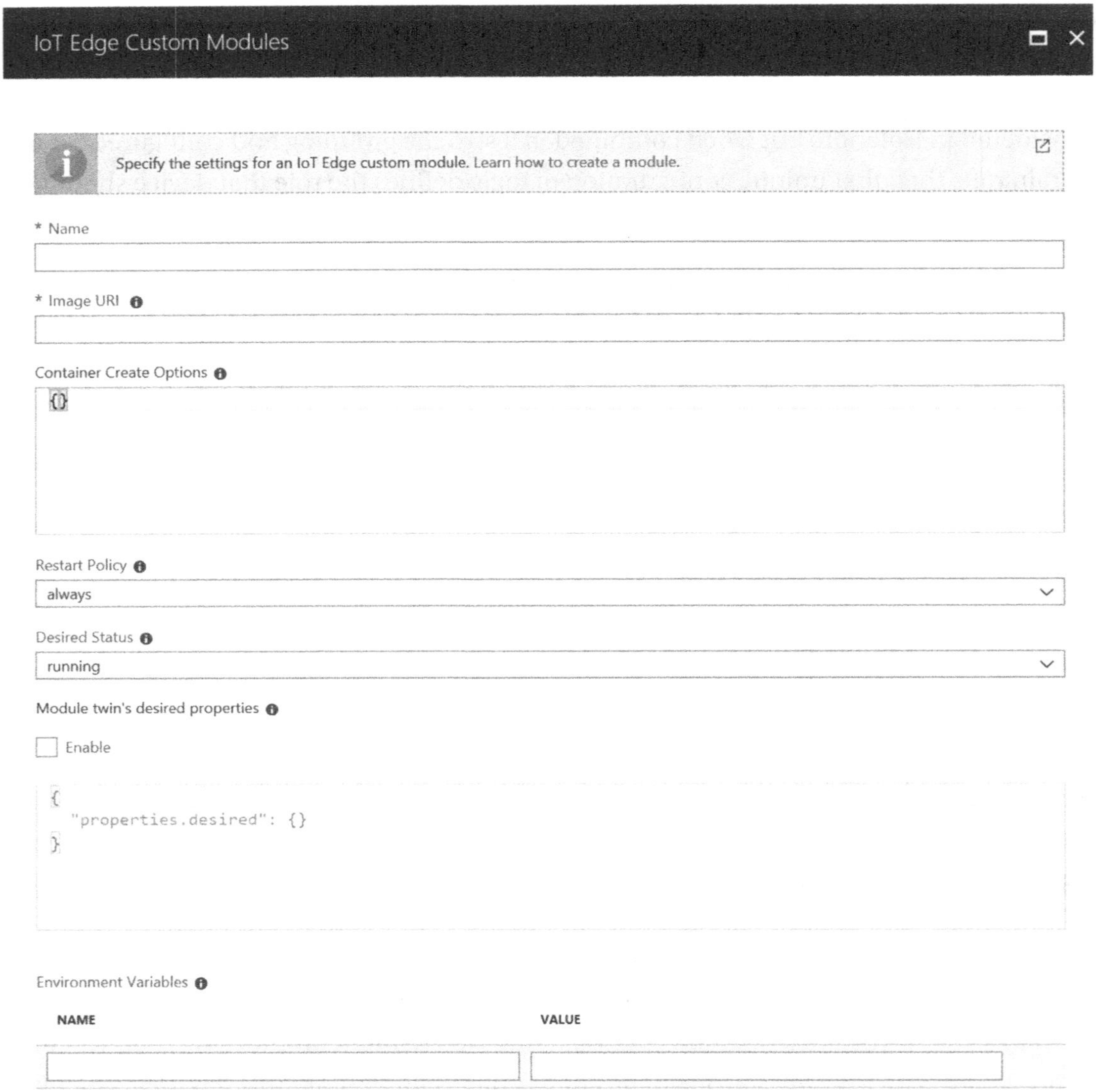

IoT Edge Custom Modules   ▫ ✕

ℹ Specify the settings for an IoT Edge custom module. Learn how to create a module.   ↗

* Name

* Image URI ℹ

Container Create Options ℹ

{}

Restart Policy ℹ

always   ⌄

Desired Status ℹ

running   ⌄

Module twin's desired properties ℹ

☐ Enable

{
    "properties.desired": {}
}

Environment Variables ℹ

NAME	VALUE

Figure 2-5. *Add module blade*

Here is an overview of the information on this blade.

- **Name**: The friendly name of the module. This will be used on the device to name the container.

- **Image URI**: The location in a container registry from which to retrieve the container image.

- **Container create options**: A single string that contains valid JSON. This single string will be passed to the container upon container instantiation and contains the initial configuration parameters where needed. Not all containers require this.

- **Restart policy**: A single value that communicates how the Edge runtime should handle restarts for the container. Valid options include:

  - **Always**: Restart the module if it stops for any reason.

  - **Never**: Never restart the module, regardless of why it stopped.

  - **On-unhealthy**: Restart the module if it crashes or is deemed otherwise unhealthy. Otherwise, do not restart it.

  - **On-failed**: Restart the module if it crashes, otherwise, do not attempt to restart it.

- **Desired status**: The initial state for the module. Most of the time, this will be set to "running" because most users will want their code to start up automatically. But there may be times when logic does not need to start up right away but needs to start up on some other trigger.

- **Module twin's desired properties**: An optional section that must be "enabled" using the checkbox. This is a simple way to set some initial configuration values when the module is deployed. The properties must all be valid JSON.

- **Environment variables**: A flat list of name/value pairs used to populate environment variables that can be consumed from within the module.

All of this information is collected and persisted in the module twin for this module. An example of the completed blade is in Figure 2-6. You should notice that only the first two fields are required. Once you have entered all the required information, press Save at the bottom and the module's twin will be updated accordingly.

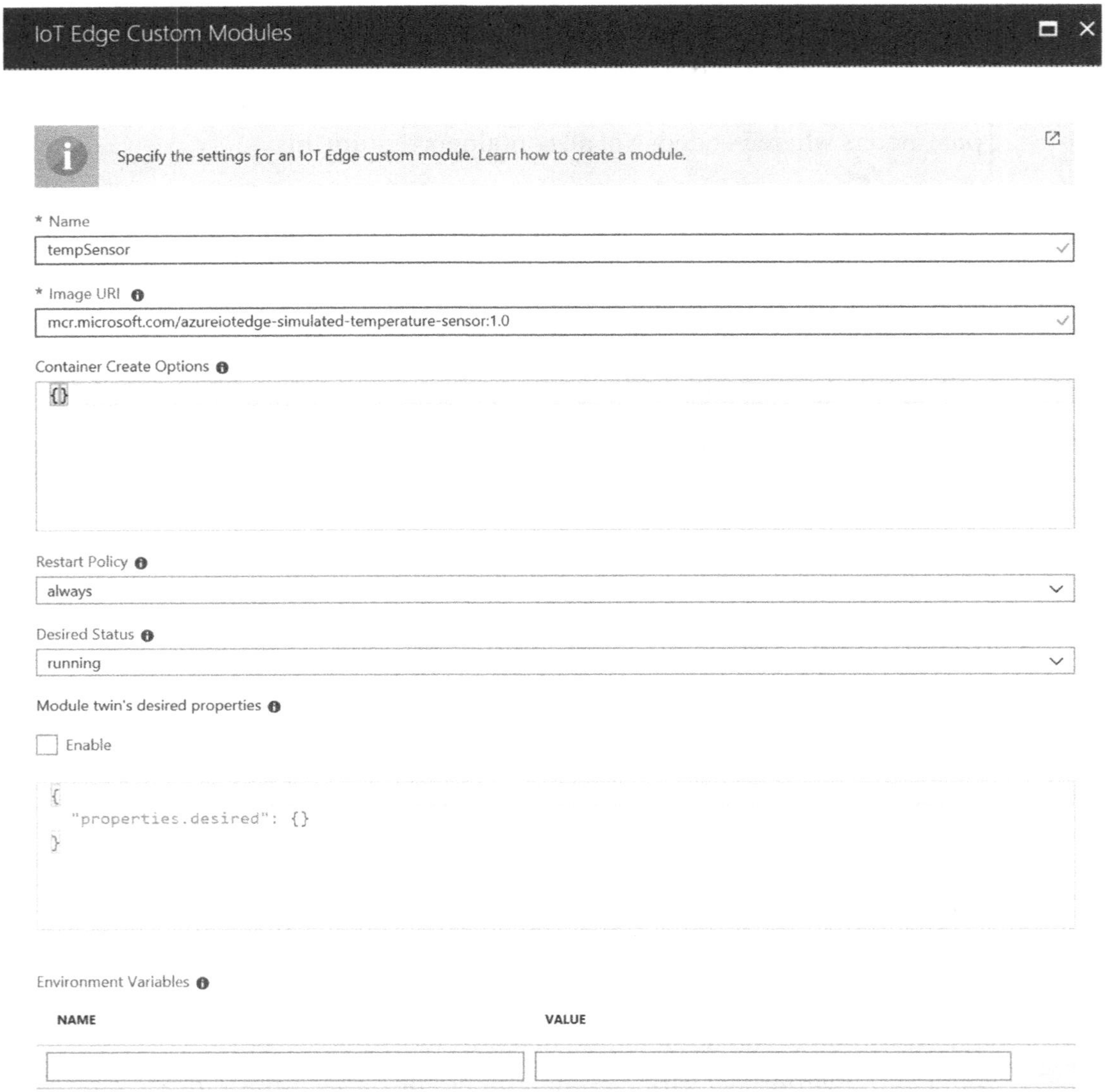

Figure 2-6. *Add an edge module*

The example module shown in Figure 2-6 is a publicly available module used to generate temperature telemetry. The module creates the telemetry internally and has no other dependencies. It is provided by Microsoft for demo and testing purposes and eliminates the upfront requirement of connecting to either a simulated or physical device to generate message traffic.

Containers

Chances are you've heard of the containerization epidemic that has been sweeping the software landscape over the past several years. Although the basic concepts that support the container model (virtualization and isolation) have been around since the early 2000s, the past five years have been a tipping point for containers as they have become mainstream. In architecting solutions, it is now common to hear of companies requiring justification for NOT using containers rather than a justification for using them.

What started out as a simple evolutionary step of virtualization has ballooned into the de facto way to guarantee a consistent execution runtime. Containers continue to spread into more and more diverse solution spaces, which demonstrates the flexibility and benefit they offer. One of the many benefits of containers is the ability to virtualize small runtime execution environments and distribute those virtualized environments more easily than an entire virtual machine. Virtual machine images are regularly 30 GB or more, while a container can often be below 100 MB. So, it should not be a huge surprise to you to find out that containers sit at the core of the IoT Edge runtime environment. When adopting a container-based approach, there are a few architectural components that you need to be aware of. There are many details you have to be aware of if you were solely responsible for managing the runtime. Luckily, IoT Hub and IoT Edge runtime handle many of these details for you, including the creation and management of the containers, but it's helpful to be aware of them at a high level when developing Edge solutions.

First, you need a runtime to actually interact and manage the containers on the target machine. The Docker runtime is an example of this. The container runtime is similar to virtual machine management software, such as Hyper-V. As the VM management solution manages the resources of the various VMs, so the container runtime manages the resources for the various containers it's managing, including starting containers, stopping containers, restarting containers, etc.

The container runtime for IoT Edge devices is a custom runtime that is based on Moby, the underlying container technology that Docker is built upon, which allows any Docker-compatible image to be used in an IoT Edge solution as long as the host device can support the space and CPU requirements of the container. This also means that any exiting Docker-based toolchain your organization might be using for development will work with the IoT Edge tooling as well.

Second, you need the actual containers. In the IoT Edge world, containers encapsulate various segments of functionality that are decoupled (called Modules, which is discussed later) and communicate through a message bus (hosted in a container called the 'edgeHub'). Because each container is decoupled and knows nothing of the other containers running on the edge device, there is great flexibility in how the containers can be configured to interact with one another. As an organization begins to grow and advance its suite of available Edge containers, custom solutions can be created much more quickly using existing containers that may be simply configured in a new and exciting way.

Note   There is a difference between a container and a container image. To clarify this difference, it is helpful to use an example from Object Oriented language. In OOAD terms, the difference between the class definition and a specific instance of that class represents the difference between a container image and a container. The container image defines how containers are built and a container is an instance of an image definition.

A third component needed when using containers is a container registry. You can think of a container registry as the bookshelf from which the container images (books) are retrieved. As container images are built, they must be stored somewhere that is accessible to the container runtime. The runtime is given instructions on which images to run (including the image version) and then gets a local copy of that image (if it does not already exist) and starts a container based on the image. To enable and automate this series of interactions between the runtime and the registry, a well-defined set of APIs must exist to interact with the container images. This is what a container registry provides. Well-known, publicly available registries include Docker Hub and the Azure Container Registry. Figure 2-7 shows how all of these components work together in a container-based architecture.

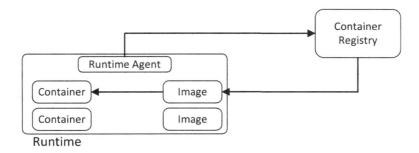

Figure 2-7. *Basic container architecture*

Modules

One of the most common IoT Edge terms is "module." An edge module is like a container image, but an edge module is more than just a container image. An edge module includes a module identity and module configuration information, which is stored in a module twin information, which is stored in a module twin. A module identity is a way to track a specific instance of a module. Imagine you need to deploy the same module more than once to a given IoT Edge device. The module identity is used to track the separate instances. This concept is used primarily in the routing of messages, which is discussed later in this chapter. Another concept specific to an edge module is a module twin. Twins are also discussed later in this chapter, but for now you should know that in addition to a *device* twin, each module in an IoT Edge solution has its own *module* twin. It's an edge specific configuration file for the module.

Edge Agent and Edge Hub

In the earlier section where we discussed containers, I referred to the container runtime multiple times and then in Figure 2-7, there is a box labeled "Runtime Agent" that was left unexplained. Both of these concepts relate to the edge runtime that is composed of two separate modules that are supplied by the Azure IoT Edge infrastructure. These two modules are (1) edgeAgent and (2) edgeHub. Together they manage, monitor, and support the custom modules that you use in your edge solutions. The edgeAgent module is responsible for retrieving the specified module images from the container registry, starting up the module, and monitoring the module. If one of the registered modules stops for some reason, the edgeAgent module restarts it. If the module continually restarts, errors, or crashes, edgeAgent will use an exponential back off approach for restarts so that resources are not constantly chewed up on the edge device. This is helpful when using a lower powered device that can be easily overwhelmed by CPU spikes.

One of the other tasks the edgeAgent handles is reporting module status to the IoT Hub. These status messages, or heartbeats, are used to enable reporting of the devices based on the last known reported state. The valid options for the status codes are:

- 200: OK

- 400: The deployment configuration is invalid

- 406: The edge device is offline or not sending status reports

- 412: The schema version in the deployment configuration is invalid

- 417: The device does not have its deployment configuration set

- 500: An error occurred in the edge runtime

You can see these status indicators in the Azure portal beside the device. Figure 2-8 shows an example of this.

DEVICE ID	RUNTIME RESPONSE	IOT EDGE MODULE COUNT
device-one	N/A	0
device-two	OK	0
device~2222	406 - The device is offline or not sending status reports	8

Figure 2-8. *Device status in Azure portal*

The first device has an "N/A" for its response code. This means the physical device has not been configured to connect to the IoT Hub instance yet.

Note   Keep in mind that the devices listed in the portal are virtual devices that are primarily placeholder entities with security information associated with it to enable bootstrapping the physical device. This means that the status will never be real time, but it should be current within a few minutes. This separation of the physical device and the virtual device also means that the virtual device can be configured and ready to go in the portal, but the physical device is not properly configured or has simply not been powered up. You must keep this in mind to know where to troubleshoot when things are not working as expected.

The "OK" beside device-two represents a "200" response from the device indicates that the device is running and working as expected. You can also see that there is a "406" response code for device-2222, which indicates the device is offline or has stopped sending status reports for some other reason.

When you think about the functions of the edgeAgent module, you should primarily think of *module management,* while that's not all it does, that is its primary focus.

The edgeHub module primarily handles the messaging responsibility between the modules on the edge device and between the edge device and the IoT Hub. This includes messages exchanged either from device-to-cloud (D2C), which is from the edge device to the IoT Hub or cloud-to-device (C2D), which is from the IoT Hub to the edge device.

As mentioned before, IoT Edge devices are based on modules. That is different than regular IoT devices. Whereas in a normal IoT scenario, the device connects directly to the IoT Hub endpoint using a device agent, and any messages it generates and transmits are only sent to the IoT Hub, in an Edge scenario, the code that needs to connect to the IoT Hub is not only running inside a virtualized container, it's isolated from the IoT Hub by the Edge runtime. To provide some relief for this challenge and also provide a consistent Azure IoT API, the edgeHub module exposes an API that is similar to the IoT Hub API. It actually serves as an IoT Hub proxy for the local edge modules. As a proxy, it exposes the same protocol endpoints as the IoT Hub and currently supports MQTT and AMQP, but not HTTP.

Another responsibility for the edgeHub module is authenticating the device with IoT Hub. IoT Hub only allows secure connections from either regular IoT devices or IoT Edge devices. So when the edge device first connects to the IoT Hub, it must authenticate itself using security information that matches the virtual device that already exists in the IoT Hub. After the initial connection has been established, security information is cached on the edge device and the IoT hub does not require authentication for future connection attempts. All of these authentication requests and exchanges are transparent to your code. You simply issue a connect request from your module code (which looks almost identical to a connect request from a regular IoT device) and the edgeHub module takes care of brokering that exchange on your behalf.

Another one of the main responsibilities of the edgeHub module is brokering the intra-module messaging. When you create and deploy a module, they are by design independent and isolated from any other module. If they were not, they could not be independently deployed containers. With this isolation comes a challenge – how does one module communicate with another module? How can I as a developer consume messages from modules that I have no visibility into and how can I send my messages to other modules that have no visibility into my module? The answer is to use a message bus.[1]

The message bus pattern has been around for a while and simply provides a way for two entities that have no knowledge of each other to communicate. This is done through a few key abstractions. One of the cornerstones of this pattern is the abstraction of the "send to" or "receive from" address. In message-oriented architectures, message publishers have to publish a message to an address or an inbox. When using message queues, the address is the location of the queue. When using HTTP, the address is the URL. In both of those instances, there is an out-of-band agreement between the publisher and the consumer about what the address will be. If that agreement is not possible, another solution is required, which is one of the solutions the message bus pattern is intended to solve. The way it addresses that problem is by abstracting the address to a generic address label or tag. The underlying storage or persistence mechanism is known only to the message bus, while publishers and consumers are able to send and receive to and from the address. The implementation of this looks like the interaction in Figure 2-9.

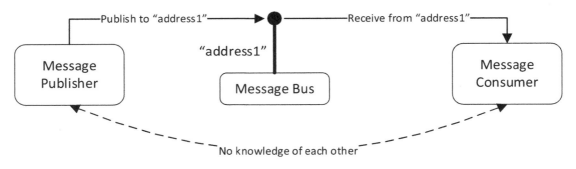

Figure 2-9. *Address abstraction in message bus pattern*

In this diagram, the publisher sends a message to a generic inbox or address location named "address1". The publisher has no idea what consumers (if any) will be receiving the messages it publishes. Additionally, the consumer registers with the message bus as a consumer of any messages that are delivered to location "address1". It is unaware of the publisher or the timing of the messages that will be delivered to the address.

---

[1]Hohpe, G., & Woolf, B. (2003). *Enterprise Integration Patterns: Designing, Building, and Deploying Messaging Solutions.* Addison-Wesley Professional.

This pattern is implemented in the edgeHub module. edgeHub provides an API for modules to send and receive messages to a generic address location. Modules do not need to know what the underlying persistence mechanism is or who the upstream or downstream modules are in the chain. Through this abstraction, modules can be chained together in various custom message workflow combinations.

Another benefit of this pattern is the way the message bus can hide the details of message delivery. Imagine the publisher in Figure 2-9 sends a message to "address1" but there is no consumer or the registered consumer is not currently running. The message bus has a responsibility to deliver that message when there is an active consumer. This message buffering can be complicated and the message bus provides welcome relief to publishers or consumers. As you would expect, the edgeHub module provides this capability. We will discuss some of the specifics about *how* it accomplishes this in the Routing section.

Device Twins

The concept of twins is not new with Azure IoT Edge, it was introduced into Azure with the IoT Hub service, but there are some specific additions related to Azure IoT Edge. Before we get to the IoT Edge specifics, we need to establish a baseline understanding of twins in general. A device twin is a JSON document, created and managed by IoT Hub. This document stores properties about the device, as well as other metadata and configuration information. The properties stored in the twin are both properties to be pushed to the device called "desired" properties as well as properties that have been collected from the device called "reported" properties. Both of these sets of properties have no enforced schema. Because of the asynchronous nature of the twin/device updates, the twin cannot be guaranteed to be always up to date, but it will always have the last reported state of the device and will be eventually consistent with the current properties on the device.

Twins enable backend service interactions through the IoT Hub APIs. Through those APIs, the metadata in a twin document can be queried, which can enable scenarios like device reporting on dashboards or monitoring of long-running jobs across many devices. This is historically very difficult to implement because it requires a real-time request to every device. With twins, the queries can happen in milliseconds, with the understanding that the result set is the last reported device state, not a real-time update from the device. Most organizations are willing to accept that latency.

The content of the twin JSON document is broken down into four areas:

1. **Identity information**: identification properties, like device ID and X509 thumbprint that are read-only and were created by the IoT Hub when the virtual device was initially created. While some of the information in this section may be known to the device through other means, the device cannot query or otherwise access the properties in this section of the twin document.

2. **Tags**: metadata created by backend services and solutions to categorize and classify devices. Examples include: the deployment location (city, building, etc.) or the attached peripherals (heat sensor, humidity sensor).

3. **Desired properties**: created or updated by backend services and solutions – used to request a configuration change be sent to the device. Updating the twin document does not immediately update the physical device. It simply initiates the change request be sent to the device from IoT Hub.

4. **Reported properties**: contains the last known state from the device for the properties specified in the "desired properties" section. These are updateable from the device but read-only and queryable from the backend services.

Figure 2-10 shows a visual representation of the twin structure.

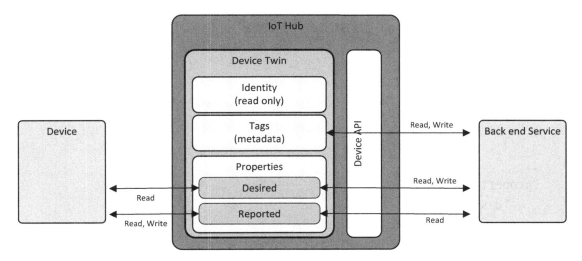

Figure 2-10. *Device twin interactions*

As shown in Figure 2-10, backend services can interact with the device twin through the device API provided by the IoT Hub. Through this API, services can read and update the device tags, read and update the desired properties, and read and query the reported properties. Additionally, the device can read (and be notified of changes to) the desired properties and read and update the reported properties. Here is a sample device twin JSON document:

```
{
    "deviceId": "device-2222",
    "etag": "AAAAAAAAAAc=",
    "status": "enabled",
    "statusReason": "provisioned",
    "statusUpdateTime": "0001-01-01T00:00:00",
    "connectionState": "connected",
    "lastActivityTime": "2015-02-30T16:24:48.789Z",
    "cloudToDeviceMessageCount": 0,
    "authenticationType": "sas",
    "x509Thumbprint": {
        "primaryThumbprint": null,
        "secondaryThumbprint": null
    },
```

```
    "version": 2,
    "tags": {
        "$etag": "123",
        "deploymentLocation": {
            "building": "43",
            "floor": "1"
        }
    },
    "properties": {
        "desired": {
            "telemetryConfig": {
                "sendFrequency": "5m"
            },
            "$metadata" : {...},
            "$version": 1
        },
        "reported": {
            "telemetryConfig": {
                "sendFrequency": "5m",
                "status": "success"
            }
            "batteryLevel": 55,
            "$metadata" : {...},
            "$version": 4
        }
    }
}
```

There are just a few restrictions imposed on any device twin document:

1. Any desired or reported property must be valid JSON.

2. The JSON for any property cannot exceed the maximum depth of 5 levels.

3. The total size of any twin document cannot exceed 8 KB in size.

Module Twins

In Azure IoT Edge, the concept of twins not only applies to the edge device, but also to every module running on that device. The edge device has a twin in addition to each module having a twin. Because all of the code and configuration happens at the module level for edge devices, there is very little interaction with the device twin for edge devices, but you should be aware that it exists. Everything you read about in the previous section regarding device twins is also true for module twins. The module twin has the same sections, the same restrictions, and the same API access model. Any device in IoT Hub can have up to 20 module twins associated with it. Here is a sample module twin – the only difference is the addition of the moduleId property.

```
{
    "deviceId": "device-2222",
    "moduleId": "moduleA",
    "etag": "AAAAAAAAAAc=",
    "status": "enabled",
    "statusReason": "provisioned",
    "statusUpdateTime": "0001-01-01T00:00:00",
    "connectionState": "connected",
    "lastActivityTime": "2015-02-30T16:24:48.789Z",
    "cloudToDeviceMessageCount": 0,
    "authenticationType": "sas",
    "x509Thumbprint": {
        "primaryThumbprint": null,
        "secondaryThumbprint": null
    },
    "version": 2,
    "tags": {
        "$etag": "123",
        "deploymentLocation": {
            "building": "43",
            "floor": "1"
        }
    },
```

```
    "properties": {
        "desired": {
            "telemetryConfig": {
                "sendFrequency": "5m"
            },
            "$metadata" : {...},
            "$version": 1
        },
        "reported": {
            "telemetryConfig": {
                "sendFrequency": "5m",
                "status": "success"
            }
            "batteryLevel": 55,
            "$metadata" : {...},
            "$version": 4
        }
    }
}
```

There are two special module twin cases worth highlighting. Since the edgeHub and edgeAgent are both modules, they both have twins. Due to the extra responsibility each of these modules have, there are properties and configuration contained in each of the twins that any edge device must be aware of. As you begin to develop an Azure IoT Edge solution, you will add information about custom modules that need to be included in the deployment. This updates the configuration in the module twin for both the edgeHub and edgeAgent modules. It should be noted that, unlike other edge modules, the module twins for these modules are not editable within the Azure portal. The twins for these modules are updated through other deployment mechanisms that are discussed later. Here is an example segment from the edgeAgent twin:

```
"properties": {
  "desired": {
    "schemaVersion": "1.0",
    "runtime": {
      "type": "docker",
```

```
"settings": {
    "minDockerVersion": "v1.25",
    "loggingOptions": "",
    "registryCredentials": {
      "myRegistry": {
      "username": "userName",
      "password": "password",
      "address": "reg.azurecr.io"
      }
        }
      }
  },
 "systemModules": {
   "edgeAgent": {
     "type": "docker",
     "settings": {
       "image": "mcr.microsoft.com/azureiotedge-agent:1.0",
        "createOptions": ""
        }
    },
    "edgeHub": {
      "type": "docker",
      "status": "running",
      "restartPolicy": "always",
      "settings": {
        "image": "mcr.microsoft.com/azureiotedge-hub:1.0",
        "createOptions": "{\"HostConfig\":{\"PortBindings\":{\"8883/
        tcp\":[{\"HostPort\":\"8883\"}],\"443/tcp\":[{\"HostPort\":
        \"443\"}]}}}"
      }
    }
  },
  "modules": {
    "moduleA": {
    "version": "1.0",
```

```
            "type": "docker",
            "status": "running",
            "restartPolicy": "always",
            "settings": {
                "image": "reg.azurecr.io/moduleA:1.0.0-amd64",
                "createOptions": ""
                }
            },
            "moduleB": {
              "version": "1.0",
                "type": "docker",
                "status": "running",
                "restartPolicy": "always",
                "settings": {
                "image": "reg.azurecr.io/moduleB:1.0.0-amd64",
                "createOptions": ""
                }
          }
        }
      }
    }
```

This snippet shows just the desired properties for the edgeAgent module twin. Take a look at the `registryCredentials` section. This should seem vaguely familiar to you. The concept of container registries and the credentials needed to connect to them was discussed in the Container section earlier in this chapter. The `registryCredentials` section keeps a listing of any container registries that need to be accessed. This configuration information is sent to the edge device for the edgeAgent to use when needed to pull down the required images.

Another significant section is the `systemModules` section. You won't have to change this information often, but it's helpful to be aware of the information in case versions for the system components are updated.

The `modules` section is where all the custom (nonsystem) modules are enumerated. With each module entry, there are a few standard settings like the `restartPolicy` and the `status`, but the most important settings are the `image` and the `createOptions` settings. These specify what container image and version to use as well as the JSON create options to pass to the container when it's starting up. The `createOptions` setting must be JSON *serialized as a string* – it cannot be the actual JSON structure. This is why the string for the edgeHub `createOptions` contains so many escaped string literals – because that value is just a string, but the *content* of that string can be parsed as valid JSON when the container runtime supplies that on the command line.

Next, let's take a look at the twin for the edgeHub module:

```
"properties": {
  "desired": {
    "schemaVersion": "1.0",
    "routes": {
      "route1": "FROM /messages/modules/moduleA/outputs/* INTO
      BrokeredEndpoint(\"/modules/moduleB/inputs/input1\")",
        "route2": "FROM /messages/modules/moduleB/outputs/upstreamOutput
        INTO $upstream"
      },
    "storeAndForwardConfiguration": {
      "timeToLiveSecs": 7200
    }
  }
}
```

Remember back to the discussion about the edgeHub module? One of the primary concerns for the edgeHub module is message routing between modules. The routes that define the message workflow are defined as part of the edge solution development workflow and then sent to the edge device as configuration for the edgeHub module twin. The edgeHub module then defines and manages the defined routes when it starts up. One special route defined in the example above is `$upstream`. It is used exactly as it is shown here and it represents the IoT Hub. So, any route that defines `$upstream` in the `INTO` clause, is defining a route to the cloud endpoint. In the next section, we will discuss edge routing in more detail. This sample was simply to illustrate where the information was maintained.

Edge Message Routing

The concept of defining message routes has existed in the IoT Hub service for a few years. Now, that concept has been included in the Azure IoT Edge runtime. We have seen the way the edgeHub module provides a generic, abstracted way for modules to communicate with each other while having no knowledge of any other module. These abstracted connections between modules happen through message routes that are defined in the edgeHub module twin, as shown in the previous section. An edge message route contains three parts: (1) a source, (2) a sink (destination), and (3) a condition. The source and sink are required and the condition is optional. In any given edge solution or deployment, many routes can exist. Figure 2-11 illustrates some possible routes between modules.

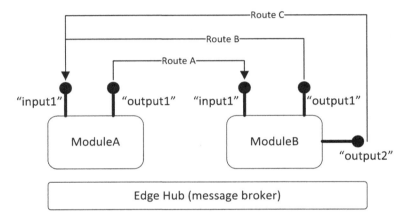

Figure 2-11. *Edge message routes*

In Figure 2-11, there are two modules and three routes defined. Let's walk through each of the three routes.

- **Route A**: Creates a path from the source "output1" in ModuleA to the sink "input1" in ModuleB.

- **Route B**: Creates a path from the source "output1" in ModuleB to the sink "input1" in ModuleA. Modules can declare both input and output addresses in the edge hub message broker.

- **Route C**: Creates a path from a second output source in ModuleB to the sink "input1" in ModuleA, the same sink used in Route B. Routes can be combined in many ways. And each module can define multiple input address and multiple output addresses.

This example shows some basic interactions with only two modules. When you apply these same concepts to a deployment with five or six modules, you can begin to see much more complex scenarios that can be configured using edge routing.

Earlier, in the twin section, you saw an example of routes as they relate to the edgeHub module twin information. Remember that each route has three components: the source, the sink, and the condition. Let's discuss each of those in more detail now. As a reminder, all routes follow this structure:

```
FROM <source> WHERE <condition> INTO <sink>
```

Source

The source of messages for any given route is used by the edgeHub module to determine where the messages originate for that route. The source can contain any mixture of the following components, provided the required order is observed:

- ***** – the wildcard character; it represents all messages from that node in the descriptor

- **Module name** – the name of the module; used to constrain the source to only a certain subset of messages from a specific module

- **Output name** – the name of a specific output used in a module; used to constrain the messages from a certain module to only one of the module's outputs

These three components are combined in various ways to describe the message source for the routes. Here are some example routes:

- **/messages/*** – All messages from any module or leaf device, regardless of output

- **/messages/modules/*** – All messages from any module, regardless of the output

- **/messages/modules/{moduleName}/*** – All messages from the named module

- **/messages/modules/{moduleName}/outputs/*** – All messages from all outputs used in the named module

- **/messages/modules/{moduleName}/outputs/{outputName}** – All messages from the named output in the named module

You might be wondering why edge routing needs a WHERE clause if the source can handle the flexibility to filter the messages. In truth, you may find that you do not need the WHERE clause. You might be able to filter the source enough that you never need it. But, think about the difference between declaratively stating what messages you want to look at, vs. deciding to make that decision to filter at runtime, based on the payload. That's one of the main differences between the approaches. If you know ahead of time that all messages from a temperature sensor need to be routed to a certain destination, then filtering the source should be sufficient. But if you need to only route temperature sensor messages that exceed a threshold, then you will have to use the WHERE clause.

Condition

The condition of the message route is optional. But, if you decide you need to use this feature, you declare the condition using the IoT Hub query language. This syntax supports operations on the systemProperties and appProperties, which both look at the header of the message, and body properties. To refer to any of these properties in the query syntax, use the following syntax:

- **System properties**: $<propertyName> ($messageId, for example) – these header values are provided out of the box to every edge implementation.

- **App properties**: <propertyName> (messageStatus, for example) – these header values are added in code by the application and are custom to the edge implementation.

- **Body properties**: $body.<propertyName> ($body.temperatureValue, for example) – these values come from the message payload and are custom to the edge implementation.

There are also functions and operators that are supported in the query syntax. Here is a sampling of some of the functions supported in route queries:

- IS_DEFINED(property): Boolean that returns true only if the property specified exists in the message

- AS_NUMBER(property): Converts the input string to a number for math operations

- LENGTH(property): Returns the length of the property value string

For a full list of supported operations, see: `https://docs.microsoft.com/en-us/azure/iot-hub/iot-hub-devguide-query-language#expressions-and-conditions`.

Here is an example route with a `WHERE` clause:

```
FROM /messages/modules/tempSensor/* WHERE IS_DEFINED(alertStatus) INTO $upstream
```

This route has as its source all messages coming from the tempSensor module. It then filters those messages to only the messages that have a **header** property for the "alertStatus" property. So any messages that do not have that custom property (which would be added in the edge code) will not be routed.

Sink

The sink is the destination for the route. There are two options for the sinks. There is a special, fixed sink that represents the IoT Hub, called `$upstream`. Any route that specifies that sink is declaring that those messages should be sent to the IoT Hub endpoint. The other option for sinks is this format:

```
BrokeredEndpoint("/modules/{moduleName}/inputs/{input1}")
```

This example sink describes the "input1" destination in the "moduleName" module. The resulting messages from the source and any conditional clause will be sent to this module for processing. If the specified input name does not exist in the module, the messages cannot be delivered. In this case, the edgeHub module stores the messages for the TTL (time to live) specified by the `storeAndForwardConfiguration.timeToLiveSecs` property of the edgeHub twin desiredProperties section. When the TTL has expired for a message, it is removed from the local queue of messages to deliver.

Edge Device Security

Security is a deep topic that we won't fully cover here, but I want to call out a few specifics you need to be aware of. First, there is an additional component running on the edge device that has been overlooked up to this point. It is the security manager service. The security manager service is the main line of defense against attacks on the edge device. It is responsible for several tasks on the edge device. These include:

- Securing the bootstrapping process of the edge device
- Verifying and validating the root of trust on the device and abstracting it from the other dependent services

- Verifying the code (modules) running on the device has not been tampered with

- Securing and storing any secrets required for cloud provisioning services

- Provisioning and storing device identity information

The security manager service is actually the service that starts the edgeAgent module we have discussed previously and handles validating every module's identity to guarantee the module code has not been altered or tampered with. And since a module cannot start up without being initiated by the security manager service, all module code running on the edge device can be trusted. The architecture of the security manager service is shown in Figure 2-12.

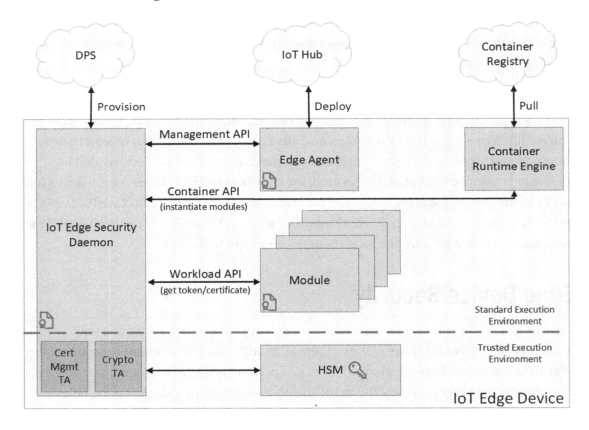

Figure 2-12. *The security manager architecture (Image from Microsoft blog post, "Azure IoT Edge Security Manager", July 29, 2018)*

Two important APIs that the security manager provides are:

1. **Management API**: This is a special API reserved just for the edge Agent module. When the edgeAgent is provisioned, the security manager service collects information about the edgeAgent module to use in verification later. The edgeAgent can then use this API to orchestrate the management of other modules on the devices. So every call to the underlying container services is actually brokered by the security manager service from the edgeAgent to the underlying container API. This allows the security manager service to perform runtime attestations on the modules running.

2. **Workload API**: This API is leveraged by all modules on the device to retrieve identity information required to contact the IoT Hub or other modules. Each module has a unique identity that is known to the security manager service and can be used to prove the module is secure.

   A related but slightly different concept in Azure IoT Edge is identity. Every device has a unique identity. Additionally, each module in an edge deployment has a unique identity. These identities are created and managed in the IoT Hub, but the necessary information is provisioned to the edge device so that the security manager service can validate and verify not only the device's identity but also the module's identity. This will be discussed later in the Security chapter.

Edge Deployments

Once you begin managing large fleets of devices, rolling out changes becomes challenging. IoT Hub offers a feature called Deployments that helps make this task less challenging. While this feature is not specific to Azure IoT Edge, there are a few IoT Edge specific features that you should be aware of. Essentially, deployments are a way to group devices and apply a common configuration manifest (configuration settings and list of modules) to that group and hand that orchestration workload off to IoT Hub. Deployments are created in IoT Hub, either through the portal, the PowerShell interface, or the API interface.

Once a deployment is defined, the IoT Hub instance continually manages the deployment, evaluating the target devices and the configuration specified, ensuring the devices always have the correct software and settings. Figure 2-13 shows the Azure portal UI where a deployment can be created.

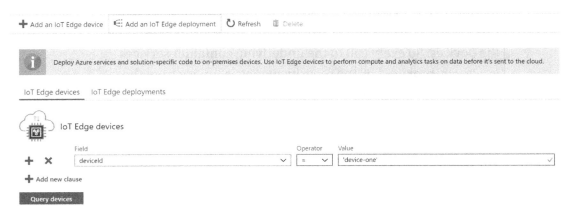

Figure 2-13. *Create a deployment in the Azure portal*

If you click the Add and IoT Edge deployment link in Figure 2-13, you will be presented with a screen containing several steps that you must complete. There are a lot of concepts mentioned in this chapter and that will be mentioned in the upcoming chapters that you need to understand before you will be able to correctly create and manage an IoT Edge deployment. But remember that all of the configuration for IoT Edge devices can and should be automated through deployments. Here is a description of the steps you can complete to create a deployment. If you don't understand all of these concepts now, just mark this section and return to this when you are ready to automate some of your edge deployments.

- **Name and label**: The name of the deployment and any metadata tags you want to associate with this deployment.

- **Add modules**: A list of the modules that should be assigned to the targeted devices. If any of the modules are housed in a secure (private) container registry, you need to provide the container registry credentials in this step as well.

- **Specify routes**: The routes that should be configured and added to the deployment manifest for the target devices.

- **Specify metrics**: A list of custom name/value pairs that should be associated with the deployment. You can provide a metric name and metric value, which can be a query against the device metadata. The metric value is continually evaluated and updated based on the progress of the devices targeted in the deployment.

- **Target devices**: A target condition (in the form of a where clause) used to identify the devices to be included in the deployment. This is a dynamic condition and is continually evaluated to detect what devices should be included and what devices should be removed from the deployment. In the target devices section, you can also provide a priority. A priority determines which deployment configuration takes precedence if there are multiple deployments in place for a specific device. The higher priority wins.

Summary

In this chapter you learned about the core concepts that are involved in an Azure IoT Edge solution. You learned about some of the differences in IoT Hub for edge devices. You examined how existing technologies like Docker, Moby, and containers are used to support the concept of edge modules, and that the edge runtime is composed of two special modules, edgeAgent and edgeHub, that each have a certain set of tasks they are responsible for. We looked at how twins are used for device management, but more specifically to IoT Edge, we saw how each module has a twin as well that follows the device twin model. We saw how edge device routing enables the ability to let decoupled modules communicate with one another. Finally, we discussed a high-level overview of the edge security manager service along with IoT deployments. If you have been following along, you should now have a solid understanding of all the concepts required to be productive with Azure IoT Edge. In the next chapter, we will be setting our development environment so that we can start building edge solutions with the right tools.

## CHAPTER 3

Azure IoT Edge Development Environment

The Azure IoT Edge platform has a robust set of tools that provides developers with a similar development experience to what they are used to, in spite of the more complicated configuration of an edge solution. The Azure IoT Edge development toolchain is based on Visual Studio or VS Code, Docker/Moby, .Net Core (for .Net apps), Azure IoT Hub, and a container registry, usually either DockerHub or Azure Container Registry (ACR). This chapter will walk you through how to set up, configure, and connect all of these separate technologies to create a cohesive development experience. For examples, we will use a Windows 10 machine, but you can use a Windows Server machine as well if needed.

One of the first things to highlight about the edge development experience is that Azure IoT Edge development work can be done in either the VS Code IDE or Visual Studio. This chapter will walk you through setting up both environments. If this is your first experience with VS Code, that is okay. This chapter will walk you through everything you need to know to configure your development environment from the beginning.

Another important point to note is that you will need access to an instance of the Azure IoT Hub service in Azure. That is required to configure and manage your edge device. So, if you do not have access to an Azure subscription, you can sign up for a free trial of Azure at: `https://azure.microsoft.com/en-us/free/`.

There is a third point to be aware of if you are running this setup process on a virtual machine. Part of this configuration process in this chapter will be configuring your development machine as an edge device. Because the edge runtime is based on virtualization technologies like Docker and Moby, installing Docker and/or Moby requires nested virtualization to be enabled in your VM. If you are running on a normal development machine, this is not required. But there will be steps to guide you on how to set that up in the section on setting up Docker.

© David Jensen 2019
D. Jensen, *Beginning Azure IoT Edge Computing*, https://doi.org/10.1007/978-1-4842-4536-1_3

Note   Additionally, if you are running this setup process using a virtual machine in Azure, you must select a Windows 10 VM size of at least **Standard D4s v3**. This size has the number of CPUs required to enable nested virtualization. If you are running on a machine that is less than that size, you should stop reading this chapter and scale up your VM as a first step.

Configure VS Code

As I mentioned earlier, IoT Edge development can be done in either VS Code or Visual Studio. In this section, we will walk through setting up VS Code to develop IoT Edge solutions. VS Code was the first IDE to support IoT Edge development and, as a result, is more mature. If you do not have VS Code installed you can install and download it from: `https://code.visualstudio.com/`. Once you have downloaded it, please run the install process. If this is your first time using VS Code, please read through the following two sections. If you are familiar with VS Code, you can skip to the section on *Configuring VS Code for IoT*.

VS Code vs. Visual Studio

VS Code is Microsoft's cross-platform, open-source Integrated Development Environment (IDE). One of the main differences between VS Code and Visual Studio is that Visual Studio was a large install, packed with lots of project and solution templates (and if you are anything like me, you only used 5 – 10% of those templates). Whereas, VS Code is a much smaller initial install (< 50MB, compared to the Visual Studio install of > 1 GB). VS Code is so much smaller because it does not have hundreds of project and solution templates included. The initial download is a very streamlined package, which does not initially support languages like C#. However, there is a vast marketplace that contains thousands of extensions. So, once you install VS Code, the most common next step is to find and install all the required extensions to support your development requirements.

Another difference between VS Code and Visual Studio is that VS Code is free. It does not require a license for private or commercial use. This can mean potentially huge savings for development shops who are used to spending several thousands of dollars for Visual Studio. This does not mean that VS Code can perform all the tasks of Visual Studio. It cannot. But if the tasks you need are supported by VS Code, then it is a great, cost-effective option.

A final difference between VS Code and Visual Studio is the cross-platform nature of VS Code. VS Code will run on Windows machines as well as Mac OS and Linux machines. Visual Studio could only run on Windows for many years, but recently Microsoft has released a version of Visual Studio that will run on Mac OS.

First Lap Around VS Code

Whenever you launch VS Code, you are presented with the welcome screen. Figure 3-1 shows what that looks like.

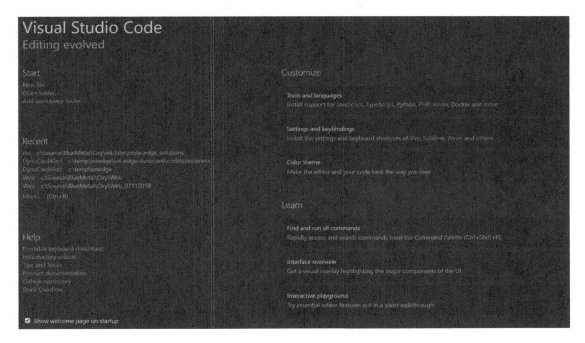

Figure 3-1. *VS Code welcome screen*

From the welcome screen, you can enable a guided tour to get more familiar with the environment. Click the "Interface overview" option in the bottom right section of the Welcome Screen. Once you click this option, you should see options appear as shown in Figure 3-2. These guides help to point out the major components of the VS Code UI.

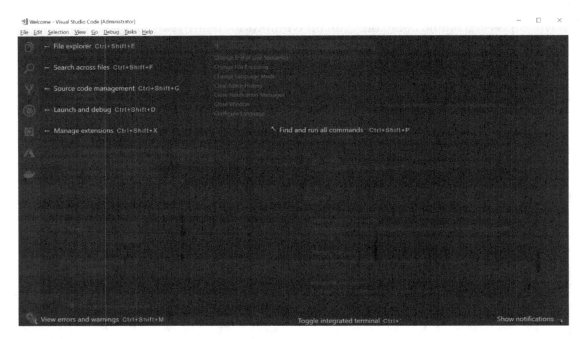

Figure 3-2. *VS Code guided interface overview*

Additionally, if you are familiar with other code editors and prefer to use the keyboard shortcuts from that editor, you have the option to mimic other editors. To do this, simply click the Settings and keybindings option under the Customize section on the welcome page. You should see a list of popular keymaps as shown in Figure 3-3.

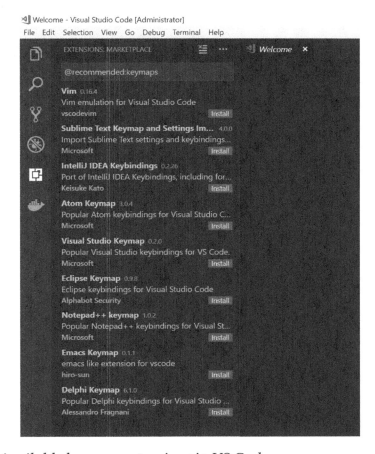

Figure 3-3. *Available keymap extensions in VS Code*

One of the main differences between Visual Studio and VS Code that we mentioned earlier is that VS Code does not include a wide variety of project templates or extensions to use with the initial install. The way you customize and enhance your VS Code experience is through the VS Code extension marketplace. Extensions and the extension marketplace are first-class concepts in VS Code and there are extensions created by companies like Microsoft as well as individuals that enable just about anything you can think of needing in a source code editor. An example of some extensions is shown in Figure 3-3. If you look at the search bar for that example, you see that the list is filtered to only include the recommended keymaps. But you can search for any keyword you need. You can also visit: `http://marketplace.visualstudio.com/VSCode` and browse all the available extensions in your browser. Figure 3-4 shows some of the most popular extensions in the marketplace for VS Code.

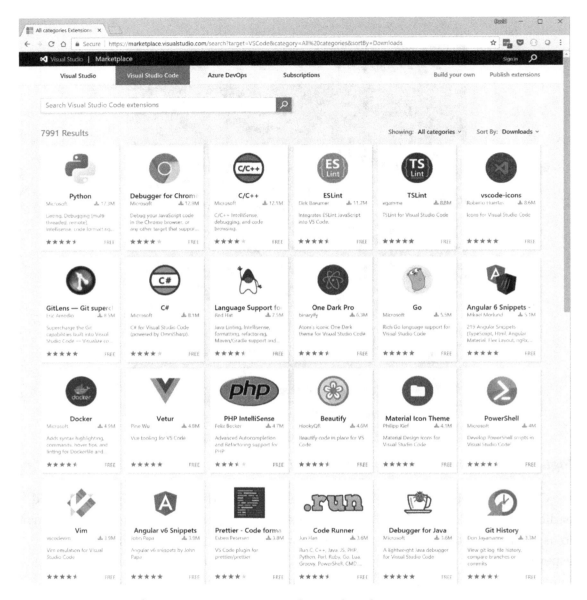

Figure 3-4. *Popular extensions in VS Code marketplace*

Configure VS Code for IoT Edge

Now that we have installed VS Code, we need to configure it for working with the Azure IoT Edge platform. If you have not already opened your instance of VS Code, open it now. You may be prompted to update it, based on how long it's been since you installed it. The product team is continually updating it. So, if it's been longer than a couple of weeks, chances are, there's an update waiting for you.

Git is the default source control option in VS Code and there is support built into VS Code for Git from the ground up. If you do not have Git installed on your machine, you will be prompted by VS Code to install it. If you see the prompt, shown in Figure 3-5, you can click the *Download Git* button which will install Git on your machine. It should be noted that this installation is not simply installing a Git plug-in into VS Code – Git is being installed as a standalone product that VS Code will then hook into.

Figure 3-5. *VS Code prompt to install Git*

When installing Git, you can choose VS Code as the default Git editor. This simply means that you will use VS Code when Git needs you to type in a message. If you do not select this option, Git will use your system's default editor. You do not have to select this option and it will not affect any of the steps that follow. But if you'd like to choose that option, select it in the dialog, as shown in Figure 3-6.

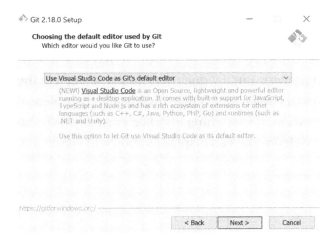

Figure 3-6. *Select VS Code as the default editor*

Once, VS Code is opened, we can begin to install the required extensions from the VS Code marketplace. We will install four VS Code extensions to help with the IoT Edge development process. Click the VS Code extensions icon on the left side of the window. Then, in the search bar, enter "azure iot". You should see a list of results similar to Figure 3-7.

Figure 3-7. *Azure IoT related extensions for VS Code*

In the list of extension search results, select the *Azure IoT Edge* extension. After selecting it in the list, you need to click the green Install button. Once that is complete, you need to install the *Azure IoT Toolkit* extension. It may install as part of the IoT Edge extension installation process. But if it does not, simply select it in the list of extensions and click the green Install button for it. Once the install is complete, click the *reload* button next to the extension. If everything installed correctly, you should see the Azure IoT Toolkit Extension welcome screen display as shown in Figure 3-8.

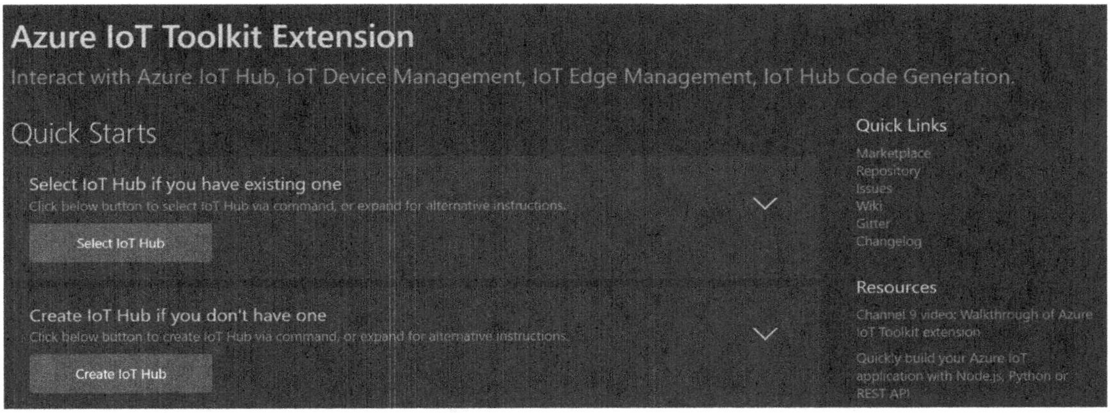

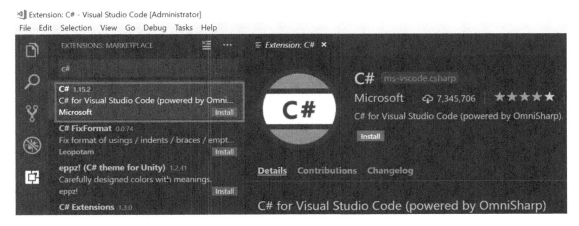

Figure 3-8. *Azure IoT Toolkit welcome screen*

Next, in the VS Code extension window, search for *C#* extensions and install the extension shown in Figure 3-9.

Figure 3-9. *C# extension*

The C# extension for VS Code gives you a native C# coding experience in VS Code, including Intellisense, refactoring/renaming, compile-time validation and more. Remember, VS Code does not natively understand C# as Visual Studio does. So, this helpful extension gives us many of the C# helps, tricks and hints in VS Code that we now rely on in Visual Studio. The upcoming examples will leverage the C# edge module template, which needs this extension.

The last VS Code extension we need to install is the Docker extension. You can search for docker in the extension search bar as shown in Figure 3-10. Once you have selected it, install it as you did with the other extensions.

Figure 3-10. *Docker extension*

Configure Visual Studio for IoT Edge

If you would like to use Visual Studio for your IoT Edge IDE and you have not installed Visual Studio 2017, you can download the Community Edition from https:// visualstudio.microsoft.com/downloads/. If you have Visual Studio installed, verify that your version is at least 15.7. This is a requirement for the Azure IoT Edge tooling. You can check your version by clicking Help ➤ About. If you have a version less than 15.7, you need to update it now before you move ahead. Additionally, check any update notifications in Visual Studio you may have to ensure you have installed all available updates for Cloud Explorer. This component needs to be up to date as well. Once you have completed any needed updates for both Visual Studio and Cloud Explorer, you should see the IoT Hubs resource type in the Cloud Explorer, as shown in Figure 3-11.

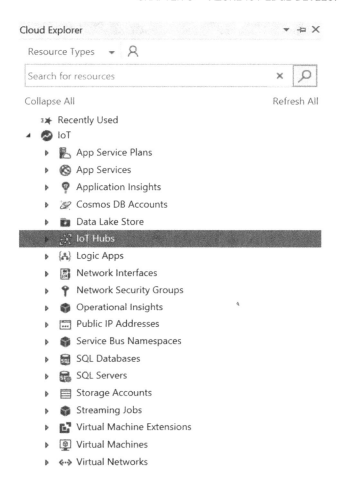

Figure 3-11. *Updated Cloud Explorer*

Once you have downloaded the installer, complete the install process. After the installer completes, launch Visual Studio to allow it to run the initial configuration process. After that completes, you can download and install the Azure IoT Edge Tools add-in for Visual Studio from here: `https://marketplace.visualstudio.com/items?itemName=vsc-iot.vsiotedgetools`, or you can go to `http://marketplace.visualstudio.com/` and search for Azure IoT Edge Tools. It should be the first result as shown in Figure 3-12.

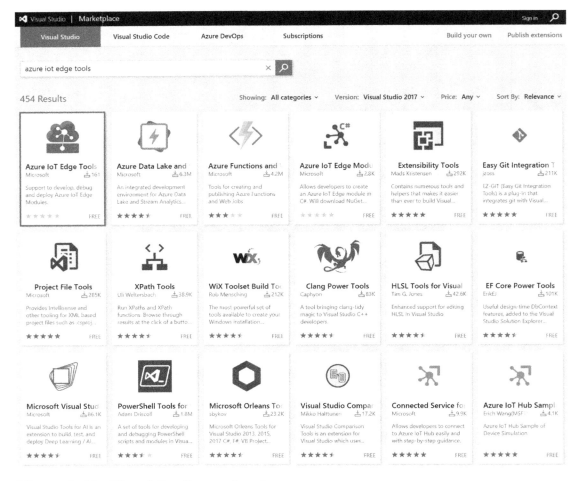

Figure 3-12. *Visual Studio marketplace*

Click "Download" and then run the VSIX installer package. You can verify that the installation completed successfully, but checking to see if you a new option in the File ➤ New Project dialog as shown in Figure 3-13.

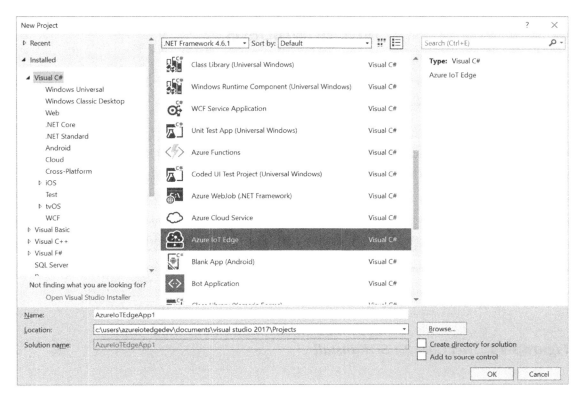

Figure 3-13. *New IoT Edge project type*

Install .Net Core 2.1

If you have not already installed the .Net Core 2.1 SDK, you will need to install it from
`www.microsoft.com/net/download`. Figure 3-14 shows the download page and which
option to select.

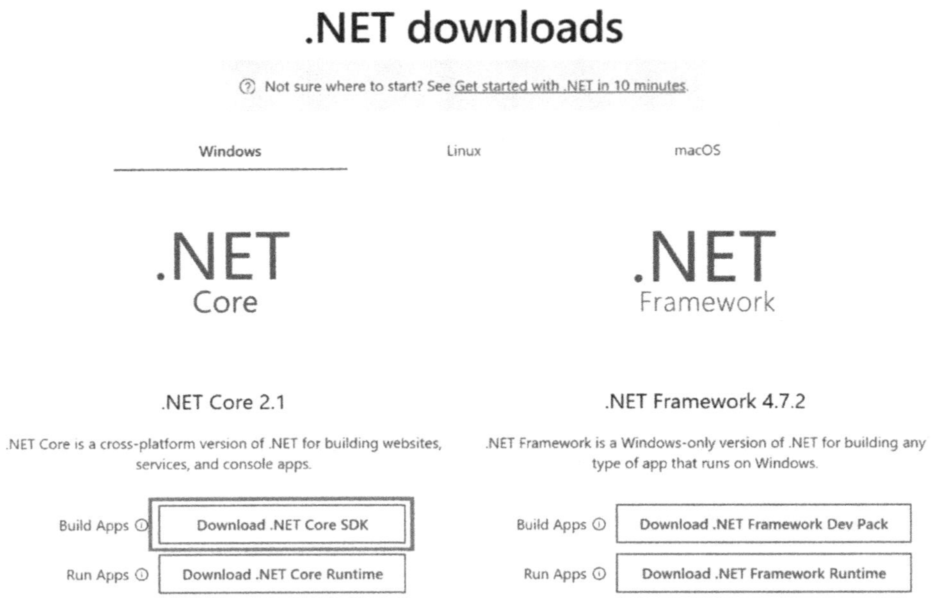

.NET downloads

⑦ Not sure where to start? See Get started with .NET in 10 minutes.

| Windows | Linux | macOS |

.NET
Core

.NET Core 2.1

.NET Core is a cross-platform version of .NET for building websites, services, and console apps.

Build Apps ⓘ [Download .NET Core SDK]

Run Apps ⓘ [Download .NET Core Runtime]

.NET
Framework

.NET Framework 4.7.2

.NET Framework is a Windows-only version of .NET for building any type of app that runs on Windows.

Build Apps ⓘ [Download .NET Framework Dev Pack]

Run Apps ⓘ [Download .NET Framework Runtime]

Figure 3-14. *.Net Core 2.1 SDK install*

Install Docker

Docker is a key component of local IoT Edge development. If you do not already have it installed, you will need that as well. I assuming you are running on a Windows development machine. If that is the case, you can install Docker Community Edition for Windows, from: `https://store.docker.com/editions/community/docker-ce-desktop-windows`. If you are running this on a Linux or Mac development machine, go to: `https://store.docker.com` and find the Community Edition that is right for your machine. If you have never downloaded Docker before or are not logged in with your Docker credentials, you will see a button, as shown in Figure 3-15, asking you to login to download Docker.

Get Docker Community Edition for Windows

Docker for Windows is available for free.

Requires Microsoft Windows 10 Professional or
Enterprise 64-bit. For previous versions get Docker
Toolbox.

Please Login To Download

Figure 3-15. *Login prompt to download Docker*

Figure 3-16 shows the Docker login dialog. If you have a Docker ID, use those credentials to login. If you do not have a login, click the *Create Account* option, as shown in Figure 3-16.

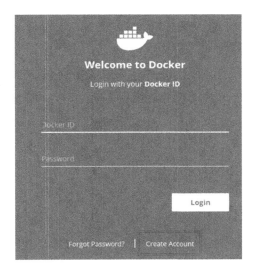

Figure 3-16. *Docker login dialog*

Occasionally, I have had trouble with the next step and the *Sign Up* button will stay disabled, even after I entered the account information. If this happens to you, just refresh your browser until you see the "I'm not a robot" captcha, as shown in Figure 3-17. Then, you should be able to proceed by entering your information.

Figure 3-17. *Docker ID creation dialog*

Once you have created a Docker account, or signed in with your existing Docker account, you should see the option to install Docker as shown in Figure 3-18.

Figure 3-18. *Docker download dialog*

After Docker has downloaded and it finishes the install, you will be prompted to restart your machine. Restart and Docker should attempt to start after you login. If you do not have virtualization enabled (or nested virtualization, if running this on a VM), you will be prompted to enable Hyper-V. As a reminder, there was a note earlier in this chapter that mentioned the minimum size required if you are running this setup process using a virtual machine in Azure. If that is you, you must select a Windows 10 VM size of at least **Standard D4s v3**. This size has the number of CPUs required to enable nested virtualization. If you did not heed the earlier warning, you need to scale your machine to at least that size before continuing. The next steps will not work on Azure VMs smaller than that size.

Regardless of the location, if you are running on any virtual machine, you must enable nested virtualization. To enable nested virtualization, use the following steps.

To enable nested virtualization on a Windows VM:

1. Launch a Powershell Window as Administrator.

2. Run the commands in Listing 3-1 from the Powershell window.

Listing 3-1. Commands to enable nested virtualization on Windows VM

```
Enable-WindowsOptionalFeature -Online -FeatureName Microsoft-Hyper-V -All
-Verbose

Enable-WindowsOptionalFeature -Online -FeatureName Containers -All -Verbose

bcdedit /set hypervisorlaunchtype Auto
```

3. Restart your machine, if you were not prompted to do so already.

Once Docker has been installed and you have enabled (nested) virtualization, you need to create a local Docker registry for holding local images as you develop. To create and start a local registry, run the command shown in Listing 3-2 from a command prompt:

Listing 3-2. Docker command to start a local registry

```
docker run -d -p 5000:5000 --name registry registry:2
```

This command starts local docker registry on port 5000. To verify that things are running as expected, from the command line run the command shown in Listing 3-3.

Listing 3-3. Docker command to list currently running containers

```
C:\> docker ps
```

If everything is running as expected, you should see the list of currently running Docker containers. It should look similar to the output in Figure 3-19.

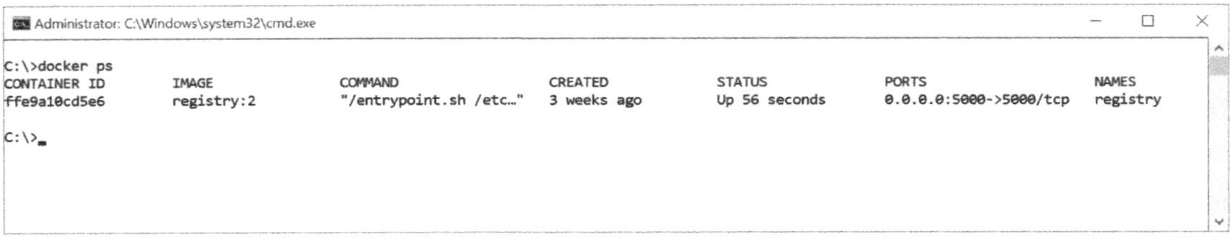

```
Administrator: C:\Windows\system32\cmd.exe                                              —    □    ×

C:\>docker ps
CONTAINER ID      IMAGE            COMMAND             CREATED        STATUS          PORTS                    NAMES
ffe9a10cd5e6      registry:2       "/entrypoint.sh /etc…"  3 weeks ago    Up 56 seconds   0.0.0.0:5000->5000/tcp   registry

C:\>_
```

Figure 3-19. *Docker registry container running*

Install the IoT Edge Emulator

One of the newer tools to the IoT Edge family of tools is the IoT Edge Dev Tool. It is
a python package that has a simulator for the Edge runtime as well as support for
debugging and testing IoT Edge modules and solutions. The dev tool allows developers
to run modules on their development machine without having to run the module/
solution in a Docker container. You must have Docker CE as well as Python (2.7/3.6)
and Pip installed. Once you have those components installed, simply run the command
shown in Listing 3-4.

Listing 3-4. Install IoT Edge Dev Tool

```
pip install --upgrade iotedgehubdev
```

Once this command completes, the dev tool is installed. We will configure it and set
it up in the next chapter.

Configure IoT Hub

The primary Azure service that manages IoT devices, including IoT Edge, is the Azure
IoT Hub. Many of the core concepts for IoT Hub were reviewed in the previous chapter.
But at this point in the process, we need to create an instance of IoT Hub, in order to
provision the security information and device metadata required to connect an actual
device to the service.

Create an IoT Hub Instance

To create an instance of the Azure IoT Hub service, log in to the Azure portal and click IoT Hub in the left navigation menu, as shown in Figure 3-20.

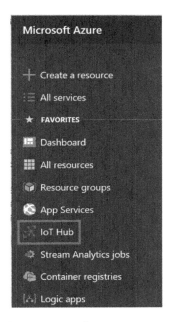

Figure 3-20. *IoT Hub in the Azure portal*

If you do not see IoT Hub in the left navigation, you can click *All Services* at the top of the left navigation panel and then enter "iot" in the search bar. IoT Hub should be in the list of the results, at which point you can click it. Once you have clicked the IoT Hub service, you will see an *Add* option at the top of the blade. Click that to follow the prompts below and create an instance of the IoT Hub service. Figure 3-21 shows the first screen in this process.

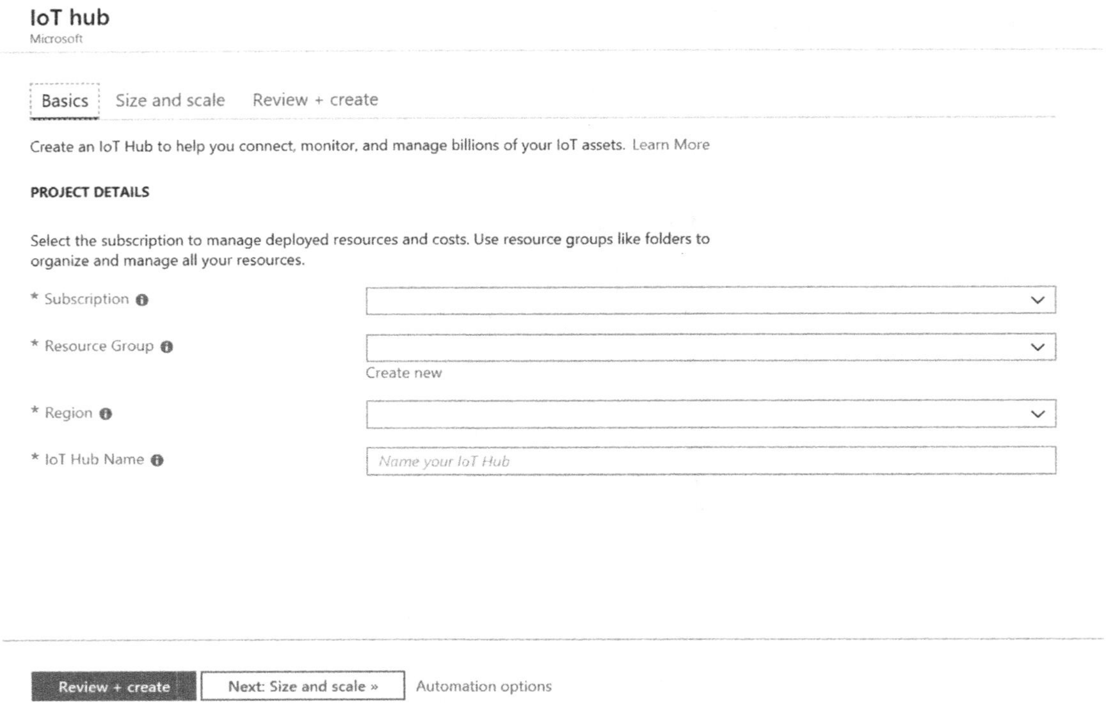

IoT hub
Microsoft

Basics | Size and scale | Review + create

Create an IoT Hub to help you connect, monitor, and manage billions of your IoT assets. Learn More

PROJECT DETAILS

Select the subscription to manage deployed resources and costs. Use resource groups like folders to organize and manage all your resources.

* Subscription ❶

* Resource Group ❶

Create new

* Region ❶

* IoT Hub Name ❶

Name your IoT Hub

Review + create   Next: Size and scale »   Automation options

Figure 3-21. *IoT Hub creation basic information*

After you enter the basic naming and location information for your instance, click *Next* at the bottom of the blade. The next screen allows you to select the size and number of IoT hub instances you need, as shown in Figure 3-22.

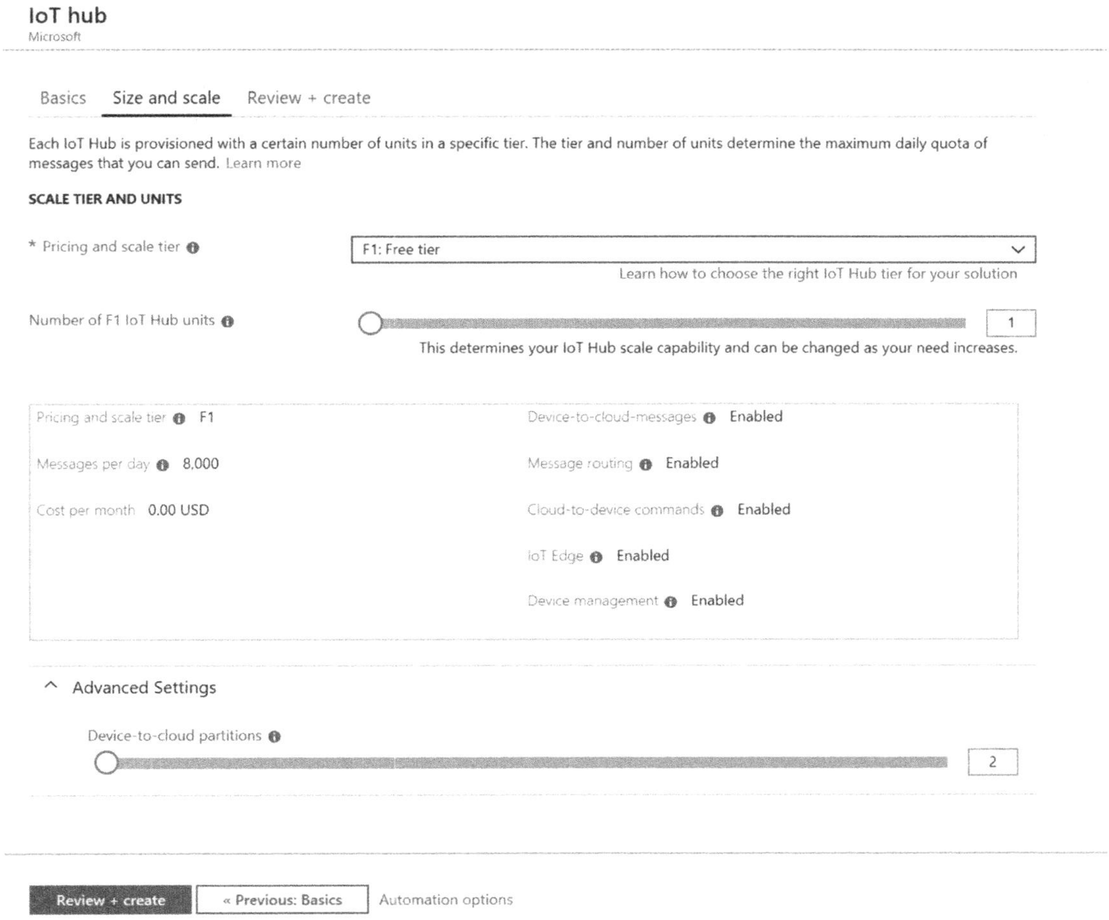

IoT hub
Microsoft

Basics   **Size and scale**   Review + create

Each IoT Hub is provisioned with a certain number of units in a specific tier. The tier and number of units determine the maximum daily quota of messages that you can send. Learn more

SCALE TIER AND UNITS

* Pricing and scale tier ⓘ

F1: Free tier   ⌄

Learn how to choose the right IoT Hub tier for your solution

Number of F1 IoT Hub units ⓘ

◯▬▬▬▬▬▬▬▬▬▬▬▬▬▬▬▬▬▬▬▬▬▬   1

This determines your IoT Hub scale capability and can be changed as your need increases.

Pricing and scale tier ⓘ F1	Device-to-cloud-messages ⓘ Enabled
Messages per day ⓘ 8,000	Message routing ⓘ Enabled
Cost per month 0.00 USD	Cloud-to-device commands ⓘ Enabled
	IoT Edge ⓘ Enabled
	Device management ⓘ Enabled

^ Advanced Settings

Device-to-cloud partitions ⓘ

◯▬▬▬▬▬▬▬▬▬▬▬▬▬▬▬▬▬▬▬▬▬▬▬▬▬   2

Review + create   « Previous: Basics   Automation options

Figure 3-22. *Azure IoT Hub size options*

Since we are targeting a development, I suggest using the Free (F1) tier, but keep in mind that there is only one free instance allowed per Azure subscription and it cannot be scaled up – meaning, when you want to scale up, you will have to create a new instance of IoT Hub at the desired level. The Free tier is the only tier with this limitation. All other tiers can be scaled up or down in place as needed. Additionally, the Free tier has a limit of 8,000 messages / day. So, if you were to run a robust test that generated a significant number of messages, you could burn through all your messages in a day. Once you have selected the size and number of IoT Hub instances you need, select the *Review + create* option and then press the "Create" button.

Add an Edge Device to IoT Hub

After your IoT Hub instance has finished deploying, navigate to your instance and select the IoT Edge blade, as shown in Figure 3-23.

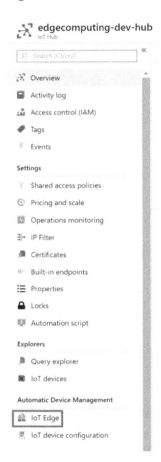

Figure 3-23.   *IoT Edge blade Azure portal*

Once you select the IoT Edge blade, you will see any edge devices you've added to this IoT Hub instance as well as the option to add a new device. This is shown in Figure 3-24.

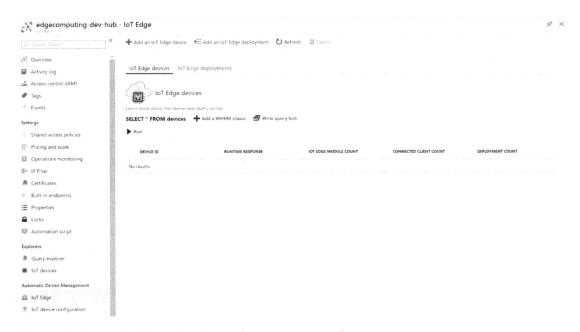

Figure 3-24. *IoT Edge details in the Azure portal*

Click the *Add an IoT Edge device* option at the top of the blade. You will be prompted to enter a unique device ID. Enter the ID and click the *Save* button. When you click the *Save* button, IoT Hub generates and provisions a set of security keys and other metadata associated with the device. Once you have created at least one edge device in the Azure portal, you are ready to connect and provision the actual device to the IoT Hub using the information (security keys, connection strings, etc.) generated in this step.

Install Azure IoT Edge SDK

Up until this point, we have been installing many of the prerequisites for the Azure IoT Edge SDK. Now we will begin installing and configuring the SDK on your target IoT Edge device. This can be your development machine or another machine. If you are not setting up your development machine at this point, you should plan on returning to this section and walking through the next few sections with your machine. Developing and debugging becomes much easier if you are able to run your edge module code locally and attach the VS Code debugger to it.

You can set up the edge SDK on either a Windows or a Linux machine. Currently, the only Linux installations supported are Ubuntu 16.06 and 18.04, but support for more installations and versions are being added. As you walk through the SDK installation process, you will see the commands for both Windows and Linux. Regardless of the platform on your machine, you can follow the steps here. It is important to note that some of the steps required for Linux installations are not required for the Windows installations because of the preexisting trust that Microsoft has with the Windows OS. So, there are a few extra small steps required for the Linux installation, just to provision the security information required to safely download Microsoft software packages.

Install the Microsoft Keys

If you are running Linux, you will need to add security information to the machine so that the Microsoft software repository feeds are trusted. Some of the software must be downloaded and installed from a trusted source that is discoverable. To enable this and add the Microsoft information, run the commands in Listing 3-5.

Listing 3-5. Ubuntu 18.04 commands to add Microsoft package sources

```
# Install repository configuration
curl https://packages.microsoft.com/config/ubuntu/18.04/prod.list >
./microsoft-prod.list
sudo cp ./microsoft-prod.list /etc/apt/sources.list.d/

# Install Microsoft GPG public key
curl https://packages.microsoft.com/keys/microsoft.asc | gpg --dearmor >
microsoft.gpg
sudo cp ./microsoft.gpg /etc/apt/trusted.gpg.d/

# Perform apt upgrade
sudo apt-get upgrade
```

The result of the commands should look similar to the output shown in Figure 3-25.

Figure 3-25. *Registering Microsoft software repository feed on Linux*

If you are running Windows, the needed trust and software source information is already included in the operating system. So, there is no need to run the Windows equivalent of these commands.

Install the Container Runtime

Once the repository feeds have been installed and configured on a Linux machine, the required IoT Edge packages can be added using the normal Linux package installation utility *apt-get*. To download these packages, run the commands in Listing 3-6. It is important to note that these commands are installing the Moby container runtime, not a full-featured implementation of Docker. Moby is the only supported container runtime for IoT Edge and should be used for production scenarios, but you can use Docker if needed in the development and testing scenarios.

Listing 3-6. Ubuntu 18.04 commands to install Moby container runtime

```
sudo apt-get update
sudo apt-get install moby-engine
sudo apt-get install moby-cli
```

The result of the commands should look similar to the output shown in Figure 3-26.

```
iotedgedev@iotedge-linux-devtest: ~                                              —    □    ×
Selecting previously unselected package aufs-tools.
Preparing to unpack .../aufs-tools_1%3a4.9+20170918-1ubuntu1_amd64.deb ...
Unpacking aufs-tools (1:4.9+20170918-1ubuntu1) ...
Selecting previously unselected package cgroupfs-mount.
Preparing to unpack .../cgroupfs-mount_1.4_all.deb ...
Unpacking cgroupfs-mount (1.4) ...
Selecting previously unselected package moby-engine.
Preparing to unpack .../moby-engine_3-az-09f5e9d_amd64.deb ...
Unpacking moby-engine (3-az-09f5e9d) ...
Setting up aufs-tools (1:4.9+20170918-1ubuntu1) ...
Setting up moby-engine (3-az-09f5e9d) ...
Adding group `docker' (GID 115) ...
Done.
Created symlink /etc/systemd/system/multi-user.target.wants/docker.service → /lib/systemd/system/docker.service.
Created symlink /etc/systemd/system/sockets.target.wants/docker.socket → /lib/systemd/system/docker.socket.
Processing triggers for ureadahead (0.100.0-20) ...
Setting up cgroupfs-mount (1.4) ...
Processing triggers for libc-bin (2.27-3ubuntu1) ...
Processing triggers for systemd (237-3ubuntu10.3) ...
Processing triggers for man-db (2.8.3-2) ...
Setting up pigz (2.4-1) ...
Processing triggers for ureadahead (0.100.0-20) ...
iotedgedev@iotedge-linux-devtest:~$ sudo apt-get install moby-cli
Reading package lists... Done
Building dependency tree
Reading state information... Done
The following NEW packages will be installed:
  moby-cli
0 upgraded, 1 newly installed, 0 to remove and 0 not upgraded.
Need to get 6318 kB of archives.
After this operation, 30.6 MB of additional disk space will be used.
Get:1 https://packages.microsoft.com/ubuntu/18.04/prod bionic/main amd64 moby-cli amd64 1.0.0-1 [6318 kB]
Fetched 6318 kB in 1s (9626 kB/s)
Selecting previously unselected package moby-cli.
(Reading database ... 56610 files and directories currently installed.)
Preparing to unpack .../moby-cli_1.0.0-1_amd64.deb ...
Unpacking moby-cli (1.0.0-1) ...
Setting up moby-cli (1.0.0-1) ...
iotedgedev@iotedge-linux-devtest:~$
```

Figure 3-26. *Installing IoT Edge container packages on Linux*

For Windows installations, the steps performed earlier that installed Docker for Windows, accomplished the same result as these commands. If you completed those steps, there are no further steps required to install a container runtime on Windows. If you did not complete those steps, please refer to that section and complete those steps now.

Install the Security Service

Now that your machine has been configured with the required perquisites, the IoT Edge security service can be installed. If you remember back to the discussion in the previous chapter, the security service is the initial service from which all other IoT Edge services are launched. It ensures all the system-level integrations are done in a secure way to prevent hacking or other forms of device tampering. To install the IoT Edge security service on Linux, run the commands shown in Listing 3-7.

Listing 3-7. Linux commands to install IoT Edge security service

```
sudo apt-get update
sudo apt-get install iotedge
```

The output from these commands should look similar to the output shown in Figure 3-27.

Figure 3-27.   *Installing the IoT Edge security service on Linux*

To install the IoT Edge security service on Windows, open a Powershell window as an Administrator and run the commands shown in Listing 3-8.

Listing 3-8.   Powershell command to install the IoT Edge security service

```
. {Invoke-WebRequest -useb aka.ms/iotedge-win} | Invoke-Expression;
Install-SecurityDaemon -Manual -ContainerOs Linux -DeviceConnectionString
'<connection-string>'
```

This command downloads a Powershell script which includes new commands related to (un)installing the security service. The Install-SecurityDaemon cmdlet can be invoked as either a manual device registration or as part of a device provisioning (DPS) workload.

Note   The Azure Device Provisioning Service (DPS) is an automated way to connect fleets of devices to Azure without having to individually configure each device. We will go into that service in detail in a later chapter.

The command line arguments for the Powershell script include:

- **Manual**: Indicates a manual device registration and will prompt for/ require the device connection string parameter.

  - **DeviceConnectionString**: Parameter that is requested only if "Manual" is specified on the command line. The value supplied should be the primary or secondary connection string for the *device*, not the IoT Hub.

Note   There are two main connection strings to be aware of in IoT Hub. The main connection string relates to overall service. There are also connection strings for each device. Pay close attention to whether instructions are requesting the IoT Hub connection string or the device connection string.

- **DPS**: Indicates the device is being automatically provisioned using the Azure Device Provisioning Service and will prompt for/require the DPS scope ID and registration ID.

  - **ScopeID**: A unique ID that indicates the device provisioning service the device should be registered to

  - **RegistrationID**: A unique ID that represents the device within the device provisioning scope

- **ContainerOS**: Specifies the type of containers to use on this machine. Valid values are "Windows" and "Linux."

Configure the Security Service

The security service creates several supporting files that are used to configure it. The main file is located at /etc/iotedge/config.yaml for Linux and C:\ProgramData\ iotedge\config.yaml for Windows. If you followed the steps above for installing the security service on a Windows machine, the Powershell script updated this file for you. If you followed the steps above for installing the security service on a Linux machine, you still need to configure the service with the device specific information.

Note   The configuration file is in YAML. Configuring an IoT Edge device does not require an in-depth knowledge of YAML, but if you are unfamiliar with the structure of a YAML and would like to read more about it, visit `http://yaml.org` for more information.

To configure the config.yaml file on a Linux machine, you can run the command in Listing 3-9 which launches the file into an editor.

Listing 3-9. Command to edit config.yaml file

```
sudo nano /etc/iotedge/config.yaml
```

Once you have the file open in the editor, look for the `provisioning` section and replace the `manual / device_connection_string` entry to be the device connection string for your device. Save and close the file, by typing `Ctrl + X`, then `Y`, then `Enter`. Once you have edited and saved the config.yaml file, you must restart the service for the changes to take effect. You can restart the service using the command in Listing 3-10.

Listing 3-10. Linux command to restart the iotedge security service

```
sudo systemctl restart iotedge
```

After the service restarts, you should be able to see information in the IoT Hub for the device. There isn't any deployment information associated with the device yet, but the device should have connected to the IoT Hub successfully. You can see an example of this by selecting the IoT Hub instance in the Azure portal and then selecting your device. The module listing at the bottom of the blade should look similar to the information in Figure 3-28. You can see the runtime status for the edgeAgent module is `running`, but there are no other running modules listed. Once you specify a deployment manifest for the device, other modules will be listed here and the status of each module will be reported. For now, if your device's information looks like Figure 3-28, you are in good shape.

Modules   IoT Edge hub connections   Deployments

| | Verify that your modules are included in the deployment, and whether your modules have been reported by the device. Click Set modules to change the modules that appear. Each device can host a maximum of 20 modules. |

NAME	TYPE	SPECIFIED IN DEPLOYMENT	REPORTED BY DEVICE	RUNTIME STATUS	EXIT CODE
SedgeAgent	IoT Edge System module	⊘ No	✓ Yes	running	-
SedgeHub	Module Identity	N/A	N/A	N/A	N/A

Figure 3-28. *IoT Hub information for the newly configured device*

As a point of reference, an entire config.yaml is included in Listing 3-11. There are some helpful comments included in the file that should help you become more familiar with the overall structure, format, and content of the file.

Listing 3-11. Example IoT Edge config.yaml file

```
###############################################################
#                    IoT Edge Daemon configuration
###############################################################
#
# This file configures the IoT Edge daemon. The daemon must be
# restarted to pick up any configuration changes.
#
# Note - this file is yaml.
# Learn more here: http://yaml.org/refcard.html
#
###############################################################

###############################################################
# Provisioning mode and settings
###############################################################
#
# Configures the identity provisioning mode of the daemon.
#
# Supported modes:
#     manual - using an iothub connection string
#     dps    - using dps for provisioning
#
###############################################################
```

```
provisioning:
  source: "manual"
  device_connection_string: "<DEVICE CONNECTION STRING HERE>"

# provisioning:
#   source: "dps"
#   global_endpoint: "https://global.azure-devices-provisioning.net"
#   scope_id: "{scope_id}"
#   registration_id: "{registration_id}"

###############################################################
# Certificate settings
###############################################################
#
# Configures the certificates required to operate the IoT Edge
# runtime as a gateway which enables external leaf devices to # securely
  communicate with the Edge Hub. If not specified,
# the required certificates are auto generated for quick start
# scenarios which are not intended for production
# environments.
#
# Settings:
#   device_ca_cert - path to the device ca cert and its chain
#   device_ca_pk   - path to the device ca private key file
#   trusted_ca_certs - path to a file with the trusted CA
#                      certificates required for Edge module
#                      communication
#
###############################################################

# certificates:
#   device_ca_cert: "<PATH TO DEVICE CA CERTIFICATE HERE>"
#   device_ca_pk: "<PATH TO DEVICE CA PRIVATE KEY HERE>"
#   trusted_ca_certs: "<PATH TO TRUSTED CA CERTIFICATES HERE>"
```

```
###############################################################
# Edge Agent module spec
###############################################################
#
# Configures the initial Edge Agent module.
#
# The daemon uses this definition to bootstrap the system.
# The Edge Agent can then update itself based on the Edge
# Agent module definition present in the deployment in
# IoT Hub.
#
###############################################################

agent:
  name: "edgeAgent"
  type: "docker"
  env: {}
  config:
    image: "mcr.microsoft.com/azureiotedge-agent:1.0"
    auth: {}

###############################################################
# Edge device hostname
###############################################################
#
# Configures the env variable 'IOTEDGE_GATEWAYHOSTNAME'
# injected into modules. Regardless of case the hostname is
# specified below, a lower case value is used to configure the
# Edge Hub server hostname as well as the environment variable
# specified above.
#
# It is important to note that when connecting downstream
# devices to the Edge Hub that the lower case value of this
# hostname be used in the 'GatewayHostName' field of the
# device's connection string URI.
###############################################################
```

```
hostname: "<ADD HOSTNAME HERE>"

###############################################################
# Connect settings
###############################################################
#
#
# Configures URIs used by clients of the management and
# workload APIs
#     management_uri - used by the Edge Agent and 'iotedge'
#                       CLI to start, stop, and manage modules
#     workload_uri  - used by modules to retrieve tokens and
#                       certificates
#
# The following uri schemes are supported:
#     http - connect over TCP
#
###############################################################

connect:
  management_uri: "http://<GATEWAY_ADDRESS>:15580"
  workload_uri: "http://<GATEWAY_ADDRESS>:15581"

###############################################################
# Listen settings
###############################################################
#
# Configures the listen addresses for the daemon.
#     management_uri - used by the Edge Agent and 'iotedge'
#                   CLI to start, stop, and manage modules
#     workload_uri - used by modules to retrieve tokens and
#                       certificates
#
# The following uri schemes are supported:
#     http - listen over TCP
#
###############################################################
```

```
listen:
  management_uri: "http://<GATEWAY_ADDRESS>:15580"
  workload_uri: "http://<GATEWAY_ADDRESS>:15581"

###############################################################
# Home Directory
###############################################################
#
# This configures the home directory for the daemon.
#
###############################################################

homedir: "C:\\ProgramData\\iotedge"


###############################################################
# Moby Container Runtime settings
###############################################################
#
# uri - configures the uri for the container runtime.
# network - configures the network on which the containers
#           will be created.
#
###############################################################

moby_runtime:
  uri: "npipe://./pipe/docker_engine"
# network: "nat"
```

Summary

In this chapter, we installed and configured all the tools necessary to develop and deploy IoT Edge solutions. We discussed the differences between VS Code and Visual Studio and walked through setting up both IDEs for IoT Edge development. In the next chapter, we will begin creating our first IoT Edge solution.

CHAPTER 4

Hello Edge

At this point in your edge computing journey, you have learned what it takes for your organization to start entertaining the edge computing paradigm, you have learned about the core concepts that enable and support the Azure IoT Edge platform, and you have configured your own development environment to begin building and deploying your edge solutions. But you have not actually built any code yet. In this chapter, we will walk through how to build your first edge solution, how to deploy it to your local development machine (which should be configured as an edge device at this point), and the iterative development process required to update the edge solution configuration. If you have not configured your development machine using the instructions in Chapter 3, this would be a good time to take care of that.

Once you have your development environment setup and ready, creating edge solutions is a straightforward process, in either VS Code or Visual Studio. As we will see, the IDEs scaffold a basic but functioning edge solution template that we can customize and modify.

As we walk through these examples, I will illustrate how to perform each task first in VS Code and then in Visual Studio. As of this writing, the VS Code tooling is more mature and handles more tasks than the tooling in Visual Studio. But the teams at Microsoft are constantly working to achieve feature parity in both IDEs. But, since there is a fairly large gap in tooling functionality at this point, I will highlight the differences between the two experiences.

© David Jensen 2019
D. Jensen, *Beginning Azure IoT Edge Computing*, https://doi.org/10.1007/978-1-4842-4536-1_4

Create a Solution Using VS Code

To create an edge solution using VS Code, first open VS Code, then press `Ctrl+Shift+P`
to open the command window, as shown in Figure 4-1.

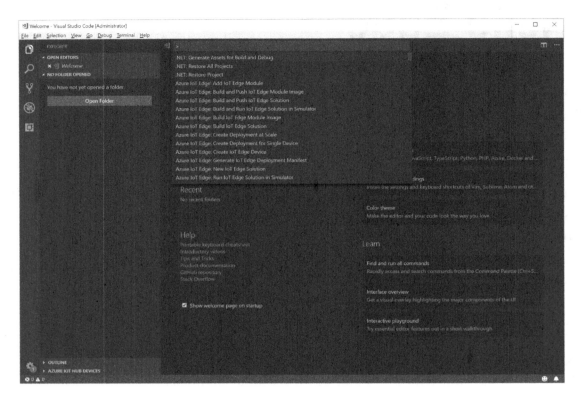

Figure 4-1. *VS Code command window*

In the command window, you can start typing "edge" and all "edge" related
commands will display, as shown in Figure 4-2.

Figure 4-2. *Azure IoT Edge related commands*

In this list, select the "New IoT Edge Solution" and press Enter. The tooling will then prompt you for the needed information: the solution root folder, the solution name, the edge module template to use during the initial solution scaffolding (we will be using the C# module template), the module name, and the address of the local docker registry you previously set up. Once you have entered all the information, your initial solution should look like the solution in Figure 4-3.

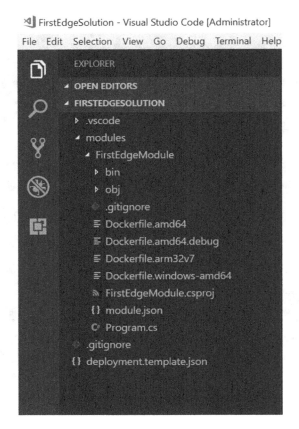

Figure 4-3. *Initial VS Code edge solution*

In this initial solution, the files and folders are organized in the recommended structure. It looks like the structure shown in Figure 4-4.

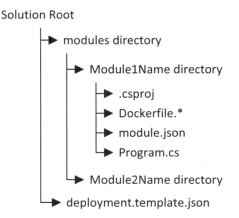

Figure 4-4. *Recommended edge solution structure*

As you look at the files in the initial solution, there are some files that should look familiar and some files that you likely have not seen before. Let's walk through a quick explanation of these files to understand how each file is used in the edge solution development process.

- **deployment.template.json** – The JSON-based template that contains all the required information for the edge runtime to download the Docker images, create the edge container modules and start them. It contains information about each edge module that should be deployed to the edge device, including the container registry and registry credentials if needed. Additionally, any Docker container create options are listed as well. Finally, any IoT Edge module-specific settings that are part of the module twin are included as well. Keep in mind that this file is merely used to generate the deployment.json file (not shown yet), which is the actual deployment instruction file.

- **Dockerfile.*** – If you have used Docker, then you should be familiar with Dockerfiles. The initially scaffolded solution includes several flavors of files for use with Docker.

  - **Dockerfile.amd64** – Dockerfile for Linux-based x86/x64 processors

  - **Dockerfile.amd64.debug** – Dockerfile for Linux-based x86/x64 processors that includes debug information and a separate container for the debugger

  - **Dockerfile.arm32v7** – Dockerfile for Linux-based ARM processors

  - **Dockerfile.windows-amd64** – Dockerfile for Windows IoT Core machines for x86/x64 processors

- **FirstEdgeModule.csproj** – The .csproj file based on .Net Core for the module. The name will vary, based on the module name you supplied during the scaffolding process. This file should be familiar to you if you have done any .Net development before now.

- **module.json** – A file that simplifies the interaction between the edge development environment and the Docker/build environment. This file simply lists all the available Docker build options and the IoT Edge plugin in VS Code inspects that file, when you issue a build command and prompts you to select the configuration you want to build. It then invokes the appropriate Docker build (and push) commands to complete the task.

- **Program.cs** – Contains the entry point for the C# module template (main()). The initial version of this file contains logic to register event handlers for the edge runtime.

Create a Solution Using Visual Studio

In this section, we will walk through the corresponding steps in Visual Studio to create our first edge solution. As a reminder, if you have not gone through the Visual Studio configuration steps in the previous chapter, please do that now. Once Visual Studio has been correctly configured, to create a solution in Visual Studio, select File ➤ New Project to launch the New Project dialog and select the Azure IoT Edge template, as shown in Figure 4-5.

Figure 4-5. *Azure IoT Edge project template in Visual Studio*

Then, select the module template you need to create, enter the required name and Docker repository and press OK, as shown in Figure 4-6. As of this writing, the only module template available in Visual Studio is C#.

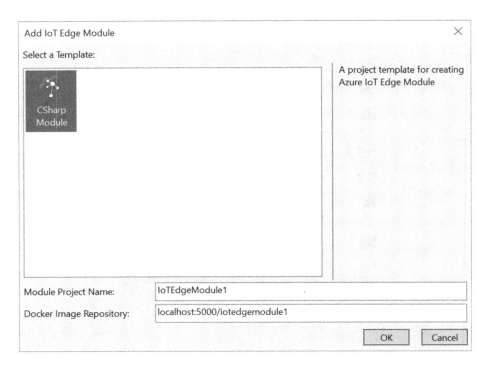

Figure 4-6. *Edge module Visual Studio module template selection*

Once the solution scaffolding has completed, the edge solution should look similar to the structure shown in Figure 4-7.

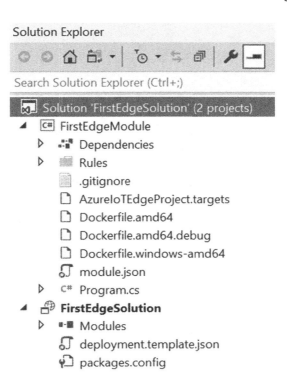

Figure 4-7. *Initial Visual Studio edge solution*

The files are the same as what we saw in the solution scaffolded in VS Code, they are just organized slightly differently in Visual Studio.

IoT Hub Connection String

In VS Code, it's helpful to connect the development environment to the IoT Hub that you previously set up. This will allow you to easily deploy your edge solutions to a device registered with the IoT Hub. This step is not required in Visual Studio, provided you previously updated the Cloud Explorer add-in and have connected it to the Azure subscription containing the IoT Hub you are working with.

To connect to the IoT Hub in VS Code, select the "Set IoT Hub Connection String" option in the IoT Toolkit extension window, as shown in Figure 4-8.

Figure 4-8. *Set IoT Hub connection string in VS Code*

This will open a command window prompt, into which you can paste the IoT connection string.

Note   Remember that there are two types of connection strings in the IoT Hub world: connection strings for the IoT Hub instance and connection strings for the device. The connection string referred to in this section is the IoT Hub instance connection string, not the device connection string.

Once you have correctly entered the service connection string, the list of devices should appear in the window.

Exploring the Solution Actions

Now that we have a general understanding of the initial project artifacts and the overall structure, we will take a more detailed look at each of the most important files and explain how to build upon the template to create a customized edge solution. All of the artifacts I have mentioned up to this point can be grouped into one of three actions: *develop*, *build*, or *deploy*. Develop includes all the C# code (or another language if you are working with another module template). Build includes the Docker files and other files used to assist in creating the Docker images. And finally, deployment includes the files used to take the Docker images, describe the inter-container message interactions and deploy that manifest to a target edge device. A high-level interaction between the groups of files can be seen in Figure 4-9.

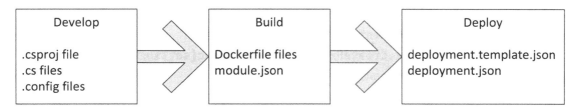

Figure 4-9. *Edge solution artifact actions*

Develop

Let's begin to examine the Develop activity by looking into the Program.cs file that was created for us as part of the initial solution. As stated earlier, this file defines the entry point for each module you will develop. There is a static void Main(string[] args) method just as in other C# applications. An example is shown in Listing 4-1.

Listing 4-1. Example Main() method

```
static void Main(string[] args)
{
    Init().Wait();

    // Wait until the app unloads or is cancelled
    var cts = new CancellationTokenSource();
    AssemblyLoadContext.Default.Unloading +=
        (ctx) => cts.Cancel();
    Console.CancelKeyPress += (sender, cpe) => cts.Cancel();
    WhenCancelled(cts.Token).Wait();
}
```

This method is mainly responsible for invoking the asynchronous Init() method, registering a cancelation event handler and then waiting for a cancelation event (shutdown) to occur. The Init() method is shown in Listing 4-2.

Listing 4-2. Example Init() method

```
static async Task Init()
{
    AmqpTransportSettings amqpSetting =
      new AmqpTransportSettings(TransportType.Amqp_Tcp_Only);
    ITransportSettings[] settings = { amqpSetting };
```

```
// Open a connection to the Edge runtime
ModuleClient moduleClient =
  await ModuleClient.CreateFromEnvironmentAsync(settings);
await moduleClient.OpenAsync();
Console.WriteLine("IoT Hub module client initialized.");

// Register callback to be called when a message
// is received by the module
await moduleClient.SetInputMessageHandlerAsync("input1",
  PipeMessage, moduleClient);
}
```

ModuleClient

In the Init method shown in Listing 4-2, we start to see some of the edge-specific code that wires up the module to the edge runtime. First, notice the line where an instance of the ModuleClient class is created. ModuleClient is the primary API used to interact with the edge runtime. There are several static method options available to create an instance of the class. The one shown in Listing 4-2 supplies the transport settings that depend on environment variables in the edge runtime for the remaining values. There are several possible ways to create a ModuleClient instance. But, all of the possible options are in one of three overloaded methods: Create, CreateFromConnectionString, CreateFromEnvironment.

- Create: Accepts some combination of the following parameters that are explicitly passed into the constructor.

  - Hostname: The fully qualified DNS name of the IoT Hub.

  - authenticationMethod: The authentication method used for this connection. Refer to the section on Authentication Methods later in this chapter.

  - gatewayHostname: The fully qualified DNS name of the gateway (in the case where you have a hierarchy of edge devices and some edge devices serve as gateways for other edge devices).

  - transportSettings: A prioritized list of the transport types and their settings. Refer to the section on transport settings later in this chapter.

  - transportType: An enumeration with the values shown in Table 4-1.

Table 4-1. *Transport Types*

Transport Type	Description
Http1	HTTP version 1 transport
Amqp	Try AMQP over TCP first and fallback to AMQP over WebSocket if that fails
Amqp_WebSocket_Only	AMQP over WebSockets only
Amqp_Tcp_Only	AMQP over native TCP only
Mqtt	Try MQTT over TCP first and failback to MQTT over WebSocket if that fails
Mqtt_WebSocket_Only	MQTT over WebSocket only
Mqtt_Tcp_Only	MQTT over native TCP only

- CreateFromConnectionString: Accepts the device connection string along with some combination of other values. If values are not supplied, the default values are used.

  - connectiongString: The device connection string from the device info in the IoT Hub.

  - transportSettings: A prioritized list of the transport types and their settings. Refer to the section on transport settings later in this chapter.

  - transportType: An enumeration with the values shown in Table 4-1.

- CreateFromEnvironment: Accepts transport settings and relies on the remainder of the required information to be retrieved from environment variables. The values of the environment variables are populated from the config.yaml described in earlier chapters.

  - transportSettings: A prioritized list of the transport types and their settings. Refer to the section on transport settings later in this chapter.

  - transportType: An enumeration with the values shown in Table 4-1.

Once you have created an instance of the ModuleClient, you can begin to interact with it and the messages being sent and received. The ModuleClient has a few groups of methods. There are methods that handle receiving and acknowledging messages from the edgeHub message broker. There are methods that handle the opening and closing of the underlying client connection. There are methods that handle registering for events that occur in the edge runtime. And there are methods that handle retrieving and updating the properties associated with the module in the module twin. Here is a breakdown of these `ModuleClient` methods into their respective group.

- ModuleClient connection management

  - OpenAsync: Opens the client transport layer

  - CloseAsync: Closes the client transport layer

- Message receipt and acknowledgment

  - AbandonAsync: Accepts a message and abandons the message to be placed back on the module message queue

  - CompleteAsync: Accepts a message and removes the message from the module message queue

- Twin property retrieval and updating

  - GetTwinAsync: Retrieves the module twin for the current module

  - UpdateReportedPropertiesAsync: Pushes updated property changes to the IoT Hub, which updates the reported values on the module twin

- Message publishing to the edgeHub broker

  - SendEventAsync: Accepts an output name and one message to publish

  - SendEventBatchAsync: Accepts an output name and a list of messages to publish

- Runtime event handling

  - SetConnectionStatusChangeHandler: Registers a callback that is invoked when the module connection state changes. The callback will be supplied a value for the current connection status as well as the reason for the state change (retry expired, SAS token expired, client closed, etc.).

- SetDesiredPropertyUpdateCallbackAsync: Registers a callback that is invoked when a desired property state is updated in the service.

- SetInputMessageHandlerAsync: Registers a callback that responds to messages specified for a specific input. This is the primary way to subscribe to an individual message topic.

- SetMessageHandlerAsync: Registers a default callback that is invoked if no individual input handler is registered or if a message is addressed to an input handler that does not exist.

- SetMethodHandlerAsync: Registers a callback for a specific, named direct method invocation.

- SetMethodDefaultHandlerAsync: Registers a default callback that is invoked if no individual method handler is registered.

IoT Hub Authentication

As you saw in the description of the `ModuleClient` class, there are several constructors that accept parameters called "authenticationMethod". These instances are class instances that implement `IAuthenticationMethod` from the `Microsoft.Azure.Devices.Client` namespace. There are several options you can choose from and it's helpful to understand the difference between the various options, to ensure you're picking the correct implementation. Before we go into detail on the different method options, let's review a couple of concepts that relate to IoT Hub security in general.

There are three main types of device security used in IoT Hub: symmetric keys, X.509 certificates, TPM (trusted platform module) chips. Within the symmetric key option, there are two sub-options: device level keys (generated when the device is added to the IoT Hub) and SAS policy keys. SAS policies allow a user to define specific permissions associated with a key. Examples of out-of-the-box SAS policies are:

- Service: Allows the service connect permission (sending and receiving messages on the service endpoints)

- Device: Allows the device connect permission (sending and receiving messages on the device endpoints)

- RegistryRead: Allows the registry read permission (reading from the device identity metadata registry)

- RegistryReadWrite: Allows the registry read and registry write permissions (reading and updating the device identity metadata registry)

- Iothubowner: Allows the device connect, service connect, registry read and registry write permissions (all of the above actions)

In a canonical IoT scenario, the IoT Hub will have a set of keys for each device registered with the service and a set of keys that relate to the SAS policies listed above. However, in IoT Edge scenarios, there are additional keys generated. In addition to the device-level keys, each IoT *module* has a set of keys. You might wonder why IoT Edge devices could not just use the device-level security concepts as regular IoT devices. Think about multiple departments within an organization that might need to build, deploy and secure modules independent of each other. In a typical factory, there are some controls that must be more secure than others. If a single IoT Edge device is deployed to a factory, it is possible for that one edge device to be connected to multiple factory machines or multiple inputs on the same machine. In this case, there could be multiple modules, each connected to a separate input. In this scenario, one department might need to secure one input differently from another. Module-level keys allow this capability.

One final concept to be aware of is the concept of tokens. Security tokens in the context of Azure IoT imply a time-constrained permission. That is, the permission will expire at some point. The previous security options do not expire. If you have the key or the certificate, you can access the resource. But, those keys can be used to generate tokens that do expire.

All of that is foundational to the edge device authentication methods available. There are eight different `IAuthenticationMethod` options you can instantiate and supply to the `ModuleClient` constructor. Here is a brief description of each.

Table 4-2. *Device authentication methods*

Authentication Method	Description
DeviceAuthenticationWithRegistrySymmetricKey	Uses the device-level symmetric key **Required**: deviceID, key
DeviceAuthenticationWithSharedAccessPolicyKey	Uses a shared access policy key **Required**: deviceID, key, policy name
DeviceAuthenticationWithToken	Uses a generated shared access token **Required**: deviceID, token
DeviceAuthenticationWithX509Certificate	Uses an X.509 certificate **Required**: deviceID, certificate
DeviceAuthenticationWithTpm	Uses SAS token from TPM interface **Required**: deviceID, TPM provider **Optional**: TTL in seconds, TTL buffer %
ModuleAuthenticationWithTokenRefresh	Uses SAS token, allows token refresh **Required**: deviceID, moduleID **Optional**: TTL in seconds, TTL buffer %
ModuleAuthenticationWithRegistrySymmetricKey	Uses module-level symmetric key **Required**: deviceID, moduleID, key
ModuleAuthenticationWithToken	Uses a generated shared access token **Required**: deviceID, moduleID, token

Transport Settings

Transport settings are used to control the communication protocol between the device and the IoT Hub endpoints. The supported protocols are AMQP, MQTT, and HTTP. The transport settings are used in conjunction with the TransportType enumeration listed in Table 4-1. The TransportType values control the behavior of how each protocol is managed. The available implementations of ITransportSettings are listed in Table 4-3.

Table 4-3. *Valid TransportSettings and TransportTypes*

Transport Setting	Valid TransportType Options
AmqpTransportSettings	Amqp, Amqp_Tcp_Only, Amqp_WebSocket_Only
Http1TransportSettings	Http1
MqttTransportSettings	Mqtt, Mqtt_Tcp_Only, Mqtt_WebSocket_only

Message Handler

To further illustrate the Develop actions, let's look at the implementation provided in the initial project that was scaffolded earlier. In Listing 4-2, the last line registers an input message handler using the delegate `PipeMessage`. The implementation of `PipeMessage` is shown in Listing 4-3.

Listing 4-3. Example input message handler

```
static async Task<MessageResponse> PipeMessage(Message message, object
userContext)
{
  int counterValue = Interlocked.Increment(ref counter);

  var moduleClient = userContext as ModuleClient;
  if (moduleClient == null)
  {
    throw new InvalidOperationException("UserContext " +
    "doesn't contain expected values");
  }

  byte[] messageBytes = message.GetBytes();
  string messageStr = Encoding.UTF8.GetString(messageBytes);
  Console.WriteLine($"Received message: {counterValue}, " +
                    Body: [{messageString}]");

  if (!string.IsNullOrEmpty(messageString))
  {
    var pipeMessage = new Message(messageBytes);
    foreach (var prop in message.Properties)
```

```
  {
    pipeMessage.Properties.Add(prop.Key, prop.Value);
  }
  await moduleClient.SendEventAsync("output1", pipeMessage);
  Console.WriteLine("Received message sent");
  }
  return MessageResponse.Completed;
}
```

In this example, the edge runtime supplies the message to the event handler and the event handler essentially creates a copy of the message and then publishes the new message to the output1 named output. The named outputs do not have to be defined anywhere. But, keep in mind any name that is specified in these output event handlers must match the name specified in any routes that are intended to publish to this input.

As we wrap up this introduction on the Develop actions in an edge solution, there is one mindset that is helpful to remember when building edge solutions. Edge development is primarily event driven. There are a few cases where it's not, but almost everything you develop for an edge solution will involve defining event handlers to process incoming events or defining output event handlers to publish an event. So, understanding the available methods on the ModuleClient class to work with the events is foundational in your journey to master edge solution development. Let's move on to discuss how to build an edge solution.

Build

Building an edge solution is a different experience than the typical experience of running and debugging within the IDE. Because an edge solution is based on Docker containers, the container images must first be built and pushed to a container registry. Then, a deployment manifest is sent to a device that pulls those images to the local device, instantiates the containers and wires them together. In this scenario, the "build" step is much more disconnected from the "run" (deploy) step than most developers are used to. In Visual Studio, VS Code or Eclipse, we are used to building, running, and launching an app all with the single press of a button. You will have to adjust, but there are some dev tools starting to emerge that make the build, deploy, and debug tasks much more approachable.

You may have noticed the Dockerfile variants that were generated as part of the initial solution creation. They may seem appropriate, given the fact that you know edge development is based on Docker and containers. But, the module.json file is probably new to you, leaving you wondering what it is and how to use it. You can think of the module.json file as one that contains a list of build configurations (Dockerfiles). So, module.json is really a wrapper around any Dockerfiles that are part of the module. You can see how this works if you right click the module.json in the edge solution you just created and select "Build IoT Edge Module Image" option. An example of this is shown in Figure 4-10.

Figure 4-10.   *Build module using module.json*

After you select the option, you will see the command window (in VS Code) prompt you to select a configuration to build. And, you should notice that the options listed are built using the of names of the `"platforms"` section of the `module.json` file. This is shown in Figure 4-11.

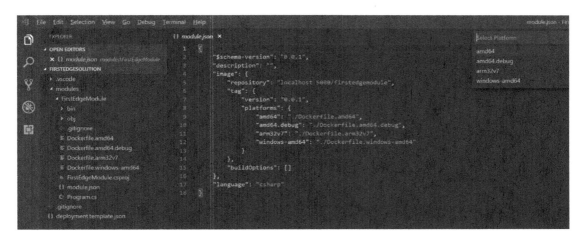

Figure 4-11. *Build options command prompt*

The only restriction for the `platforms` section is that it must be valid JSON. Which means if you have several Dockerfiles and need to name them something meaningful to your process or team, you have the freedom to rename those labels. You may also have multiple values point to the same Dockerfile if you need that flexibility. Think of the `platforms` section as a list of the valid build configurations you need to support. When you select one of the options to build, the VS Code tooling will initiate the docker commands to complete a docker build using the referenced Dockerfile.

Additionally, if you select the "Build and Push IoT Module Image" option from the menu in Figure 4-10, the VS Code tooling will not only build the image, it will tag the image with the value listed as the `repository` value and push the image to that repository. So, in the example shown in Figure 4-11, after a successful image build of the amd64 configuration, the image would be tagged as `localhost:5000/firstedgemodule:0.0.1-amd64` and pushed to the local repository. The pattern for the tag value is shown in Listing 4-4, which shows the values from the `module.json` JSON structure:

Listing 4-4. Docker tag format from module.json properties

```
{repository}:{tag.version}-{tag.platform}
```

Now, let's briefly look at these same commands using the Visual Studio tooling. In Visual Studio, the context menus are connected to the IoT Edge project (.iotedgeproj extension). When you right click that project, you will see the menu displayed in Figure 4-12.

Figure 4-12. *IoT Edge build menu in Visual Studio*

One of the first things to observe is that the tooling is expecting a certain set of platforms in the module.json file. You cannot rename those platforms as you can in VS Code. Another difference to be aware of in Visual Studio is that when you build using the tooling, you are dealing with the IoT Edge project, not the individual modules. The side of effect of this is that you must include any modules you want to build into that project first. If you aren't sure if your module will be built, you can expand the `Modules` node in the Solution Explorer, as shown in Figure 4-13.

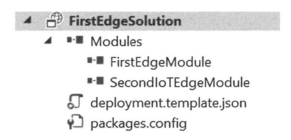

Figure 4-13. *Module list in IoT Edge project*

There are options on the context menu to add edge projects to this orchestration project and you can remove projects as well if needed. The end result of coordinating the build process through a single project is that, for any single build operation, all projects in the list of this IoT Edge project must be built with the same configuration. For example, if there are two projects in your edge solution and you want to build a debug version for one of them, you will have to first remove the project you do not want to debug, then build the debug image, using the context menu options shown in Figure 4-12.

All of this inflexibility in the Visual Studio tooling is likely due to how immature it is. At the time of this writing, the roadmap for this tooling is not clear. But Microsoft is working toward feature parity between VS Code and Visual Studio.

Deploy

The third action supported in an edge solution is deploying the code to an edge device. Just to be clear on the prerequisites for the deploy activities, let's review what must be completed in order to deploy. You must have coded and developed at least one module and built it into a Docker container image. Additionally, you must have pushed that image to a container registry, either a hosted container registry or a local registry. Once you have the images ready, you are ready to assign the deployment manifest to an edge device. When the edge runtime has the deployment manifest, it will handle pulling the images to the device, starting the containers and managing the health of the containers.

The deployment manifest file is named `deployment.json` and it is generated from the `deployment.template.json` file that is included in the initial edge solution.

Generating the manifest is a single easy step using the tooling in either VS Code or Visual Studio. An example generating the manifest in VS Code is shown in Figure 4-14.

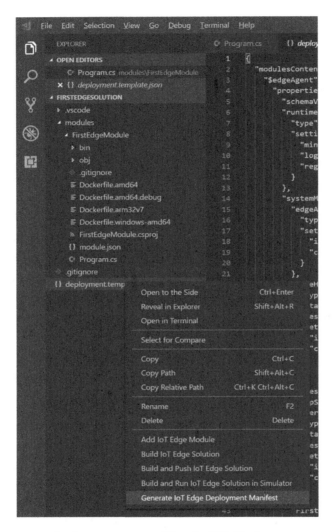

Figure 4-14. *Generate deployment manifest in VS Code*

The result of this is a `deployment.json` file in the config directory of the solution root directory. Now, let's examine both the deployment template and the generated deployment manifest files. You can click the `deployment.template.json` file to view the contents, but it might be easier to understand the structure through a visualization. A high-level view of the file can be seen in Figure 4-15.

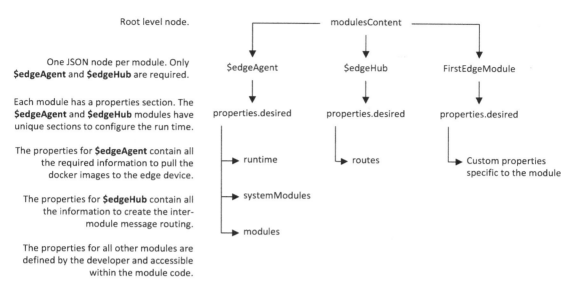

Figure 4-15. *Visual summary of the edge deployment manifest file*

The $edgeAgent and $edgeHub have specialized property sections in the manifest and those sections must be understood to properly configure your edge device. Tables 4-4 and 4-5 list the $edgeAgent and $edgeHub specific properties, respectively.

Table 4-4. *$edgeAgent properties*

Property Name	Description
runtime.type	Must always be "docker."
runtime.settings.minDockerVersion	The minimum Docker version required for this deployment.
runtime.settings.loggingOptions	The Docker logging options to use for the $edgeAgent container.[1]
runtme.settings.registryCredentials	The user name, password and address for any container registries the run time needs to access. There can be one or many sets of credentials.
systemModules.edgeAgent	Module information defined in Table 4-6.
systemModules.edgeHub	Module information defined in Table 4-6.

---

[1]To read more about the Docker logging options, visit https://docs.docker.com/config/containers/logging/configure

Table 4-5. *$edgeHub Properties*

Property Name	Description
routes	A list of name/value pairs of routes. The name of the route can be free form. The value of the route must follow the route definition guidelines described in the Core Concepts chapter.

Table 4-6. *Module Information JSON Structure*

Property Name	Description
type	Must be "docker."
status	For the system modules ($edgeHub, $edgeAgent), it must be "running." For custom modules, it can be: • Stopped: After being deployed, the module will remain idle until called upon to start by you or another module. • Running: This is the default option. The module will start running immediately after being deployed.
restartPolicy	For the system modules ($edgeHub, $edgeAgent), it must be "always." For custom modules, it can be: • Never: The module never restarts if it shuts down for any reason. • On-failed: The module restarts if it crashes, but not if it shuts down cleanly. • On-unhealthy: The module restarts if it crashes or returns an unhealthy status. It's up to each module to implement the health status function. • Always: The module always restarts if it shuts down for any reason.
settings.image	The URI to the module image.
settings. createOptions	Stringified JSON containing the options for the creation of the container.[2]

As you begin to look in your solution's deployment.template.json file, you should see a JSON segment that looks like the code in Listing 4-5.

---

[2]To read about all the available create options, visit https://docs.docker.com/engine/api/ v1.32/#operation/ContainerCreate

Listing 4-5. Module information in deployment.template.json

```
"FirstEdgeModule": {
  "version": "1.0",
  "type": "docker",
  "status": "running",
  "restartPolicy": "always",
  "settings": {
    "image": "${MODULES.FirstEdgeModule.amd64}",
    "createOptions": "{}"
  }
}
```

The entry for the module image location is a variable that maps to a build configuration in the module.json file. When you generate the deployment manifest as shown in Figure 4-14, any variables that exist in the deployment.template.json file will be replaced with the literal values from the module.json file into the generated deployment.json file. For example, in the code shown in Listing 4-5, if the corresponding module.json file looks like the code in Listing 4-6, the resulting entry in the generated deployment.json file would be localhost:5000/firstedgemodule:0.0.1-amd64.

Listing 4-6. module.json file

```
{
    "$schema-version": "0.0.1",
    "description": "",
    "image": {
        "repository": "localhost:5000/firstedgemodule",
        "tag": {
            "version": "0.0.1",
            "platforms": {
                "amd64": "./Dockerfile.amd64",
                "amd64.debug": "./Dockerfile.amd64.debug",
                "arm32v7": "./Dockerfile.arm32v7",
                "windows-amd64": "./Dockerfile.windows-amd64"
            }
        },
```

```
        "buildOptions": []
    },
    "language": "csharp"
}
```

The tooling uses the repository and the specified build platform in module.json to construct the image URI for deployment.json. Variable substitutions are also allowed in module.json. Substitution of variables is most helpful when build CI/CD pipelines for IoT Edge solutions.

Once you have a generated deployment manifest, right click the file in VS Code and you will see options similar to Figure 4-16.

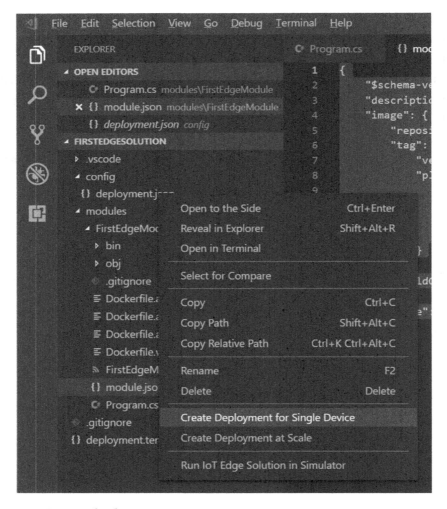

Figure 4-16. *Create deployment options*

For now, select the option to create a deployment for a single device. VS Code will prompt you to select a device from the devices connected to the configured IoT Hub. Creating a deployment at scale will be discussed in the chapter on the Device Provisioning Service. When you select the device to target for the deployment, the IoT Hub translates the single deployment manifest file into module twins for each of the modules listed in the manifest, including the twin for edgeHub and edgeAgent, and updates the twins accordingly. Once the twins have been updated, the edge runtime is notified there are changes and it pulls down the twin information and updates, creates, or removes modules as needed, based on the module name and version number.

The tooling support for edge deployment in Visual Studio is slightly different than VS Code. To generate the deployment manifest in Visual Studio, right click the IoT Edge Project in the solution explorer, as shown in Figure 4-17.

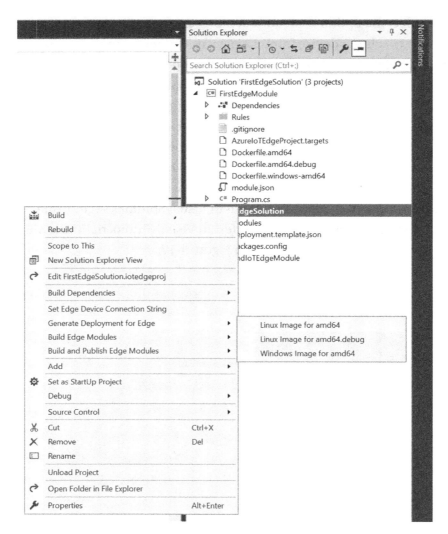

Figure 4-17. *Generate deployment manifest in Visual Studio*

This generates the `deployment.json` file to the same `./config` directory, but the file is not visible in the solution explorer as it was in VS Code. To deploy this generated file to a single device, navigate to the device in the Cloud Explorer window and right click the device, as shown in Figure 4-18.

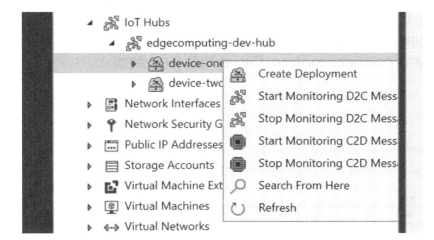

Figure 4-18. *Create a single device deployment in Visual Studio*

When you select the Create Deployment option, Visual Studio will open up a File Explorer window in the directory where generated manifest is stored. Simply select the file and the tooling will enforce the same updates behind the scenes as VS Code.

Running Your Solution

Now that you are familiar with the content of the edge solution and the main types of actions you can perform using the tooling in either VS Code or Visual Studio, let's deploy our initial edge solution and verify that's working. To do this, make sure you have built each individual module image and pushed the image to a container registry (localhost:5000 is a good place to start for local development). Additionally, make sure you have generated the deployment manifest and then deploy that manifest to a single device. Make sure that you target the device you set up in the previous chapter when you configured your development environment. Figure 4-19 show the output from building and pushing my custom module to the local Docker registry.

Note   Keep in mind that your container registry must be accessible from your edge device. Otherwise, the edge runtime on the device will not be able to pull the needed images. So, if you are pushing your images to the local Docker registry (localhost:5000), you must use the edge runtime on the machine hosting that local registry. If you are deploying your edge solution to a different device from your development machine, the container registry must be in a publicly available location (Azure Container Registry or Docker Hub, for example).

```
---> Using cache
---> 29aa1fff1f49
Step 10/12 : RUN useradd -ms /bin/bash moduleuser
---> Using cache
---> e9f22eb857b8
Step 11/12 : USER moduleuser
---> Using cache
---> 8aef2ec17f81
Step 12/12 : ENTRYPOINT ["dotnet", "FirstEdgeModule.dll"]
---> Using cache
---> b76f46360134
Successfully built b76f46360134
Successfully tagged localhost:5000/firstedgemodule:0.0.1-amd64
SECURITY WARNING: You are building a Docker image from Windows against a non-Windows Docker host. All files and directories added to bu
The push refers to repository [localhost:5000/firstedgemodule]
61b5581f71bb: Pushed
2a731d10f21a: Pushed
4ffcd604408c: Pushed
deb1fcb724d8: Pushed
e67e29c96730: Pushed
3e992aa287e9: Pushed
237472299760: Pushed
0.0.1-amd64: digest: sha256:32d1f5037e15c30da13482f575020ed1f22808448dbc8b873bca4d329611e76c size: 1789
PS C:\Users\iotedgedev\Documents\FirstEdgeSolution> ▌
```

Figure 4-19. *VS Code output from building and pushing custom module*

Make sure the edge runtime service is running. To check this, run one of the following commands:

- Linux: `sudo systemctl status iotedge`

- Windows: `Get-Service iotedge`

Once you have assigned the deployment manifest to the edge device, the edge runtime will start to pull the images and create Docker containers based on those images. You can see what containers are currently running by running the command: `docker ps`. If you are running the initial edge solution we have been working with throughout this chapter, the output will look like the output in Figure 4-20.

```
PS C:\Users\iotedgedev> docker ps
CONTAINER ID   IMAGE                                                    COMMAND                CREATED         STATUS          PORTS                                                                            NAMES
bf603ce907f    mcr.microsoft.com/azureiotedge-hub:1.0                   "/bin/sh -c 'echo \"$…" 46 seconds ago  Up 41 seconds   0.0.0.0:443->443/tcp, 0.0.0.0:5671->5671/tcp, 0.0.0.0:8883->8883/tcp            edgeHub
9c6cacbb7da1   mcr.microsoft.com/azureiotedge-simulated-temperature-sensor:1.0  "/bin/sh -c 'echo \"$…" 51 seconds ago  Up 46 seconds                                                                                    tempSensor
be3920a541bd   localhost:5000/firstedgemodule:0.0.1-amd64               "dotnet firstedgemod…"  50 seconds ago  Up 53 seconds                                                                                    FirstEdgeModule
b6519962c365   mcr.microsoft.com/azureiotedge-agent:1.0                 "/bin/sh -c 'echo \"$…" 3 minutes ago   Up 5 minutes                                                                                     edgeAgent
ffe8a10cd5e6   registry:2                                               "/entrypoint.sh /etc…"  2 months ago    Up 31 minutes   0.0.0.0:5000->5000/tcp                                                           registry
PS C:\Users\iotedgedev> _
```

Figure 4-20. *docker ps output*

You should see four running edge modules and a fifth line for the local registry if you have it running. The Temperature Sensor module (tempSensor) is a module provided by Microsoft that generates telemetry to test with. This eliminates the need to connect to either a physical or virtual device to start handling messages and data. Additionally, the

C# module template we used in our first edge solution is ready to handle the telemetry generated by this tempSensor module. To view this data, run the command in Listing 4-7.

Listing 4-7. Viewing module output

```
docker logs -f tempSensor
```

The docker logs command displays the console output for the module specified. The output for the tempSensor module looks like the sample in Listing 4-8.

Listing 4-8. tempSensor output

```
Sending message: 238, Body: [{"machine":{"temperature":100.29815234851478,"
pressure":10.033966723248518},"ambient":{"temperature":21.250450821942859,"
humidity":26},"timeCreated":"2018-11-10T04:47:58.3126199Z"}]
```

Next, we can look at the output from our custom module, which is configured to process the telemetry generated from the tempSensor module. To view its' output, run the command in Listing 4-7, but specify the name of your module (FirstEdgeModule), rather than tempSensor. You should see output similar to what is shown in Listing 4-9.

Listing 4-9. FirstEdgeModule output

```
Received message: 315, Body: [{"machine":{"temperature":102.57867492541149,
"pressure":10.293773092768397},"ambient":{"temperature":21.076086747262668,
"humidity":25},"timeCreated":"2018-11-10T04:54:26.7116022Z"}]
Received message sent
```

Just to refresh your memory the code that is generating this output is shown in Listing 4-10.

Listing 4-10. Custom event handler method

```
static async Task<MessageResponse> PipeMessage(Message message, object
userContext)
{
  int counterValue = Interlocked.Increment(ref counter);

  var moduleClient = userContext as ModuleClient;
  if (moduleClient == null)
```

115

```
  {
    throw new InvalidOperationException("UserContext doesn't"+
          " contain expected values");
  }

  byte[] messageBytes = message.GetBytes();
  string msgString = Encoding.UTF8.GetString(messageBytes);
  Console.WriteLine($"Received message: {counterValue}, " +
                    Body: [{messageString}]");

  if (!string.IsNullOrEmpty(messageString))
  {
    var pipeMessage = new Message(messageBytes);
    foreach (var prop in message.Properties)
    {
      pipeMessage.Properties.Add(prop.Key, prop.Value);
    }
    await moduleClient.SendEventAsync("output1", pipeMessage);
    Console.WriteLine("Received message sent");
  }
  return MessageResponse.Completed;
}
```

This simple method accepts the message from the generated telemetry module, prints out that message, then creates a new message, copying all of the properties from the original message. Then, it sends that message to the output1 named address. Refer to the previous section on routing if you need to be reminded. Lastly, the routes that were added to the initial solution as part of the scaffolding process are shown in the Listing 4-11.

Listing 4-11. Initial deployment manifest routes

```
"routes": {
"FirstEdgeModuleToIoTHub":
"FROM /messages/modules/FirstEdgeModule/outputs/*
INTO $upstream",
```

"sensorToFirstEdgeModule":
```
"FROM /messages/modules/tempSensor/outputs/temperatureOutput
INTO
BrokeredEndpoint(\"/modules/FirstEdgeModule/inputs/input1\")"
}
```

As a quick refresher, the sensorToFirstEdgeModule route sends messages coming from the temperatureOutput in the tempSensor module and sends those messages to input1 in the FirstEdgeModule module. The event handler for input1 was registered to be the PipeMessage method shown in Listing 4-10. The FirstEdgeModuleToIoTHub route takes the messages sent to any output of the FirstEdgeModule and routes those messages to the IoT Hub ($upstream).

Summary

In this chapter, we looked at how to create an initial edge solution using the tooling in both Visual Studio and VS Code. We examined the parts of the initially scaffolded solution, including the custom C# code, the module.json file, and both the deployment.template.json and deployment.json files. We discussed the three main activities the development tooling enables – develop, build, and deploy – and discussed the related steps to each one of those activities. Finally, we looked at how to deploy the edge solution, verify it is running, and look at the module output in the docker logs. In the next chapter, we will take this knowledge and begin to make some changes to our solution and learn how to debug edge solutions as well.

CHAPTER 5

Developing and Debugging Edge Modules

Hopefully, you're starting to feel more comfortable understanding IoT Edge solutions, modules, and their related code and configuration files. Last chapter, we took a detailed look at how Azure IoT Edge solutions are structured, along with much of the tooling involved to develop, build, and deploy edge solutions and modules. In this chapter we will further examine the development and debugging experience, using the tooling in VS Code and Visual Studio and some command line utilities. The tooling we looked at last chapter is a great start for creating, building, and deploying your edge solutions, but there's more to the development process than that. As an edge solution developer, you need to be able to add additional modules and debug your solution. Fortunately, there are some great tools we can leverage to help us with this process.

Edge Development Process

As you gain experience in developing edge solutions, you will begin to see there are several tasks that you do repeatedly. A common iterative development process is shown in Figure 5-1.

119

© David Jensen 2019
D. Jensen, *Beginning Azure IoT Edge Computing*, https://doi.org/10.1007/978-1-4842-4536-1_5

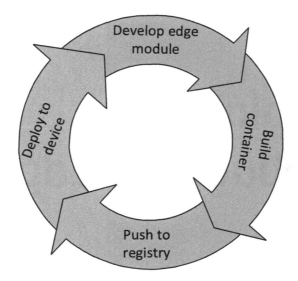

Figure 5-1. *Common edge development process*

This diagram illustrates the core actions we discussed in the last chapter and how they feed each other during the development process. This dev/test process is more involved than you may be used to when developing web apps, desktop apps, or utility console apps. In those cases, you are able to run the code in a local runtime environment, so running and testing your code changes are a simple "F5" press away. In order to develop and test your edge solutions, you must make your code changes, then you must build the container and push that container to a container registry. Finally, after the container is in a container registry, you can deploy the container to the edge device, where your testing must occur. This process holds true, even if the edge device you're testing on is your local development machine. This process is more cumbersome and error-prone than we are used to when developing solutions. An immediate feedback loop is key to developing software that is more bug-free. The edge development process just described does not have a tight feedback loop and, as a result, has the potential to introduce bugs.

However, there are some tools that are now available to help this process and make it less cumbersome by speeding up the feedback loop. These tools are: Azure IoT Edge Dev Tool and Azure IoT EdgeHub Dev Tool (a.k.a. the edge simulator). In the next two sections, we will review both of these tools to demonstrate some ways they can help simplify the edge dev/test process.

Azure IoT EdgeHub Dev Tool

The first tool we will look at that is helpful in the edge development and debugging process is the edge simulator, officially known as the Azure IoT EdgeHub Dev Tool. It simulates the local edge runtime environment, without requiring an active connection to an IoT Hub instance[1] which also eliminates the requirement to publish deployment manifests through IoT Hub. It also does not require us to push our edge module image to a container registry. We do still have to *build* the edge module image, but it can remain locally on our development machine. These are a few of the ways this simulator tool simplifies the process of development and testing our modules before publishing them. It is very useful for creating a test environment where we can isolate the testing of our module code and not have to worry so much about the configuration of the edge runtime environment and all of the other dependencies that must be in place for our edge solutions to run properly.

When running the simulator from the command line, there are four different commands you can use: `setup`, `start`, `stop`, and `modulecred`. We will discuss each of these in this section.

Before you use the simulator, you must install it. The simulator utility is a python pip package that can be installed using the command in Listing 5-1.

Listing 5-1. Install edgeHub simulator

```
pip install --upgrade iotedgehubdev
```

In case this isn't obvious, you must have python (2.7 or 3.5+, 3.5+ is recommended) and pip installed in order to install this package. After you have those prerequisites installed and you run the above command, you should see output similar to Listing 5-2.

Listing 5-2. iotedgehubdev installation output

```
Collecting iotedgehubdev
  Using cached https://files.pythonhosted.org/...iotedgehubdev-0.5.0-py2.
py3-none-any.whl
Collecting ply (from jsonpath-rw->iotedgehubdev)
```

---

[1]Your device must still exist in an IoT Hub instance to generate the security keys and configuration strings associated with it.

```
   Using cached https://files.pythonhosted.org/.../ply-3.11-py2.py3-none-
any.whl
Collecting decorator (from jsonpath-rw->iotedgehubdev)
   Using cached https://files.pythonhosted.org/.../decorator-4.3.0-py2.py3-
none-any.whl
Installing collected packages: ply, decorator, jsonpath-rw, iotedgehubdev
Successfully installed decorator-4.3.0 iotedgehubdev-0.5.0 jsonpath-
rw-1.4.0 ply-3.11
```

This output has been abbreviated for readability. Additionally, you may see warnings about the iotedgehubdev script being installed into a directory that is not on the PATH environment variable. In order for you to easily access this tool from any context on your development machine, *I highly recommend adding that directory to your PATH variable*. Once you have completed these steps, you are ready to configure the simulator. Configuring the simulator involves setting the device connection string so the simulator knows what device it is simulating. To configure it, run the command in Listing 5-3.

Listing 5-3. Configure the simulator

```
iotedgehubdev setup -c "<edge-device-connection-string>"
```

You must use double quotes around the edge device connection string. An easy way to get the device connection string is to right click the device in the list of IoT devices in the VS Code tooling and select "Copy Device Connection String" as shown in Figure 5-2.

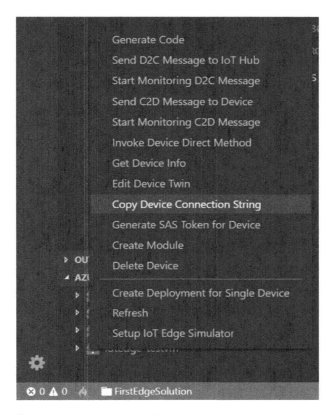

Figure 5-2. *Copy device connection string*

You can also use the option at the bottom of Figure 5-2 to "Setup IoT Edge Simulator." This will automatically copy the connection string for the device and run the `setup` command for it.

Keep in mind, the simulator utility is still in beta and might have some bugs. If you run the `setup` command and see an error that looks similar to this: "`ERROR:` `Error: string length needs to greater than or equal to 1 and less than 64` `characters.`", you can add a default value for the gateway argument (`-g "target"`) and that should resolve the issue. You should see the message: "`Setup IoT Edge Simulator` `successfully.`"

Before we move on to actually running the simulator utility, let's discuss the two ways to interact with the simulator. The first way is to run the simulator in *solution* mode. In this mode, you supply a deployment manifest (`deployment.json`) and let the utility host the modules listed in your solution. This is helpful if you have a multi-module solution and your testing involves messages being exchanged between the modules. This option uses the modules listed in the deployment manifest and starts the containers, which will follow the normal startup process in the module. Any messages that are created and sent through the edgeHub message broker, either from an attached device or telemetry that is generated in the module (like the temperature sensor), will be sent as normal. The benefit of running in solution mode is that no container registry or edge runtime were required.

The second way to use the simulator is to run it in *single module* mode. In this mode, only one module is hosted in the simulator and when you execute the start command, you specify the "inputs" you want to expose through the simulator's API ("input1", "input2", etc.). In single module mode, a local HTTP endpoint is created that allows you to send HTTP POST messages to it. These messages are translated into device messages and sent to your module through the inputs you specified, which allows your module input message event handler to execute as if a message was received from the edgeHub message broker. This can be extremely helpful when used with a tool like *curl* or *Postman* so that you can save your test messages and easily replay them to your module to test the module's logic. Each of these simulation scenarios requires unique steps, so we will examine each mode in the following sections.

Solution Mode

To run the simulator in solution mode, use the command in Listing 5-4. The "-d" option is used to specify the location of the deployment template file. Running the simulator in solution mode is very similar to running the solution in the edge runtime. You simply specify the deployment manifest and the simulator starts up all the modules and they all run through the normal startup process.

Listing 5-4. Simulator solution deployment command

```
iotedgehubdev start -d "<pathto/deployment.json>"
```

It might be helpful to think of *solution* mode as *attach* mode. In solution mode, since the simulator starts the entire solution and the modules are running in their respective containers as normal, the way you must debug your custom module is by attaching the debugger, which is different from single module mode. We will look at how to use the tooling to attach using the debugger later in this chapter.

Because the tooling must be able to attach to the debugger in the module containers, you must specify the debug version of your module in the deployment.json file used. Debug images are not the default image used in the template when the solution is created, so you will have to change the modules, as shown in Listing 5-5. Additionally, any images you build to use with the simulator must be built in debug mode.

Listing 5-5. Debug module reference in deployment.template.json file

```
"FirstEdgeModule": {
    "version": "1.0",
     "type": "docker",
     "status": "running",
  "restartPolicy": "always",
  "settings": {
    "image": "${MODULES.FirstEdgeModule.amd64.debug}",
    "createOptions": "{}"
 }
}
```

Single Module Mode

If running the simulator in solution mode can be thought of as *attach* mode, running it in single module mode should be thought of as *launch* mode. When the simulator is run in single module mode, the simulator does not automatically start your modules. Instead, it starts two other modules. The two modules/containers are:

- **edgeHubDev:** Built from the mcr.microsoft.com/azureiotedge-hub image. It is a replacement (dev) version of the edgeHub container that can run on your local machine without the security agent. This enables it to broker messages without the rigorous security constraints in the regular edge runtime.

- **Input:** Built from the mcr.microsoft.com/azureiotedge-testing-utility image. It creates an HTTP endpoint with a REST API that accepts messages POSTed to its API and passes those messages on to the edgeHubDev container.

Once these modules are up and running, your custom module code can be launched and, using the configured module information, the edgeHubDev runtime will be invoked as if it was running within the edge runtime, even though it is running natively on your development machine (not in a container).

To run the simulator in single module mode from the command line, use the "-i" option to specify the inputs you want to test in your module (you can specify multiple inputs as a comma-separated list). Two examples are shown in Listings 5-6 and 5-7.

Listing 5-6. Simulator single module mode with single input and default port

```
iotedgehubdev start -i "input1"
```

Listing 5-7. Simulator single module mode with two inputs and port number specified

```
iotedgehubdev start -i "input1,input2" -p 55000
```

In Listing 5-6, the default of 53000 will be used with a single input exposed named input1. The example shown in Listing 5-7 will use the port specified in the value of the "-p" argument, 55000 and will expose two inputs names input1 and input2.

In single module mode, because the edge runtime is not in control of the environment, there are some module requirements that are absent. One of these requirements is a set of environment variables. The two environment variables required by any module are: EdgeHubConnectionString and EdgeModuleCACertificateFile. The values for these environment variables can be constructed using the modulecred command line argument. modulecred is used to set the module connection string that should be used when the simulator is started. To set the default module configuration, run the command in Listing 5-8.

Listing 5-8. modulecred set default configurations

```
iotedgehubdev modulecred
```

In the output, look for the segment "ModuleId=target". This is the default Module ID that is set when no module ID is specified as an argument to the modulecred command. To configure the connection to use the module you want to test, run the command shown in Listing 5-9.

Listing 5-9. Set a module using modulecred

```
iotedgehubdev modulecred -m "<module name>"
```

The output of this command should contain a connection string with the value you just specified in the "<module name>" parameter (include the double quotes) for the ModuleId property and a path to the certificate file. An example of the output is shown in Listing 5-10.

Listing 5-10. modulecred command output

```
C:\Users\iotedgedev>iotedgehubdev modulecred -m "FirstEdgeModule"
EdgeHubConnectionString=HostName=<iothubname>.azure-devices.net;GatewayHost
Name=target;DeviceId=<deviceName>;ModuleId=FirstEdgeModule;SharedAccessKey=
<key>
EdgeModuleCACertificateFile=C:\ProgramData\iotedgehubdev\data\certs\edge-
device-ca\cert\edge-device-ca.cert.pem
```

If you are running these commands from the command line, you must set the environment variables, but as we will see later, there are a few shortcuts to setting them in the VS Code and Visual Studio tooling.

Once the simulator has been started and the two single mode test containers have been started and the two environment variables have been set (using the values from the modulecred command), you are ready to start your module. Your module must be started natively as if it were running on your local machine, not in a container. This means you must run the dotnet build command in the module directory to compile the bits.

After you have compiled your code, start the code inside the module (not the module container), which is usually done by starting the debugger in an IDE. Once this is done, you can pass a message to the configured module by supplying the input name and the message body content to pass to the input in the module. An example invocation of the utility is displayed in Listing 5-11.

Listing 5-11. Example temperature telemetry simulator invocation

```
curl --header "Content-Type: application/json" --request POST --data
'{"inputName": "input1","data":"[{\"machine\":{\"temperature\":
100.29815234851478,\"pressure\":10.033966723248518},\"ambient\":
{\"temperature\":21.250450821942859,\"humidity\":26},\"timeC
reated\":\"2018-11-10T04:47:58.3126199Z\"}]"}' http://localhost:53000/api/
v1/messages
```

This example uses the curl command line tool to invoke the request, but any HTTP client (like Postman) will work. The example shown in Listing 5-11 represents a message that might be sent from the tempSensor module. A simpler message is shown in Listing 5-12, which shows a simple "hello world" message.

Listing 5-12. Example "hello world" simulator invocation

```
curl --header "Content-Type: application/json" --request POST --data
'{"inputName": "input1","data":"hello world"}' http://localhost:53000/api/
v1/messages
```

As you look at both of these example invocations, there are two parameters that will change for your unique scenario. The first is the inputName value. This name must match the name of the registered message handler you are trying to test (and one of the input names that was supplied to the start command). Second, the value of the data parameter should be the actual JSON message content that you want to pass to your module. If you are running this on a Windows machine, you should surround the data param value with double quotes and ensure the message payload (data content) is valid JSON, with the embedded double quotes escaped. The examples shown must be run from a Git bash window. The result of passing the command in Listing 5-11 or Listing 5-12 is {"message":"accepted"}. This simply signifies that the message was correctly processed through the simulator. There may be additional output from your code.

Azure IoT Edge Dev Tool

The second tool we will look at is the Azure Edge Dev Tool. The Azure IoT Edge Dev Tool is a python utility that is capable of performing much of the functionality discussed in the previous chapter (and more) from the command line. With this tool, you can create and manage all of the edge solution resources, including the Docker runtime and the edge simulator as well as the Azure resources required for edge solutions, like IoT Hub. Here is a partial list of the functionality it supports:

- Create new edge solutions

- Add new modules to existing edge solutions

- Monitor messages sent from the edge to IoT Hub

- Deploy edge solutions to an edge device

- Manage IoT Hub

- Manage the local Docker environment

- Manage the edge simulator

Listing 5-13 shows the usage output of the utility, which gives an idea of the tasks that can be performed with this tool.

Listing 5-13. iotedgedev usage output

```
Options:
  --version   Show the version and exit.
  -h, --help  Show this message and exit.

Commands:
  add       Add a new module to the solution
  build     Build the solution
  deploy    Deploy solution to IoT Edge device
  genconfig Expand environment variables and placeholders in
            *.template.json and copy to config folder
  init      Create a new IoT Edge solution and provision
            Azure resources
  log       Open a new terminal window for EdgeAgent, EdgeHub
            and each Edge module and save to LOGS_PATH
  monitor   Monitor messages from IoT Edge device to IoT Hub
  new       Create a new IoT Edge solution
  push      Push module images to container registry
  setup     Setup IoT Edge simulator. This must be done
            before starting
  start     Start IoT Edge simulator
  stop      Stop IoT Edge simulator
  docker    Manage Docker
  iothub    Manage IoT Hub and IoT Edge devices
  simulator Manage IoT Edge simulator
  solution  Manage IoT Edge solutions
```

Each of these commands has a set of subcommands that perform specific operations under each of the command areas. The complete list[2] is too long to include here, but one example is the list of solution subcommands shown in Listing 5-14.

Listing 5-14. iotedgedev solution subcommands

```
Usage: iotedgedev solution [OPTIONS] COMMAND [ARGS]...

  Manage IoT Edge solutions

Options:
  -h, --help  Show this message and exit.

Commands:
  add        Add a new module to the solution
  build      Build the solution
  deploy     Deploy solution to IoT Edge device
  e2e        Push, deploy, start, monitor
  genconfig  Expand environment variables and placeholders in
             *.template.json and copy to config folder
  init       Create a new IoT Edge solution and provision
             Azure resources
  new        Create a new IoT Edge solution
  push       Push module images to container registry
```

Getting Started with the IoT Edge Dev Tool

Now that you are aware of this command line tool, you need to know how to install it and start using it. There are two ways to get started with the tool: (1) use a preconfigured container image that already has all the required tools and dependencies installed or (2) manually install all the required tools and utilities on your development machine. We will walk through both options.

---

[2]The complete list of commands and subcommands can be viewed at https://github.com/Azure/iotedgedev/wiki/command-list.

Using the Preconfigured Container

In case this wasn't obvious, to run the preconfigured container, you must first install Docker (refer to Chapter 3 for help on how to do that). Once you have Docker installed, you will need to download the image from the Microsoft registry on Docker Hub using this location: `microsoft/iotedgedev`. Once you have pulled the image, you can create a container from that image and start it as you would any other container. Listing 5-15 shows a single command that pulls the image and starts the container.

Listing 5-15. Docker command to start iotedgedev container

```
docker run -ti -v /var/run/docker.sock:/var/run/docker.sock -v <local
solution folder>:/home/iotedge microsoft/iotedgedev
```

This command not only starts the container but maps a local folder to a folder in the container. In the place where you see the reference to the local folder, you need to supply the path of the folder on your machine where you would like the generated edge solution files to exist. When this command executes, the result will be a running Docker container, and your cursor will be on container's command prompt, ready to execute any of the tool's commands.

Manually Installing the Requirements

If you would like to understand the ins and outs of the `iotedgedev` tool, including how to set it up, this section will walk through the steps required to configure this tool manually, from scratch. Here are the prerequisites that must be present on any device where you want to run the tool:

- Docker (refer to Chapter 3 for installation help)
- Python 3.6+ and pip
- Azure CLI 2.0
- Azure CLI IoT extension
  - For example: `az extension add –name azure-cli-iot-ext`
- For Linux machines only, Docker Compose

- Install edge module specific dependencies. If you're creating a C# module, you need the .Net runtime. If you're creating a Java module, you need the JDK and Maven. Here is a list of the module specific requirements:

    - C# – .NET Core SDK (2.1+ is recommended)

    - Python – Git, Cookiecutter

    - Node.js – Node.js, Yeoman, Azure IoT Edge Node.js module generator

    - Java – SDK, Maven

Once all of the required dependencies are installed, you are ready to install the tool itself, using pip. Here is the most common example of how to install it: `pip install -U iotedgedev`.

IoT Edge Dev Tool Initial Commands

After the tool is installed, either in the prebuilt container or using the manual steps, there are a few initialization commands that are helpful to be aware of. Here are a few of those initial commands along with an explanation of what the command accomplishes.

- `iotedgedev setup`: This command sets up the IoT Edge Simulator and must be run before starting the simulator.

- `iotedgedev init`: This command runs both `iotedgedev new` and `iotedgedev iothub setup`, which creates a new edge solution and sets up your Azure resources in a single command.

- `iotedgedev build`: This command builds all the module images that need to be built in the edge solution.

- `iotedgedev start`: This command starts the simulator in either solution mode or single module mode (for more details on this, refer to the Azure IoT EdgeHub Dev Tool section).

Later in this chapter, we will walk through using the tool and experiment with a few of the command line options that are helpful in different debugging scenarios.

Using the IoT Edge Dev Tool

Now that you have the Dev Tool installed, let's walk through how to create and manage a solution using the tool. When using the iotedgedev command line tool, one of the first things you need to do is create your local edge solution. The two most common ways to do this are either the `iotedgedev init` command or the `iotedgedev new` command. The `new` command creates and configures a new local edge solution with a reference to the `tempSensor` module we have already seen as well as a custom module that consumes messages from the `tempSensor` module. This command yields the same result as the "new solution" commands we have already used in the VS Code and Visual Studio tooling. An example of the output from the `new` command is shown in Listing 5-16.

Listing 5-16. Output from iotedgedev new command

```
C:\Users\iotedgedev\edgesolution2>iotedgedev new .

========================================================
======== CREATING AZURE IOT EDGE SOLUTION: . ========
========================================================


================================================================
==  IOTEDGEDEV SOLUTION ADD FILTERMODULE --TEMPLATE CSHARP  ==
================================================================


========================================
======== ENVIRONMENT VARIABLES ========
========================================

Environment Variables loaded from: .env (C:\Users\iotedgedev\
edgesolution2\.env)


============================================
======== ADDING MODULE FILTERMODULE ========
============================================


====================================================
=== DOTNET NEW -I MICROSOFT.AZURE.IOT.EDGE.MODULE ===
====================================================
```

Restoring packages for C:\Users\iotedgedev\.templateengine\dotnetcli\
v2.1.403\scratch\restore.csproj...
  Installing Microsoft.Azure.IoT.Edge.Module 2.3.0.
  Generating MSBuild file C:\Users\iotedgedev\.templateengine\dotnetcli\
  v2.1.403\scratch\obj\restore.csproj.nuget.g.props.
  Generating MSBuild file C:\Users\iotedgedev\.templateengine\dotnetcli\
  v2.1.403\scratch\obj\restore.csproj.nuget.g.targets.
  Restore completed in 390.43 ms for C:\Users\iotedgedev\.templateengine\
  dotnetcli\v2.1.403\scratch\restore.csproj.

Usage: new [options]

Options:
  -h, --help   Displays help for this command.
  -l, --list   Lists templates containing the specified name. If no
                      name is specified, lists all templates.
  -n, --name   The name for the output being created. If no name is
                      specified, the name of the current directory is used.
  -o, --output   Location to place the generated output.
  -i, --install   Installs a source or a template pack.
  -u, --uninstall   Uninstalls a source or a template pack.
  --nuget-source   Specifies a NuGet source to use during install.
  --type   Filters templates based on available types.
                      Predefined values are "project", "item" or "other".
  --force   Forces content to be generated even if it would
                      change existing files.
  -lang, --language   Filters templates based on language and specifies the
                      language of the template to create.

Templates	Short Name	Language	Tags
Console Application	console	[C#], F#, VB	Console
Class library	classlib	[C#], F#, VB	Library
IoT Edge Module	aziotedgemodule	[C#], F#	Console
Unit Test Project	mstest	[C#], F#, VB	MSTest
NUnit 3 Test...	nunit	[C#], F#, VB	NUnit
NUnit 3 Test Item	nunit-test	[C#], F#, VB	NUnit

xUnit Test Project	xunit	[C#], F#, VB	xUnit
Razor Page	page	[C#]	ASP.NET
MVC ViewImports	viewimports	[C#]	ASP.NET
MVC ViewStart	viewstart	[C#]	ASP.NET
ASP.NET Core...	web	[C#], F#	Empty
ASP.NET Core Web mvc		[C#], F#	MVC

Examples:

```
    dotnet new mvc --auth Individual
    dotnet new classlib --framework netcoreapp2.1
    dotnet new --help
```

```
========================================================================
= DOTNET NEW AZIOTEDGEMODULE -N FILTERMODULE -R
${CONTAINER_REGISTRY_SERVER}/FILTERMODULE =
========================================================================

The template "Azure IoT Edge Module" was created successfully.

Processing post-creation actions...
Running 'dotnet restore' on filtermodule...
  Restoring packages for C:\Users\iotedgedev\edgesolution2\modules\
  filtermodule\filtermodule.csproj...
  Generating MSBuild file C:\Users\iotedgedev\edgesolution2\modules\
  filtermodule\obj\filtermodule.csproj.nuget.g.props.
  Generating MSBuild file C:\Users\iotedgedev\edgesolution2\modules\
  filtermodule\obj\filtermodule.csproj.nuget.g.targets.
  Restore completed in 2.9 sec for C:\Users\iotedgedev\edgesolution2\
  modules\filtermodule\filtermodule.csproj.

Restore succeeded.
ADD COMPLETE

AZURE IOT EDGE SOLUTION CREATED

C:\Users\iotedgedev\edgesolution2>
```

Some of the output of the code in Listing 5-16 has been abbreviated for readability sake, but the end result remains that the command indicates it completed successfully.

The iotedgedev init command does everything the iotedgedev new command does but additionally creates and configures the Azure cloud resources that are required for an end-to-end solution. Example output from the init command is shown in Listing 5-17.

Listing 5-17. Output from iotedgedev init command

```
==============================================================
= IOTEDGEDEV NEW . --MODULE FILTERMODULE --TEMPLATE CSHARP =
==============================================================


======================================================
======== CREATING AZURE IOT EDGE SOLUTION: . ========
======================================================
[duplicate output from iotedgedev "new" command removed]

AZURE IOT EDGE SOLUTION CREATED

==========================================================
======== IOTEDGEDEV IOTHUB SETUP --UPDATE-DOTENV ========
==========================================================


================================
======== AUTHENTICATION ========
================================

Retrieving Azure CLI credentials from cache...

Azure CLI credentials found.

==============================
======== SUBSCRIPTION ========
==============================

Retrieving Azure Subscriptions...
```

```
Subscription Name          Id
----------------------     -----------------------------------
Visual Studio Enterprise   00000000-1111-2222-3333-444444444444
Subscription One           00000000-1111-2222-3333-555555555555
```

Select an Azure Subscription Name or Id: [00000000-1111-2222-3333-444444444444]:

```
=====================================
======= SETTING SUBSCRIPTION ========
=====================================
```

Setting Subscription to 00000000-1111-2222-3333-444444444444'...

```
========================================
======= RESOURCE GROUP LOCATION ========
========================================
```

Enter a Resource Group Location: (australiaeast, australiasoutheast, brazilsouth, canadacentral, canadaeast, centralindia, centralus, eastasia, eastus, eastus2, japanwest, japaneast, northeurope, northcentralus, southindia, uksouth, ukwest, westus, westeurope, southcentralus, westcentralus, westus2) [westus]: eastus

```
================================================
======= SETTING RESOURCE GROUP LOCATION ========
================================================
```

Setting Resource Group Location to 'eastus'...

```
===============================
======= RESOURCE GROUP ========
===============================
```

Retrieving Resource Groups...

```
Resource Group             Location
----------------------     ----------
iotedge-development        eastus
iotedgedev-rg2             eastus
```

Enter Resource Group Name (Creates a new Resource Group if not found):
[iotedgedev-rg]:

```
================================================
======== SETTING RESOURCE GROUP NAME ========
================================================
```

Setting Resource Group Name to 'iotedgedev-rg'...

Checking if Resource Group 'iotedgedev-rg' exists...

Resource Group iotedgedev-rg does not exist.
Creating Resource Group 'iotedgedev-rg' at 'eastus'...

```
============================
======== IOTHUB SKU ========
============================
```

Enter IoT Hub SKU (F1|S1|S2|S3): (F1, S1, S2, S3) [F1]: s1
Error: invalid choice: s1. (choose from F1, S1, S2, S3)
Enter IoT Hub SKU (F1|S1|S2|S3): (F1, S1, S2, S3) [F1]: S1

```
====================================
======== SETTING IOT HUB SKU ========
====================================
```

Setting IoT Hub SKU to 'S1'...

```
=========================
======== IOT HUB ========
=========================
```

Retrieving IoT Hubs in 'iotedgedev-rg'...

Enter the IoT Hub Name (Creates a new IoT Hub if not found): [iotedgedev-
iothub-000000]:

```
=================================
======== SETTING IOT HUB ========
=================================
```

Setting IoT Hub to 'iotedgedev-iothub-000000'...

Checking if 'iotedgedev-iothub-000000 IoT Hub exists...

Could not locate the iotedgedev-iothub-000000 in iotedgedev-rg.
Creating 'iotedgedev-iothub-000000 in 'iotedgedev-rg' with 'S1' sku...

Creating IoT Hub. Please wait as this could take a few minutes to
complete...

```
=============================
======== EDGE DEVICE ========
=============================
```

Retrieving edge devices in 'iotedgedev-iothub-000000'...

Enter the IoT Edge Device Id (Creates a new Edge Device if not found):
[iotedgedev-edgedevice]:

```
====================================
======== SETTING EDGE DEVICE ========
====================================
```

Setting Edge Device to 'iotedgedev-edgedevice'...

Checking if 'iotedgedev-edgedevice' device exists in 'iotedgedev-
iothub-000000'...

Could not locate the iotedgedev-edgedevice device in iotedgedev-
iothub-000000 IoT Hub in iotedgedev-rg.
Creating 'iotedgedev-edgedevice' edge device in 'iotedgedev-
iothub-000000'...

```
=====================================
======== CONNECTION STRINGS ========
=====================================
```

Retrieving 'iotedgedev-iothub-000000' connection string...

Retrieving 'iotedgedev-edgedevice' connection string...

```
IOTHUB_CONNECTION_STRING="HostName=iotedgedev-iothub-000000.azure- devices.
net;SharedAccessKeyName=iothubowner;SharedAccessKey=<key>"
DEVICE_CONNECTION_STRING="HostName=iotedgedev-iothub-21dedd.azure-devices.
net;DeviceId=iotedgedev-edgedevice;SharedAccessKey=<key>"

Successfully backed up C:\Users\iotedgedev\edgesolution\.env to
C:\Users\iotedgedev\edgesolution\.env.backup
Updated current .env file
```

This output shows the prompts and the process used to create all the required cloud resources. One of the benefits of using this command is that all of the connection strings and other generated keys, etc. are added to the .env file in the solution directory, which allows any other iotedgedev commands to use those details as context.

Once you have created a solution, using any of the tooling we have reviewed in this chapter or an earlier chapter, you can use the iotedgedev build command. The build command uses the values stored in the .env file and runs the docker build process for all containers in the solution. The output from the build command is shown in Listing 5-18.

Listing 5-18. Output from iotedgedev build command

```
C:\Users\iotedgedev\edgesolution2>iotedgedev build

=======================================
======== ENVIRONMENT VARIABLES ========
=======================================

Environment Variables loaded from: .env
(C:\Users\iotedgedev\edgesolution2\.env)


==================================
======== BUILDING MODULES ========
==================================

BUILDING MODULE: filtermodule
PROCESSING DOCKERFILE:
C:\Users\iotedgedev\edgesolution2\modules\filtermodule\Dockerfile.amd64
BUILDING DOCKER IMAGE: localhost:5000/filtermodule:0.0.1-amd64
Step 1/12 : FROM microsoft/dotnet:2.1-sdk AS build-env
 ---> 6baac5bd0ea2
```

```
Step 2/12 : WORKDIR /app
 ---> Using cache
 ---> 9fcaf5af70ec
Step 3/12 : COPY *.csproj ./
 ---> Using cache
 ---> a3403af9c2e4
Step 4/12 : RUN dotnet restore
 ---> Using cache
 ---> 83a24a48e971
Step 5/12 : COPY . ./
 ---> 96e000f659b8
Step 6/12 : RUN dotnet publish -c Release -o out
 ---> Running in 493f3d616c1d
Microsoft (R) Build Engine version 15.8.169+g1ccb72aefa for .NET Core
Copyright (C) Microsoft Corporation. All rights reserved.

  Restoring packages for /app/filtermodule.csproj...
  Generating MSBuild file /app/obj/filtermodule.csproj.nuget.g.props.
  Generating MSBuild file /app/obj/filtermodule.csproj.nuget.g.targets.
  Restore completed in 10.27 sec for /app/filtermodule.csproj.
  filtermodule -> /app/bin/Release/netcoreapp2.1/filtermodule.dll
  filtermodule -> /app/out/
 ---> 66bc85f4dc78
Step 7/12 : FROM microsoft/dotnet:2.1-runtime-stretch-slim
 ---> 0b74f72810f3
Step 8/12 : WORKDIR /app
 ---> Using cache
 ---> f60d36bbd085
Step 9/12 : COPY --from=build-env /app/out ./
 ---> Using cache
 ---> b206e921ee70
Step 10/12 : RUN useradd -ms /bin/bash moduleuser
 ---> Using cache
 ---> 969910b22653
Step 11/12 : USER moduleuser
 ---> Using cache
```

```
 ---> e0e6f1311693
Step 12/12 : ENTRYPOINT ["dotnet", "filtermodule.dll"]
 ---> Using cache
 ---> 6bce366fdc14
Successfully built 6bce366fdc14
Successfully tagged localhost:5000/filtermodule:0.0.1-amd64
BUILD COMPLETE


========================================
======== PROCESSING CONFIG FILES ========
========================================

Expanding 'deployment.template.json' to 'config\deployment.json'
```

The next logical step in the process after we have created and built the new edge solution is to start/run the solution. But, one thing to be aware of when running solutions using the iotedgedev utility is that it delegates all of the runtime commands to the simulator command utility we examined earlier in this chapter. In fact, the setup, start, and stop commands all directly correspond to the iotedgehubdev setup, start, and stop commands. For this reason, the iotedgedev setup command must be run before any of the simulator commands can be run, but if you have already configured the simulator using the iotedgehubdev setup command, then that is all that's required. Both commands configure the same tool. But if you want to combine two commands, you can use the --setup command line option with the start command and the iotedgedev utility will run both the simulator setup and start commands for you.

Once you have configured the simulator (refer to the earlier sections if you need help with this), you can run iotedgedev start to start the solution in solution mode. Listing 5-19 shows an example of this.

Listing 5-19. Output of iotedgedev start command

```
C:\Users\iotedgedev\edgesolution2>iotedgedev start


========================================
======== ENVIRONMENT VARIABLES ========
========================================

Environment Variables loaded from: .env
(C:\Users\iotedgedev\edgesolution2\.env)
```

```
================================================================
======== STARTING IOT EDGE SIMULATOR IN SOLUTION MODE ========
================================================================

Pulling edgeHubDev ... done
Creating edgeHubDev ... done
Creating tempSensor   ... done
Creating filtermodule ... done
IoT Edge Simulator has been started in solution mode.
```

This output should look familiar to you, based on the previous sections about the simulator utility. The result of this start command is that the modules in your edge solution will now be running, in the simulated edge runtime environment.

Note   As a reminder, you can create a new edge solution using the IDE or CLI tooling, build the solution and run the solution using the simulator, all without needing an instance of the IoT Hub.

To stop the running edge solution, you use the iotedgedev stop command, which should be fairly obvious at this point. An example of the output from running the stop command is shown in Listing 5-20.

Listing 5-20. Output from iotedgedev stop command

```
C:\Users\iotedgedev\edgesolution2>iotedgedev stop


========================================
======== ENVIRONMENT VARIABLES ========
========================================

Environment Variables loaded from: .env
(C:\Users\iotedgedev\edgesolution2\.env)
```

```
================================================
======== STOPPING IOT EDGE SIMULATOR ========
================================================

Stopping filtermodule ... done
Stopping tempSensor    ... done
Stopping edgeHubDev     ... done
Removing filtermodule ... done
Removing tempSensor    ... done
Removing edgeHubDev     ... done
Network azure-iot-edge-dev is external, skipping
IoT Edge Simulator has been stopped successfully.
```

You can see in the output that the utility not only stops the running containers, but it also removes the containers. This helps keep things clean between runs of the simulator. Each time the simulator starts, it will create new instances of the required containers.

There are several other commands that are available with the iotedgedev utility, but I want to point out just a few that are very helpful.

- Monitor: This command monitors the messages sent to your IoT Hub endpoint. This is a difficult thing to monitor because there are no log files for these outgoing messages, so without this utility, you have to configure the cloud resources to view the data, which can be more difficult to trace.

- solution push: Pushes all of the solution images to the configured container registry.

- solution deploy: Deploys the solution manifest to the configured edge device. The default values are pulled from the .env file.

- solution e2e: This command combines several commands into one larger, orchestrator command. The e2e command runs the solution push, deploy, start, and monitor commands back to back, giving you, the developer, an easy way to push your solution to your local development edge device.

Debugging Edge Solutions

Up until this point, we have investigated some tools and utilities that help us to run our edge solutions locally, but we have not used them in a debugging scenario yet. In this section, we will walk through how to use the tooling in VS Code and Visual Studio along with the simulator to debug our edge solutions. We will debug our solutions using the edge simulator, so if you have not configured that yet, please take this opportunity to do that.

VS Code Debugging Overview

Debugging edge solutions in VS Code is not difficult, but it is probably different than the debugging flow you're used to. One of the first differences is the location of the debugging settings. In VS Code, from the root solution directory, there should be a .vscode directory that the IDE uses to store settings and other user-specific information. In the FirstEdgeSolution that we created in the previous chapter, there should be a launch.json file in the .vscode directory as shown in Figure 5-3.

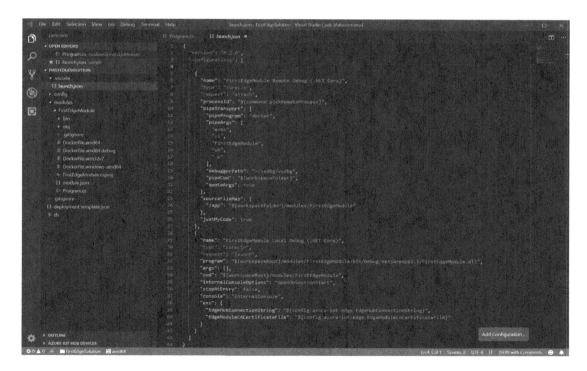

Figure 5-3. *Debugging settings in VS Code*

Launch.json is a JSON file that contains an array of launch configurations. Launch configurations are groups of settings that provide an easy way to switch from one debugging scenario to another. Additionally, you can add and remove configurations to suit your needs. To add an additional configuration, click the "Add Configuration" in the bottom right corner of the editor window shown in Figure 5-3. When you click that option, the editor will display a list of available preconfigured configurations for you to select from. For our debugging, VS Code has already added two configurations that are specific to our edge solution when we created the solution, so we do not need to add another configuration at this time.

The two configurations VS Code has prefilled for us are named "FirstEdgeModule Remote Debug (.NET Core)" and "FirstEdgeModule Local Debug (.NET Core)". One primary distinction to notice is that the "remote" configuration is an "attach" configuration and the "local" configuration is a "launch" configuration. You can see this represented in the request property of the JSON configuration. If you remember back to our discussion on the simulator, we said that running the simulator in "solution" mode was equivalent to "attach" mode and running the simulator in "single module" mode was equivalent to running the simulator in "launch" mode. The meaning of "attach" and "launch" from that discussion is identical to the meaning in these debugging configurations. So, when debugging with the simulator using solution mode, you will use the remote debug (attach) option and when debugging with the simulator in single module mode, you will use the local debug (launch) option.

VS Code Debugging in Solution Mode

Debugging in solution mode in VS Code is very straightforward. Once you have the edge solution open in VS Code, simply right click the deployment.template.json file and select the "Build and Run IoT Solution in Simulator" option, as shown in Figure 5-4. You can also access this command in the command window (Ctrl+Shift+P) and search for "Azure IoT Edge: Build and Run IoT Solution in Simulator."

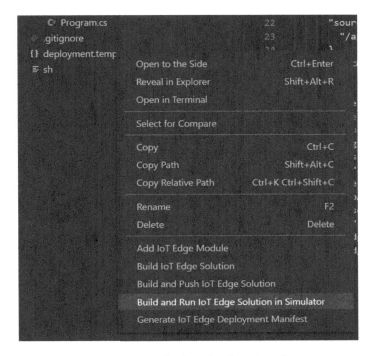

Figure 5-4. *VS Code option to run solution in the simulator*

This single command does four things to help make your interaction with the simulator easier:

1. Build the solution module images

2. Generate the `deployment.json` file from the `deployment.template.json` file

3. Start the simulator in solution mode and pass a reference to the generated deployment manifest file

4. Monitor the output of the solution edge modules in the VS Code terminal window

Once all of these steps complete, your solution will be running in the simulator and you will be able to view the messages flowing between the modules. An example of this output is shown in Listing 5-21.

Listing 5-21. Module output from running solution in the simulator

```
edgeHubDev          | Initialized AMQP connection handler
edgeHubDev          | Opened link Events
FirstEdgeModule     | IoT Hub module client initialized.
edgeHubDev          | Processing subscription ModuleMessages
edgeHubDev          | Opened link ModuleMessages
edgeHubDev          | Opened link MethodReceiving
edgeHubDev          | Processing subscription Methods
edgeHubDev          | Opened link MethodSending
tempSensor          | Successfully initialized module client
edgeHubDev          | Processing subscription ModuleMessages
tempSensor          | Sending message: 1, Body: [{"..."}]
FirstEdgeModule     | Received message: 1, Body: [{"..."}]
FirstEdgeModule     | Received message sent
tempSensor          | Sending message: 2, Body: [{"..."}]
FirstEdgeModule     | Received message: 2, Body: [{"..."}]
FirstEdgeModule     | Received message sent
```

This output had been modified for readability, but it shows the module name on the left side and the abbreviated message payload on the right. It is extremely helpful to see the combined view of messages across all running modules. And one additional feature that can't be conveyed in this text is that the module is also color coded so it's easier to trace your messages in the output window, even when there are a lot of messages flowing through the output window.

This is all very helpful, but it's still not actually debugging. So far, we have only started our solution in the simulator and started monitoring the module output. In order to debug, we need to attach our VS Code instance to the running instance of our solution in the simulator. To do this, click the Debug icon in VS Code, as shown in Figure 5-5, which will display the Debug view.

Figure 5-5. *Debug icon in VS Code*

At the top of the screen in the Debug view, you should see an option to select the correct launch configuration and then start the debugger. An example of this is shown in Figure 5-6.

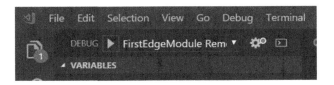

Figure 5-6. *Debugger launch options*

Because we are running the simulator in solution mode, we need to use the "attach" debugger configuration, which is the Configuration named `<Module Name> Remote Debug (.NET Core)`. Make sure that configuration is selected in the selection list and then click the button to start debugging. You will be presented with a list of processes running in the container, like the list shown in Figure 5-7. Select the `dotnet` process, which should be the top item in the list.

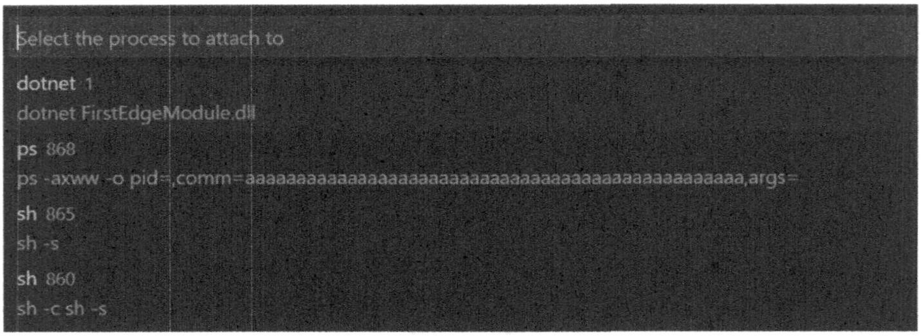

Select the process to attach to

dotnet 1
dotnet FirstEdgeModule.dll

ps 868
ps -axww -o pid=,comm=aaaaaaaaaaaaaaaaaaaaaaaaaaaaaaaaaaaaaaaaaaaaaaaaaaaa,args=

sh 865
sh -s

sh 860
sh -c sh -s

Figure 5-7. *Debugger process list*

As a reminder, when VS Code builds the debug version of your module image, it includes the required debugging information (symbols, etc.) and handles opening the correct ports into the container. Because of that groundwork, VS Code is able to retrieve this list of processes running in the container.

Once you select dotnet in the list, the debugger will attach to the process in the container and you will be able to set breakpoints in the code and inspect the data, just as you would for a locally running application. Any breakpoints you set should be set before you attach the debugger. Breakpoints set after you attach are not as consistent as breakpoints set before you attach.

Once you hit a breakpoint in your code, you have access to inspect local variables, watch windows and call stack information. Figure 5-8 shows an example of the debugging view with an active breakpoint in the temperature sensor solution we have been working with up until this point. If you look at the messages in the output window at the bottom of Figure 5-8, you will see that messages are continuing to flow from the tempSensor module, but because the breakpoint has the FirstEdgeModule execution paused, there are no messages being processed in it. If you were to remove the breakpoint and let the execution run again, you would see several messages flowing through the FirstEdgeModule very quickly because while execution was paused, the simulator was queueing the messages coming from the other modules (which is the edge runtime's behavior).

Figure 5-8. *Breakpoint in VS Code debugger*

An important detail to be aware of is that while we are using the simulator in our example debugging scenarios, you are not required to use the simulator to debug. You can connect to the actual edge runtime on an edge device. Most of the time, this is helpful when a developer has configured their development machine as an edge device and wants to connect to the containers running in that environment. The only requirement to enable that is the edge device must still be running the debug version of your module's image. Don't forget there are two places you must change to use the debug version. First, you need to build the debug version of the container using the `Dockerfile.amd64.debug` Docker build file (or a similar debug Dockerfile) and push the debug image to a container registry. Second, you must change the deployment manifest to point to that debug image. This is the step that gets overlooked most often. Once the debug image has been pushed to the registry and the deployment manifest has been updated, the edge runtime on the device will pull the debug image, start the debug-enabled container and you will be able to attach to the container just as if you were using the simulator.

VS Code Debugging in Single Module Mode

The second method for debugging edge solutions[3] with the simulator is *single module mode*. In this mode, the entire solution is not started – a single module interface is exposed. Which means any messages that normally flow between two edge modules will not be flowing. Single module mode gives you a simple way to pass messages to your module to test the logic of your code, without the complications of the asynchronous, message-driven edge runtime, which severely complicates debugging and troubleshooting. Single module mode is to solution mode what a synchronous, single-threaded application is to an asynchronous, multi-threaded application. It is much simpler to trace the logic when things are synchronous and single-threaded.

To debug a single module, open the command window and select the option "Start IoT Edge Hub Simulator for Single Module," as shown in Figure 5-9.

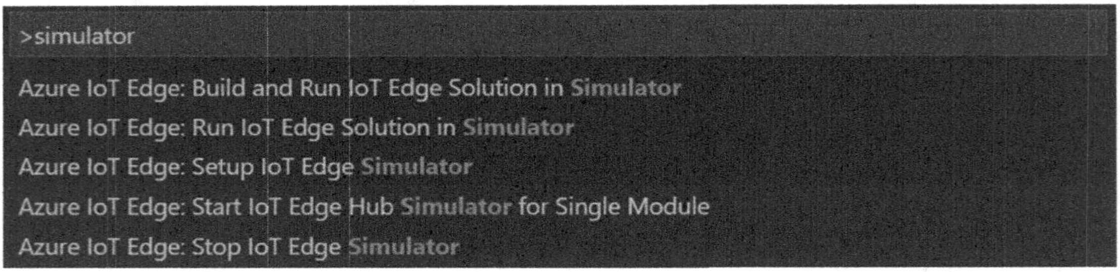

```
>simulator

Azure IoT Edge: Build and Run IoT Edge Solution in Simulator
Azure IoT Edge: Run IoT Edge Solution in Simulator
Azure IoT Edge: Setup IoT Edge Simulator
Azure IoT Edge: Start IoT Edge Hub Simulator for Single Module
Azure IoT Edge: Stop IoT Edge Simulator
```

Figure 5-9. *Start simulator in single module mode*

This command starts the two containers that make up the single module simulation environment (refer to that section earlier in this chapter for more details). The output from starting the simulator in single module mode displayed in the VS Code terminal window is shown in Listing 5-22.

---

[3]Remember that in both cases of solution mode and single module mode, the setup command must be run. That configuration step is a prerequisite.

Listing 5-22. Single module mode start command output

```
$ iotedgehubdev start -i "input1"
IoT Edge Simulator has been started in single module mode.
```
Please run `iotedgehubdev modulecred` to get credential to connect your
module.
```
And send message through:

        curl --header "Content-Type: application/json" --request
        POST --data '{"inputName": "input1","data":"hello world"}'
        http://localhost:53000/api/v1/messages

Please refer to https://github.com/Azure/iot-edge-testing-utility/blob/
master/swagger.json for detail schema
$
```

In the output in Listing 5-22, you can see the tool is instructing us to run the modulecred command that we discussed earlier. This command builds the connection strings and credentials needed for our single module to run properly. But, the value of the connection strings must be added to the runtime environment when our module is launched. To help with this, there is another command in the VS Code tooling. In VS Code, open the command prompt, and type "Set Module Credentials to User Settings." This command runs the modulecred command uses the values from that command to add an environment variable section in the appropriate debugger configuration. The result of this command is shown in Listing 5-23.

Listing 5-23. Launch.json environment variable section for Local Debug configuration

```
{
 "name": "FirstEdgeModule Local Debug (.NET Core)",
 "type": "coreclr",
 "request": "launch",
 "program": "${workspaceRoot}/modules/FirstEdgeModule/bin/Debug/
  netcoreapp2.1/FirstEdgeModule.dll",
 "args": [],
 "cwd": "${workspaceRoot}/modules/FirstEdgeModule",
 "internalConsoleOptions": "openOnSessionStart",
```

```
"stopAtEntry": false,
"console": "internalConsole",
"env": {
  "EdgeHubConnectionString": "${config:azure-iot-edge.
  EdgeHubConnectionString}",
    "EdgeModuleCACertificateFile": "${config:azure-iot-edge.
    EdgeModuleCACertificateFile}"
  }
}
```

The effect of these entries being in this debugger configuration is that the VS Code tooling will populate the values of these environment variables when the debugging session starts. This step is not needed when running the simulator in solution mode because the simulator is able to account for when it starts the solution containers. But, in single module mode, because the code is run natively on your machine, not in a container, the environment variables must be added to the local environment.

To run your module code, you need to compile the module code on your development machine. To be clear, this does mean you need to build the container image. You need to compile the code that runs inside the container on your local machine. To do that, in the terminal window of VS Code, change to the folder where your module's .proj file is and run `dotnet build` to build the .Net Core application. Next, add a breakpoint in your module's code, wherever needed. Then, navigate to the VS Code debug view by clicking the debug icon shown in Figure 5-5 and select the `<module name>` `Local Debug (.Net Core)` debugger configuration. Once you have built your code and have the breakpoint set, selected the local debug configuration, click the start debugging button and your code will initialize. You will know your code correctly initialized when you see the message: "`IoT Hub module client initialized.`"

However, don't expect your code or breakpoints to be invoked just yet. All that has happened is the `Init` operation ran as part of the startup routine. No event handling code has run because there have not been any events sent to your locally running code yet. You have to explicitly invoke your code using either the curl command line utility or Postman, a common API testing utility. To illustrate how the pieces fit together in single module mode, review the diagram in Figure 5-10.

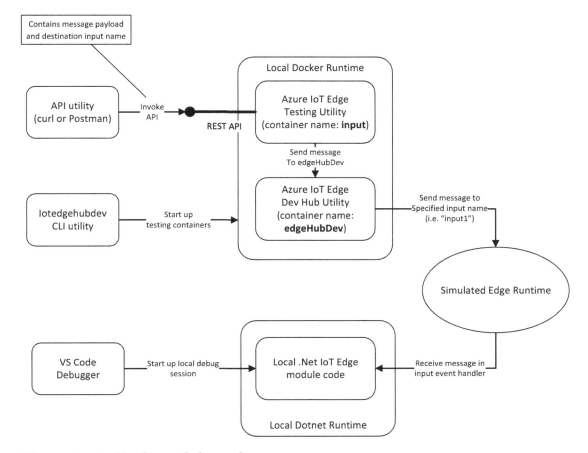

Figure 5-10. _Single module mode components_

Let's briefly review the flow of commands and messages that are illustrated in Figure 5-10.

1. The _iotedgehubdev start_ command starts the two local Docker containers, input and edgeHubDev.

2. The input container hosts a local web API to accept messages.

3. The local debugger starts the edge module code natively on the development machine, not in a container.

4. An API utility like curl or Postman is used to send a request with the device message payload and the destination input name.

5. In the `input` container, messages are transformed into IoT Edge device messages and passed to the `edgeHubDev` container, which is a simulated version of the `edgeHub` container.

6. The `edgeHubDev` container sends messages in the simulated edge runtime to the input name that was specified in the API request.

7. The locally running module event handling code receives the message and the processes the message as if it came from the edge runtime.

Once you have everything up and running, you should be able to issue the command shown in Listing 5-24 and get back the response: `"{"message":"accepted"}"`.

Listing 5-24. curl command to invoke the simulator

```
$ curl --header "Content-Type: application/json" --request POST --data
'{"inputName": "input1","data":"hello world"}' http://localhost:53000/api/
v1/messages
```

Additionally, the breakpoint you set in your module code should have been reached and you should see debugging information, similar to what is shown in Figure 5-11.

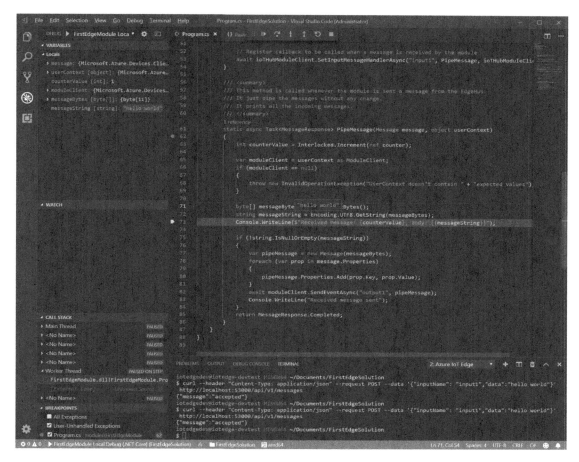

Figure 5-11. *VS Code debugging view in single module mode*

Visual Studio Debugging

Debugging IoT Edge solutions in Visual Studio is a little more straightforward than VS Code. However, if you are using Visual Studio, the setup and configuration steps must be done using the command line utilities. Visual Studio does not yet support all of the integrated tooling that VS Code does. In Visual Studio, to debug in single module mode, set the module project as the startup project in the Visual Studio solution explorer, as shown in Figure 5-12.

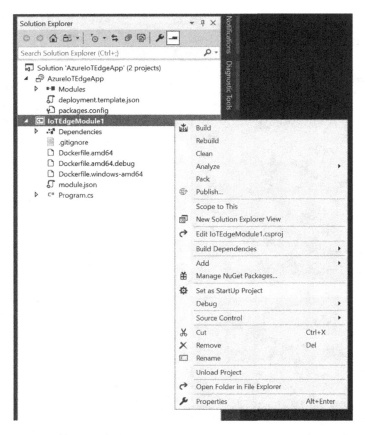

Figure 5-12. *Set a single module as startup project in Visual Studio*

Once you have set the startup project, start the debugger. When it starts, a command window will display showing "IoT Hub module client initialized." Once that appears, you can invoke the test URL using curl or Postman, just as you did with VS Code. Figure 5-13 shows the result of the "hello world" message being passed to the module.

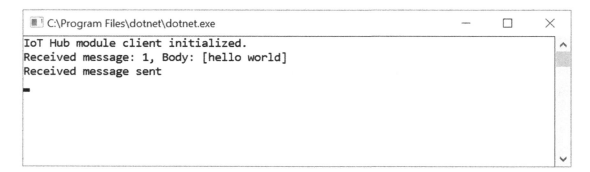

Figure 5-13. *Visual Studio single module mode console output*

To debug in solution mode in Visual Studio, you need to set the IoT Edge Project as the startup project, as shown in Figure 5-14.

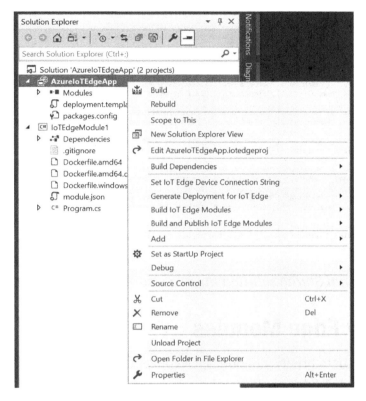

Figure 5-14. *Set IoT Edge project as startup project in Visual Studio*

After that, start the debugger by pressing F5. When you debug in solution mode in Visual Studio, you should see a separate console window open for each one of your edge module projects, each one displaying the console output for that module as it processes messages. For our sample solution, the simulator starts with the `tempSensor` telemetry generator module and our custom C# module. So, there will only be one console output window and it should display the output of the incoming telemetry being generated. An example of this is shown in Figure 5-15.

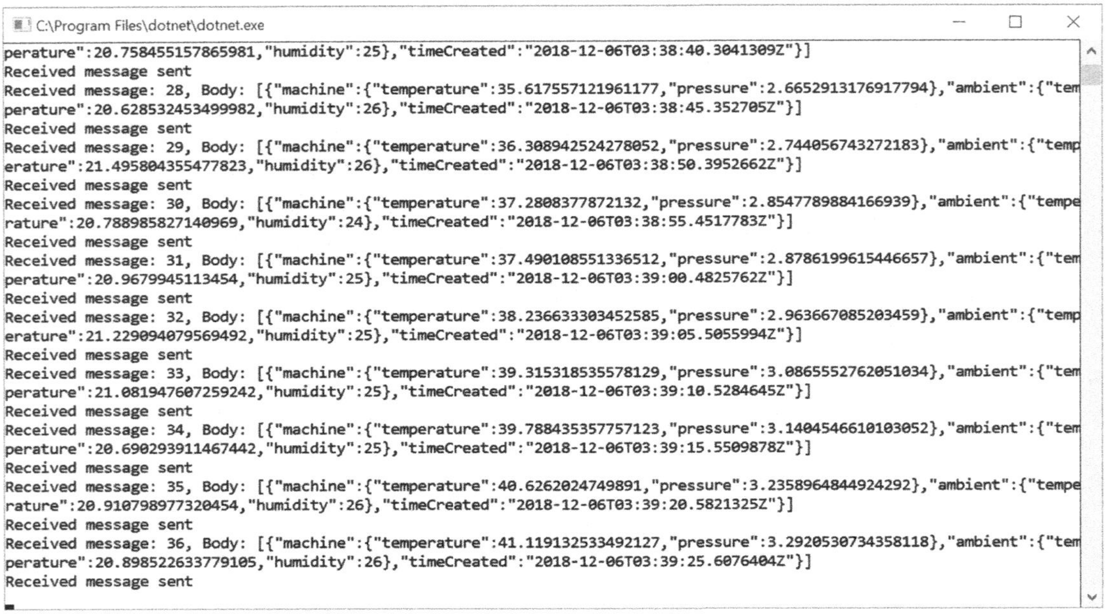

Figure 5-15. *Visual Studio solution mode console output*

Third Party Edge Modules

Another topic I want to briefly mention is the concept of third party edge modules. Because the Azure IoT Edge platform is based on containers, it is feasible that you might leverage a container someone else has developed in your edge solution. For instance, if you need to connect your edge server to a sensor that only communicates over a serial cable using an old or obscure protocol, it'd be great if you didn't have to write that code yourself, but could leverage some existing utility modules. And in fact, there are many modules that have been built that can be reused. So, I want to briefly make you aware of a few of the more popular ones and describe how you would use them.

First, remember that any container you use must exist in a container registry. This means that any third party code must have already been pushed to a public container registry, like DockerHub, or you must build the code and push to a container registry you have access to.

Modbus Edge Module

One example of a third party module that solves a common problem for many edge developers is the modbus edge module developed by Microsoft. The container can be utilized using this DockerHub container registry address and version tag: mcr.microsoft.com/azureiotedge/modbus:1.0. This module has the ability to communicate with sensors using the modbus protocol,[4] over either a serial cable or an ethernet connection. The module then translates those low-level messages into JSON-based messages that are published to another module, usually your custom module, to process the incoming messages. In this scenario, you can connect to sensors that rely on an older protocol, but consume that data in an edge solution to give it new life. Let's look at what the deployment.json section would look like for that modbus module. An example is shown in Listing 5-25.

Listing 5-25. Modbus module section in deployment.json file

```
"modbus": {
  "version": "1.0",
  "type": "docker",
  "status": "running",
  "restartPolicy": "always",
  "settings": {
  "image": " mcr.microsoft.com/azureiotedge/modbus:1.0",
  "createOptions": ""
 }
}
```

You can see that this is just like any other module in your deployment manifest, with the exception that you don't have any local code behind the module. To consume messages from this module, you also need to route the messages from the named output and specify a named input into your custom module code. An example route in the deployment manifest is shown in Listing 5-26.

---

[4]For more information on the modbus protocol, visit http://modbus.org.

Listing 5-26. Deployment manifest route for modbus module output

```
"modbus": "FROM /messages/modules/modbus/outputs/modbusOutput INTO
BrokeredEndpoint(\"/modules/myModule/inputs/modbusInput\")"
```

This route routes messages from the modbusOutput named address into the name input address modbusInput in your custom code. Given the fact that you have to route messages into your code using a known, named output address and once you have routed the messages, you have to be able to parse them, any third party modules must provide some documentation to communication the name of the output address as well as the schema of the messages it produces. For this modbus module, all the needed documentation can be found on the associated GitHub page.[5]

One last piece of configuration that is needed for this module is the configuration in the deployment manifest that relates to the module twin. A sample of this is shown in Listing 5-27.

Listing 5-27. Sample modus module configuration

```
"modbus": {
  "properties.desired": {
    "PublishInterval": "10000",
    "SlaveConfigs": {
      "Slave01": {
        "SlaveConnection": "192.168.10.10",
        "TcpPort": "502",
        "HwId": "Pump1",
        "Operations": {
          "Op01": {
            "PollingInterval": "10000",
            "UnitId": "1",
            "StartAddress": "35749",
            "Count": "57",
            "DisplayName": "Batch1"
          },
```

---

[5]https://github.com/Azure/iot-edge-modbus.

```
      "Op02": {
        "PollingInterval": "10000",
        "UnitId": "1",
        "StartAddress": "35806",
          "Count": "50",
          "DisplayName": "Batch2"
        }
      }
    }
  }
}
```

The specifics of this config are not in scope for this discussion. But I will point out two settings to show how easy it is to start communicating using this module. The SlaveConnection and TcpPort properties are all that is needed to connect this edge module to a modbus sensor over ethernet. If you set those properly, when the edge solution starts up, you will see traffic flowing without having to implement the modbus protocol.

The point you should walk away with is that third party modules can be added to your edge solution just as easily as the custom code we've looked at. You just have to be aware of the specific requirements (configuration, message input/output names, message schema) for the module.

OPC UA Edge Module

Another commonly used edge communication module is an OPC UA module, also built by Microsoft. This edge module can be used with this container registry address and tag: mcr.microsoft.com/iotedge/opc-publisher:latest. This module can connect to an OPC UA[6] endpoint and transform the message into a JSON message that can be consumed by your custom module code. Similar to the modbus module in the previous section, you simply have to know the IP of the OPC endpoint, the correct format for the route, and the structure of the incoming messages. If you need to leverage the OPC

---

[6]https://opcfoundation.org/about/opc-technologies/opc-ua/.

UA module in your solution, a snippet of the deployment manifest required for this container is shown in Listing 5-28.

Listing 5-28. OPC UA module section in the deployment manifest

```
"opc_client": {
  "version": "1.0",
  "type": "docker",
"status": "running",
"restartPolicy": "always",
"settings": {
  "image": "mcr.microsoft.com/iotedge/opc-publisher:latest",
  "createOptions": "{\"Cmd\": [ \"publisher\", \"--di=60\", \"--to\",
  \"--aa\", \"--si=1\", \"--op=150\", \"--oi=150\" ]}"
  }
}
```

This module is similar to the modbus config section, but it includes the create options property. This is a JSON string that is passed to the container when it starts up. In this example, these create options are command line options that the OPC Publisher code uses. To see a full list of the options, visit: `https://github.com/Azure/iot-edge-opc-publisher`. To leverage this module in your solution, you will also need to create a route from the output of this module to the input of your module. Listing 5-29 shows an example of how to do this.

Listing 5-29. Deployment manifest route for OPC UA module output

```
"opc": "FROM /messages/modules/opc_client/* INTO
BrokeredEndpoint(\"/modules/myOpcModule/inputs/opcInput\")"
```

This listing shows the output of the OPC module (`opc_client`) and the input of the custom module (`opcInput`) in a similar way to the route we saw in the modbus example.

Note   The output route of the OPC UA Publisher edge module is slightly different than other modules. There is no named output. It is just a wildcarded route source. The example shown here is the exact way it should be represented in any other solutions you create.

The configuration of this module is done through a separate file named `publishedNodes.json`, not in the deployment manifest. More information about that configuration file, the configuration options available and this module, in general, can be found at the GitHub address above.

Third party modules all require some special research and discovery to understand the nuances of each one and how to effectively leverage them. But, hopefully, you have a better understanding of how third party modules can be used to more quickly build edge modules. It's helpful to think about edge modules as building blocks for future solutions in your organization. The better the design is for the modules you build, the more they will be able to reuse, which speeds up the development and deployment for those solutions. This reuse and management of developed edge resources usually lead to the creation of a team who manages the catalog of edge modules for an organization. This team can then make other teams aware of existing functionality that is available, saving time and money.

For more information on edge modules available from Microsoft like the two protocol module examples we just reviewed, visit *https://azuremarketplace. microsoft.com/en-us/marketplace/apps* and click *Internet of Things*, then *IoT Edge Modules* in the left navigation. Both of the modules we discussed are on that list. But Microsoft is actively working on building edge modules containers that encapsulate cloud functionality that can be run on the edge. Currently, Stream Analytics, Storage, SQL DB, and Machine Learning are all edge modules that can be run in your edge solution.

Summary

In this chapter, we discussed the development process for edge solutions and how a couple of utilities can simplify that workflow. We looked at the `iotedgehubdev` simulator utility as well as the `iotedgedev` utility that exposes a command line interface to create and manage all aspects of edge solutions and the related development process. We then looked at the configuration and setup required to use these command line tools and what tooling is available in VS Code and Visual Studio. With a firm grasp of these tools, your edge solution development experience should be much more efficient.

Lastly, we looked at two examples of third party edge modules built by Microsoft that can be included in our edge solutions in minutes, with minor configuration. Third party modules are a powerful addition to many edge solutions, saving time and money in the development costs.

In the next chapter, we will look at enabling some advanced capabilities on the edge by looking at how to run advanced analytics modules in an IoT Edge solution.

CHAPTER 6

Analytics on the Edge

One of the driving forces for edge computing is the ability to run analytics on edge devices. Companies who have spent years creating and improving their algorithms or machine learning models that are used in their backed batch processing workflows are trying to understand how they can leverage that existing intellectual property in new ways and in new areas using the edge. In many cases, the batch processing paradigm imposes intolerable delays throughout the rest of the dependent systems, which motivates companies to look for ways to speed up the path to get the answers they want. The faster the results (results, not just data) are generated, the faster the business can react. So, companies have started introducing edge solutions that place this advanced logic (algorithms and models) as close to the source of the data as possible, which enables decisions to be made in real time, rather than having to wait on decisions until the data has been processed by backed batch processes.

But there is another, newer, use case that has been gaining momentum over the past couple of years. That use case is the use of third party advanced analytic modules in brand-new solutions. Companies that have no existing intellectual property in the form of machine learning models or proprietary algorithms are now investigating and deploying solutions that leverage models and algorithms built by companies that specialize in that field. For example, a retail company that deploys customer-facing kiosks in their retail stores might decide to deploy a speech recognition solution so that customers can ask for help without having to navigate the kiosk's user interface. In addition, that same company might decide to convert the speech it detects into text so that the text could be analyzed for patterns and common questions.

This may sound like a straightforward solution, but chances are this *retail* company has not spent any time or money building speech recognition or speech-to-text models. Rather than invest the resources required to develop those assets, it makes

© David Jensen 2019
D. Jensen, *Beginning Azure IoT Edge Computing*, https://doi.org/10.1007/978-1-4842-4536-1_6

more sense for them to leverage this logic from a third party that has created language understanding models and published them in a reusable format. This way, the retail company can continue to focus on their core business, while at the same time, deploy a compelling solution to their stores without having to become experts in language understanding algorithms.

In this chapter, we will discuss the different options available to package existing models or algorithms into edge modules as well as leverage prebuilt edge modules containing models that have been trained and curated and are available for purchase or through an open-source license.

Azure Cognitive Services

For a few years, Microsoft has been building and improving a set of APIs known as the Cognitive Toolkit (CNTK). The Cognitive Toolkit is a collection of different pretrained AI models that are available to integrate into any custom application. These services are now offered on the Azure platform under the name Azure Cognitive Services and are grouped into five different categories.[1] Figure 6-1 shows the landing page for the Azure Cognitive Services.

---

[1]To view the complete list of Azure Cognitive Services, visit https://azure.microsoft.com/en-us/services/cognitive-services/directory/.

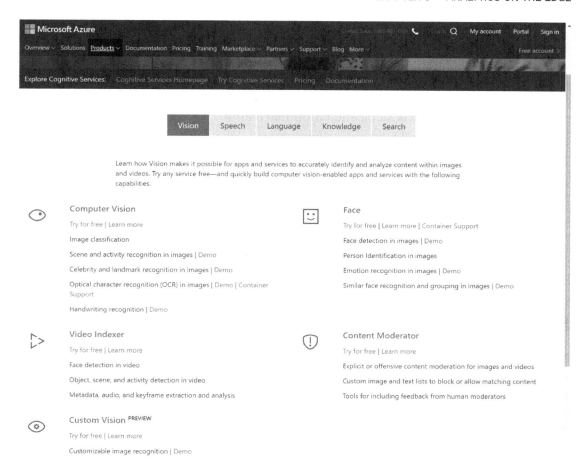

Figure 6-1. *Azure Cognitive Services landing page*

To help you understand the available services here is a list of the Azure Cognitive Services with a short description of each service.

Vision API

The Vision API is a category of cognitive services that all focus on automated image or video recognition.

- **Computer vision:** Recognizes significant elements in images. Some examples include tagging (generating metadata) from object detected in an image, landmark and celebrity recognition, handwriting detection, optical character recognition (OCR) which is detecting text characters in an image.

- **Video indexer:** Detects faces in video and other key events in video. Examples include object and scene detection in video, metadata generation from video files based on objects, scenes, and activities identified in the video.

- **Face API:** Detects facial and emotional features. Examples include detecting general faces, identifying specific people in an image, detecting emotions being expressed in the picture.

- **Content moderator:** Scans image and/or video feed sources for offensive content. Examples include automatically moderating media files during upload to sharing sites like forums or social media.

- **Custom vision:** Image recognition that can be trained and tuned to a user's specific use case. Examples include license plate recognition.

Speech API

Much like the Vision API, the Speech API is a collection of services that focus on speech recognition. The goal of speech services is to automate and replicate the natural interactions of humans through speech.

- **Speech to text:** Transcribes speech to text that is customizable and can be adapted for unique vocabularies and accents

- **Text to speech:** Converts regular text to speech and includes voice fonts for adjusting the output

- **Speaker recognition:** Identifies and verifies specific speakers based on their voice input

- **Speech translator:** Translates speech real-time and can be automated and customized for specific scenarios

Language API

The Language API is an advanced set of text analytical services that move beyond just dealing with text and use text to infer linguistic context.

- **Text Analytics:** Extracts key phrases from the text, detects the sentiment of textual phrases

- **Bing Spell Check:** The multilingual spell check service used by the Bing search engine

- **Language Understanding:** Contextualized language understanding which allows applications to respond specifically to a highly contextualized interaction

- **Translator Text:** Detects languages and can automatically translate languages, including custom vocabulary

- **Content Moderator:** Scans text for potentially offensive content, based on the context

Knowledge API

The Knowledge API is a single service that powers some of the interactions behind the Bot Framework from Microsoft.

- **QnA Maker:** Extracts questions with corresponding answers from unstructured text, supports the creation of a knowledge base from collections of questions and answers

Search API

The Search API is a collection of many of the Bing-nuanced search services.

- **Bing Web Search:** Supports safe (filtered) web searching and location-specific web searching

- **Bing Custom Search:** A custom search engine which can be used for a custom collection of data

- **Bing Video Search:** Returns video search results based on the entered criteria

- **Bing Image Search:** Returns images search results based on the entered criteria

- **Bing Local Business Search:** Returns local business search results based on the specified area of interest

- **Bing Visual Search:** Searches for related images based on an input set of images used as the search criteria

- **Bing Entity Search:** Returns search results for named entities (people, organizations, etc.) with curated and detailed information about the entity

- **Bing News Search:** Returns news results based on relevance and the current trending topics

- **Bing Autosuggest:** Returns autocomplete or query suggest results based on the partial search criteria entered

In addition to just the initial offerings, the services can be chained together. So, for example, you could spell check text and filter for offensive content before translating. This workflow strings the Spell Check, Content Moderator, and Translation services together as shown in Figure 6-2.

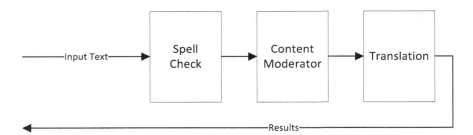

Figure 6-2. *Chain of cognitive services used in advanced workflow*

Cognitive Services Containers

As I mentioned earlier, all of the services just described are available on the Azure platform as a web API that can be scaled to support any level of traffic your application or integration needs can generate. In addition to that, Microsoft has also begun to release a subset of the Cognitive Services in Docker containers, so they are portable and can be leveraged in more scenarios than the web APIs supported.

A use case mentioned earlier in this chapter that described a retail company trying to deploy a customer-facing kiosk. If the solution depended on an HTTP call to the Azure service for each and every utterance, the solution would be extremely chatty (with network traffic, not human chattiness) and would experience significant delays with the slightest of network latency. So, a better solution would be to have the AI speech models hosted locally. With the model hosted locally, the solution can provide almost immediate feedback and can maintain a level of consistency that is not attainable with working with cloud services from an on-premises solution.

However, there is a great deal of work that goes into packaging these APIs into a portable container. So, all of the aforementioned services are not yet available in a container format. Here is a list (as of the writing of this book) of the services that are available as a container.[2]

- **Key phrase extraction:** The key phrase extraction logic from the Text Analytics API within the Language API category mentioned earlier. Key themes are identified and extracted from the input text.

- **Language detection:** The language detection logic from the Text Analytics API within the Language API category mentioned earlier. Detects the language used in the input text for over 100 languages.

- **Sentiment analysis:** The Sentiment Analysis API logic from the Text Analytics API within the Language API category mentioned earlier. Detects the sentiment, either positive (1) or negative (0), for each input text document.

- **Face:** The Face Detection API from the Vision API category mentioned earlier. Detects human faces in images, compares two faces against each other, and searches for similar faces in a known facial database.

- **Recognize text:** The Text Recognition API from the Computer Vision API in the Vision API category mentioned earlier. Detects text in images and extracts the text contained in the image. Currently, this API only supports the English language.

- **LUIS:** Allows users to load their custom LUIS (Language Understanding) applications in a container. LUIS apps enable natural language interactions through various client-facing endpoints.

---

[2]Visit https://docs.microsoft.com/en-us/azure/cognitive-services/cognitive-services-container-support for a list of the current containers supported.

- **Custom vision:** Allows a user to run a custom-built model that has been trained in the Custom Vision workspace. Custom vision models can be trained to detect any objects in images, and recently the Custom Vision API has added the ability to detect logos.

The list of Cognitive Services available in containers continues to grow. Microsoft's goal is to enable and make available as many of these services in a reusable container. So, if the Cognitive Service you need is not listed above, keep checking the list referenced earlier. It is continually changing.

Using a Cognitive Service Container

Up to this point, we have only listed and discussed the available containers and some of the functionality each of these containers possesses. Now, we need to walk through what's required to actually use one of these containers.

To get started, there are a few things that must set up in the Azure portal.

Note   This section also assumes the requirements specified in earlier chapters are still present on your machine. VS Code, the IoT Edge simulator, and the IoT Edge runtime are all required for the following sample.

The first thing you need to set up is a Cognitive Services resource. You can create this by clicking the *Create a resource* link in the top left corner of the Azure portal. In the search bar, enter cognitive services, as shown in Figure 6-3.

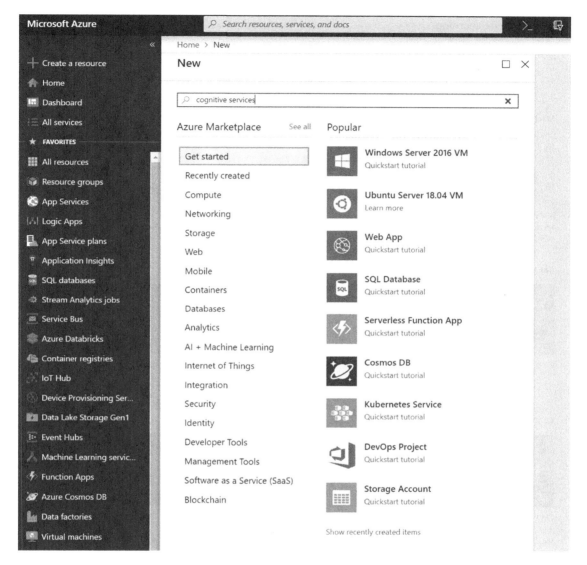

Figure 6-3. *Create Cognitive Services resource in Azure*

Once this resource is provisioned, you can begin to create individual Cognitive APIs. When you Cognitive Service resource has provisioned, open it and click the *Add* button in the top left corner. You should see something similar to the screen shown in Figure 6-4.

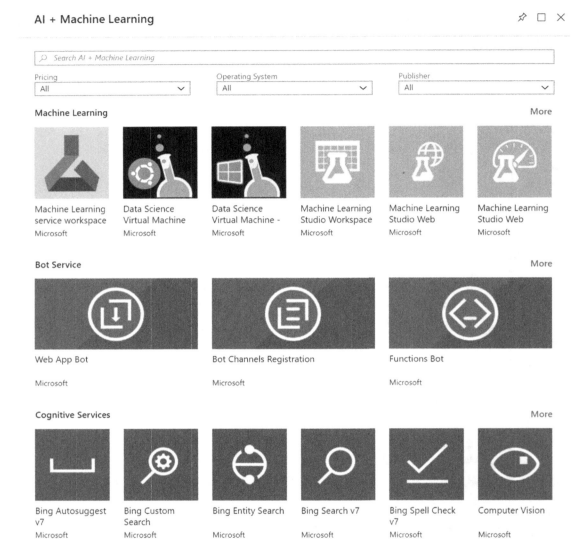

Figure 6-4. *List of available Cognitive Services*

At the bottom of this screen, you should see a list of services that seem familiar, based on the discussion so far. If you click *More* next to *Cognitive Services*, you can see the full list of available services that can be provisioned in Azure.

When working with the Cognitive Services containers, there is a pattern you must follow to enable the functionality in the container. We will pick one container and walk through that process, but you should know that the same process holds true for the other containers as well.

For our example, select Text Analytics from the list of Cognitive Services. You will need to select a region and resource group among a handful of other basic information. Once you enter that criteria, wait for the resource to finish provisioning. Once it completes, you should see a screen similar to the figure shown in Figure 6-5.

Figure 6-5. *Text Analytics resource overview*

Now that you have provisioned the Azure resources, the associated billing and security information are in place and can be used to configure the container. You see, any of the Cognitive Service containers must be configured/connected to a provisioned Azure resource so that the billing and usage can be calculated correctly.

Because we are focused on IoT Edge scenarios, I will show how to pull the text analytics sentiment container into an edge solution, configure it, and issue a simple HTTP call to test the container. This will walk you through the basic building blocks of working with the Cognitive Services containers which you can then apply to your specific scenario.

We will start with a new edge solution in VS Code. So, open VS Code and use the Ctrl+Shift+P combination to create a new edge solution. It should look like the screen shown in Figure 6-6.

Figure 6-6. *New VS Code edge solution*

Enter a solution name as shown in Figure 6-7.

Figure 6-7. *Edge solution name*

Next, enter the module template as an existing module with the full image URL. It is the bottom option in the list shown in Figure 6-8.

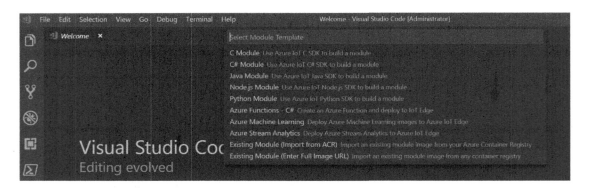

Figure 6-8. *Edge module template type*

After you select that template type, enter the module name for the cognitive services container. The next prompt asks you to enter the full path, including tags for the container image. For the Text Analytics Sentiment container, enter the URL shown in Listing 6-1.

Listing 6-1. Cognitive container image URL

```
mcr.microsoft.com/azure-cognitive-services/sentiment:latest
```

All of the Microsoft cognitive containers follow a similar pattern. They are all hosted by Microsoft under the location/tag: `mcr.microsoft.com/azure-cognitive-services` and you will have to find the name of the container and tag you need to add to the end of that image URL. After you have entered the full image URL, hit enter and your edge solution should be scaffolded out. Click the `deployment.template.json` file (which you should be familiar with from our previous discussions in the earlier chapters. The modules section of the deployment file should look like the snippet in Listing 6-2.

Listing 6-2. Modules section from the generated deployment file

```
"modules": {
        "tempSensor": {
          "version": "1.0",
          "type": "docker",
          "status": "running",
          "restartPolicy": "always",
          "settings": {
            "image": "mcr.microsoft.com/azureiotedge-simulated-
            temperature-sensor:1.0",
            "createOptions": {}
          }
        },
        "SentimentContainer": {
          "version": "1.0",
          "type": "docker",
          "status": "running",
          "restartPolicy": "always",
          "settings": {
            "image": "mcr.microsoft.com/azure-cognitive-services/
            sentiment:latest",
            "createOptions": {}
          }
        }
```

```
        }
      }
    }
```

You can see that the edge solution has not only added our sentiment container but also included the tempSensor container. Since we don't need that for this example, let's remove that from the deployment file. Additionally, we don't need any message routes, because we are only going to run the web host in our container and not route any messages to the IoT Hub or to any other containers. In the routes sections, remove the two listed routes so that the $edgeHub config section looks like the snippet in Listing 6-3.

Listing 6-3. Empty route section in the deployment file

```
"$edgeHub": {
      "properties.desired": {
        "schemaVersion": "1.0",
        "routes": { },
        "storeAndForwardConfiguration": {
          "timeToLiveSecs": 7200
        }
      }
    }
```

The last thing we need to configure in the deployment file is the startup configuration settings for the sentiment container. All of the Cognitive Services containers will need these same configuration steps. There are three configuration parameters we need to set:

- Eula: Set to the literal value "accept"

- Billing: Set to the billing endpoint retrieved from the Azure portal

- ApiKey: Set to the value of the key retrieved from the Azure portal

The billing endpoint value can be found on the Overview page of the Cognitive Service in the Azure portal, as shown in Figure 6-9.

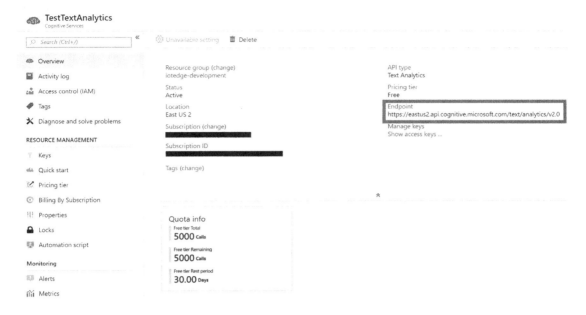

Figure 6-9. *Azure billing endpoint*

The ApiKey can be found in the Keys section of the resource in the Azure portal. Once you have located both of these configuration values, add a section of JSON into the createOptions section that looks like Listing 6-4.

Listing 6-4. Cognitive container createOptions

```
"createOptions": "{\"Env\": [\"Eula=accept\",\"Billing={BILLING-
ENDPOINT}\",\"ApiKey={API-KEY}\"],\"HostConfig\": {\"PortBindings\":
{\"5000/tcp\": [{\"HostPort\": \"8080\"}]}}}"
```

We are adding a port mapping in this section as well so that when we point a browser at port 8080 on the host machine, the container runtime will redirect that request to port 5000 in the container.

Once you have added these configuration parameters, right click the deployment. template.json file and run the solution in the simulator. You should see output similar to that shown in Listing 6-5.

Listing 6-5. Edge simulator console output

```
Sentiment   |
Sentiment   | Logging to console.
```

```
Sentiment    | Submitting metering to 'https://eastus2.api.cognitive.
               microsoft.com/text/analytics/v2.0'.
Sentiment    | WARNING: No access control enabled!
Sentiment    | Hosting environment: Production
Sentiment    | Content root path: /
Sentiment    | Now listening on: http://0.0.0.0:5000
Sentiment    | Application started. Press Ctrl+C to shut down.
```

At this point, you should be able to navigate to port 8080 (or whatever port you specified in the container port mapping) and see the welcome screen shown in Figure 6-10.

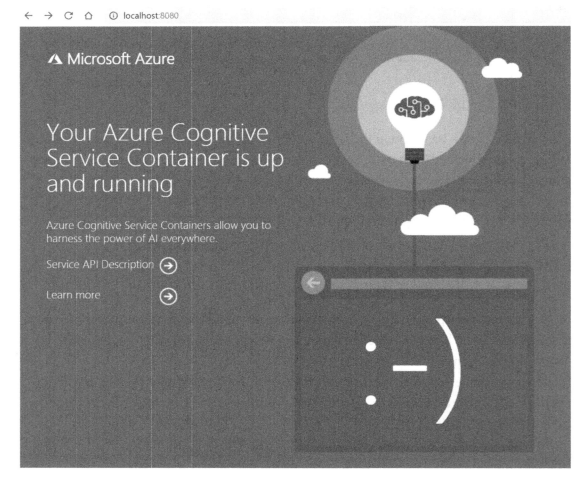

Figure 6-10. *Cognitive container welcome screen*

Now, click the link for the Service API Description and you will be able to view the Swagger[3] definition for the API. The Swagger information for our container should look like the screen shown in Figure 6-11.

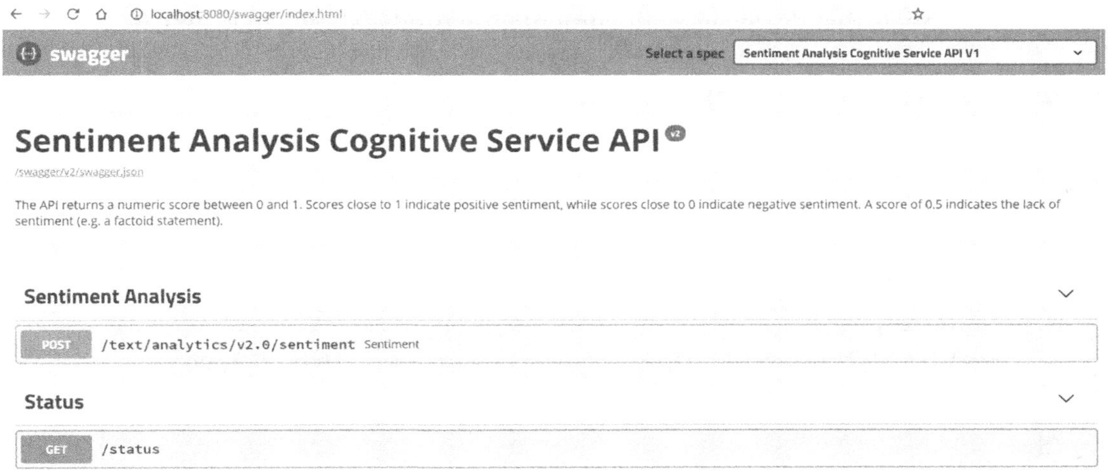

Figure 6-11. *Container Swagger screen*

You can check the status of the container by clicking the *GET* section and then click *Try it out*. Once you click *Try it out*, an *Execute* button will appear and you can invoke that method on the container. The results should look like the output shown in Listing 6-6.

Listing 6-6. Sentiment Analysis API response

```
{
  "service": "sentiment",
  "apiStatus": "Valid",
  "apiStatusMessage": "Api Key is valid."
}
```

---

[3]Swagger is a utility used to document REST APIs and you can find out more about it at https:// swagger.io/.

183

The next thing to try is the actual sentiment request. If you click the *POST* section in the Swagger screen and click *Try it out*, an *Execute* button will appear as before and if you click that, the model will be invoked. Keep in mind the first time, the model takes much longer because there are some initial tasks that must be run. In case you didn't notice it, the sample request that the Swagger documentation used is shown in Listing 6-7.

Listing 6-7. Sample sentiment request

```
{
  "documents": [
    {
      "language": "en",
      "id": "1",
      "text": "Hello world. This is some input text that I love."
    },
    {
      "language": "fr",
      "id": "2",
      "text": "Bonjour tout le monde"
    },
    {
      "language": "es",
      "id": "3",
      "text": "La carretera estaba atascada. Había mucho tráfico el día de
      ayer."
    }
  ]
}
```

And the result of the sample request is shown in Listing 6-8.

Listing 6-8. Sample sentiment response

```
{
  "documents": [
    {
      "id": "1",
      "score": 0.9869070649147034
    },
    {
      "id": "2",
      "score": 0.8401265144348145
    },
    {
      "id": "3",
      "score": 0.334433376789093
    }
  ],
  "errors": []
}
```

The score shows how positive or negative the phrase is (within the range of 0 to 1). The lower the score, the more negative it is.

Next Steps with Cognitive Services Containers

In the previous section, we learned the basics of how to use and startup the Cognitive Services containers. In order to use this in a production environment, you would need to add some additional modules to your edge solution. Most likely, you'll need a custom edge module that will control the flow of the events occurring at the edge. If you had a scenario where a customer-facing kiosk was deployed and you wanted to capture their comments about a new product line and determine of their comments were either positive or negative, you would deploy two Cognitive Services containers and a third custom container to orchestrate the workflow. The high-level architecture would look something like the diagram shown in Figure 6-12.

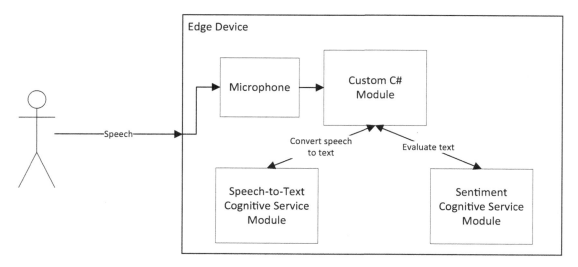

Figure 6-12. *Possible architecture for customer kiosk solution*

The custom C# module, in this case, would have to capture the audio and send the audio to the speech-to-text module through a local web request. The result of that web request would be submitted to the sentiment module for evaluation. Then, the custom logic in the C# code would respond based on whether the customer's response was either positive or negative.

This is a simple example only meant to help explain when, where and how the suite of Cognitive Services containers can be leveraged in your real-world solutions.

Azure Machine Learning Service

Everything up until this point has been geared toward models and containers that Microsoft has built and we are just consuming them. What if we need some custom logic built into our own container? If you have existing models or algorithms that need to be packaged into a container, the Azure Machine Learning (ML) service is the solution.

The Azure ML service is the latest in Azure ML tooling and replaces the previous tooling known as the ML workbench. It also provides an environment for you to prepare your data, experiment using Jupyter notebooks and finally build your model or algorithm into a container that can be pushed to a container registry and later deployed to your edge device. If you'd like to learn more about this service, you can read about it at `https://azure.microsoft.com/en-us/services/machine-learning-service/` and if you are interested in seeing some sample notebooks and how to use them to build and deploy a containerized model, visit `https://github.com/Azure/MachineLearningNotebooks`.

Summary

In this chapter, we learned about the suite of ready to use models called Azure Cognitive Services. We learned about how to access those containers and how to pull them into an edge solution. We also learned how to test the edge module once it's deployed and how we can combine the cognitive services into highly advanced interactions in a relatively short amount of time. Finally, we discussed the path forward for custom ML models and algorithms. The Azure Machine Learning service provides all the tools necessary to create, train, test, and deploy your custom models.

In the next chapter, we will look at how to provision devices at scale using the Device Provisioning Service (DPS).

CHAPTER 7

Device Provisioning Service

In this chapter, we shift our focus away from the edge platform and processing and take a look at one of the cloud services that supports any production-scale IoT scenario in Azure. This service is the Device Provisioning Service (DPS). The DPS is a service that connects to the IoT Hub service and the goal of the DPS is to validate the security information on a device and connect the device to the correct IoT Hub instance automatically. When dealing with hundreds or thousands of devices, it is not practical to manually configure them. The DPS exists to automate the device provisioning (bootstrapping) process and it is compatible with IoT and IoT Edge devices. Here are a few scenarios where using the DPS can be extremely useful:

- Single IoT Hub scenarios such as automatically connecting devices to IoT Hub without having to hardcode the IoT Hub connection string, updating the device security keys used to connect to IoT Hub

- Multi IoT Hub scenarios such as dynamically assigning devices to an IoT Hub instance to load balance the devices, assigning devices to an IoT Hub instance based on the geographic location of the device, assigning devices to an IoT Hub instance based on the owner of the device (multitenancy)

Let's take a look at how the DPS automates these scenarios and simplifies much of the configuration required to connect our edge devices to the IoT Hub service.

© David Jensen 2019
D. Jensen, *Beginning Azure IoT Edge Computing*, https://doi.org/10.1007/978-1-4842-4536-1_7

Device Provisioning Workflow

The DPS uses a predefined set of steps, the device provisioning workflow, to configure IoT and IoT Edge devices to an IoT Hub instance. In this section, we will take a look at that workflow and discuss the requirements for the various steps. Figure 7-1 shows a high-level view of this workflow.

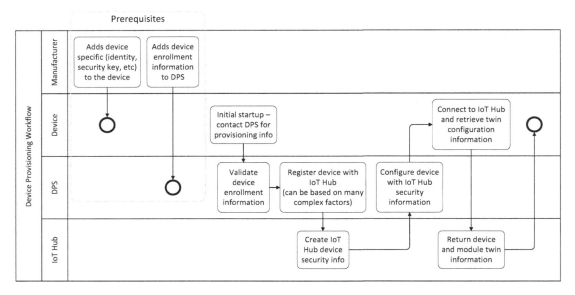

Figure 7-1. *Device provisioning workflow*

Let's examine this workflow in more detail to understand what's happening at each step.

- **Prerequisites:** The first two steps labeled as prerequisites are performed by the manufacturer.

    - The manufacturer must provision the security information on the device. This is something like an X.509 certificate or a key provisioned to a TPM. Additionally, the connection information for the DPS must be written to the device. It is recommended that this information is managed during the manufacturing process, rather than statically assigned in the device code.

    - The manufacturer must add the correct security information to the DPS enrollment list. This information is used to validate the identity of the device when it initially connects to the DPS.

- **DPS workflow:** The normal provisioning workflow starts when the device boots up for the first time.

  - Using the DPS connection information the device was given during the manufacturing process, it will connect to the DPS instance.

  - The DPS will validate the device identity/security information it received in the initial connect request against the security information associated with that device in the enrollment list. This is the information populated during the second prerequisite mentioned earlier.

  - Once the DPS has validated the device, it will register the device with the correct IoT Hub instance. Complex logic can be used in this step to determine the IoT Hub instance to assign the device to, which is one of the main benefits of the DPS – complex provisioning business rules can be implemented and automated.

  - After the device has been registered with its IoT Hub instance, the DPS sends the IoT Hub connection information to the device.

  - When the device receives the IoT Hub connection information, it will attempt the initial connection to the IoT Hub. During this initial connection, the device twin and, in the case of IoT Edge devices, module twin, information will be sent to the device.

  - Finally, the twin information is used on the device to complete the device configuration. In the case of IoT Edge devices, this includes pulling down the initial container images from the container registries and starting up the edge runtime, based on the module configurations (module twins).

Device Provisioning Service Concepts

The Device Provisioning Service introduces its users to some concepts that might be new, especially if you do not have any experience with device manufacturing. During the manufacturing process (as I mentioned earlier), the manufacturer has a step that must be performed for the DPS to be able to validate the identity of the device and allow the device to auto-register. And the process varies based on whether the device will use X.509 certificates or TPMs for security. Let's see how this manufacturing relates to the way devices are provisioned by the DPS by reviewing a couple of concepts that the DPS relies on enrollments and allocation policies.

DPS Enrollments

The concept of device enrollment in the DPS is fairly straightforward. You can think of enrollment similar to a class roster in school – a list of every possible member that might join. In a classroom, the roster represents the complete list of allowed students, any of which may or may not show up to the class that day. In DPS terms, the enrollment is the list of allowed devices that are permitted to register, but some of them may not have registered (shown up to class) yet. This enrollment list (roster) is built from the information the manufacturer sends to the DPS. The requirement for any enrollment is that the identity of the device attempting to enroll must be verifiable, also known as attestation. If a device identity cannot be attested, it will not be allowed to continue in the provisioning process.

In the DPS, there are group enrollments and individual enrollments. The type of enrollment you chose really depends on the way you secure your devices. If you are using TPMs, then you must use individual enrollments because the device's security information and identity are based on its individually unique keys. TPMs can't use a common signing root like certificates, so each individual device identity must be added to an enrollment list.

If you are using certificates, you can use either group or individual enrollments, depending on how you have set up your certificate management solution. If you have a common root or intermediate certificates in the certificate chain that can be used to attest multiple devices. Then, that common cert can be uploaded to the DPS and used to define an enrollment group. Once that is done, any device presenting a leaf (individual) certificate that has been signed by the root or an intermediate certificate for that group will be granted access. One of the nice things about the DPS provisioning process is that each enrollment group can assign devices to different IoT Hubs if needed. So, if you are a service provider and have a different intermediate signing certificate for different customers, you can use the customer intermediate signing certificate to define a DPS enrollment group and assign all devices in that group to a dedicated instance of IoT Hub. But, if you do not have any shared signing certificates in the certificate chain, you may still use individual certificates to create an individual enrollment.

One of the other attributes associated with both group and individual enrollments is the initial device twin state. Once you define the initial device twin state in an enrollment group, the DPS pushes that information to the correct IoT Hub instance so that the device receives that configuration during the initial startup/bootstrapping process. This is extremely powerful when you couple it together with the concepts we've discussed earlier – IoT Hub automated deployments.

Note   Remember from the Core Concepts chapter that deployments are defined by a condition in the device twin that continually and dynamically identifies the devices that should be included in the deployment based on the twin attributes. Setting the initial twin state as part of the enrollment can feed devices directly into deployments that have been set up in the IoT Hub.

With these features, the DPS helps to facilitate an automated workflow where the initial state of the device is set in the DPS based on the enrollment and then the IoT Hub detects that state and completes the device updates based on what has been configured in the IoT Hub deployments for that device. Additionally, for IoT Edge devices, you can include the modules and the complete deployment manifest as part of the deployment group. This functionality enables completely automated device bootstrapping workflows like the one shown in Figure 7-2.

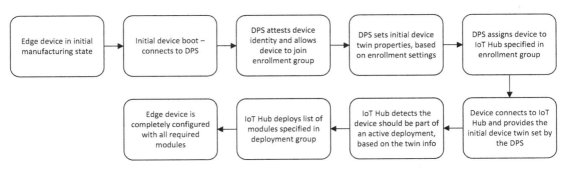

Figure 7-2. *Example automated device provisioning workflow*

DPS Allocation Policies

Devices are assigned to an IoT Hub by the DPS through an allocation policy. Allocation policies can be set at the service level or at the enrollment level. The default allocation policy is set at the service level and can be one of three options:

- **Lowest latency:** The DPS assigns devices to the IoT Hub that is geographically closest to the device location.

- **Evenly weighted distribution:** This is the default setting; devices are distributed evenly across all the linked IoT Hubs.

- **Static configuration:** Devices are assigned based on the allocation policy in the device's enrollment group.

Devices that need an allocation policy different than the default, service-level, policy can use an allocation policy that applies to the device enrollment. In an enrollment (individual or group), the list of IoT Hubs available for the enrollment can be filtered and the enrollment allocation policy will be used on the filtered list of IoT Hubs. This allocation policy will override the service level policy, no matter what the service level allocation policy is. Additionally, the allocation policies in enrollments have a fourth option:

- **Custom:** This allocation policy uses an Azure Function. With this policy, any logic that can be coded in a Function can be used to determine which IoT Hub to assign the devices to.

Reprovisioning

Reprovisioning is the process of sending a device through the provisioning process we have described a second, third (or more) iteration. When this happens, a decision must be made about the device's IoT Hub twin information that may have been significantly updated since the initial provisioning. The three options are:

- **Reprovision and migrate data:** The device assigned to the updated IoT Hub and the device twin is migrated from the current IoT Hub to the new IoT Hub.

- **Reprovision and reset to initial config:** The device is assigned to the updated IoT Hub and the initial config from the DPS enrollment for the device replaces the current device twin.

- **Never reprovision:** Do not allow this process to occur. This means that once a device is provisioned it will have to be manually reprovisioned if that is ever needed.

Device Provision Service Setup

There are a few ways to create and configure an instance of the DPS. You can use the Azure portal, the Azure command line interface (CLI) or ARM templates. In this section, we will walk through using the Azure portal to set up a DPS instance and connect it to our IoT Hub instance.

In the portal, click the "Create a resource" link and search for the IoT Hub Device Provisioning Service, as shown in Figure 7-3.

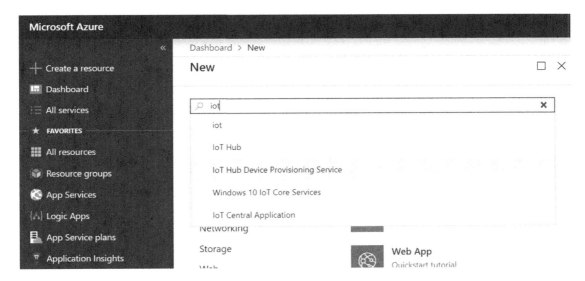

Figure 7-3. *Search for DPS resource in the Azure portal*

After you select the Device Provisioning Service, click the *Create* button at the bottom of the screen. The next screen, shown in Figure 7-4, prompts you to enter the name of the DPS instance as well as the location, resource group, and Azure subscription to use.

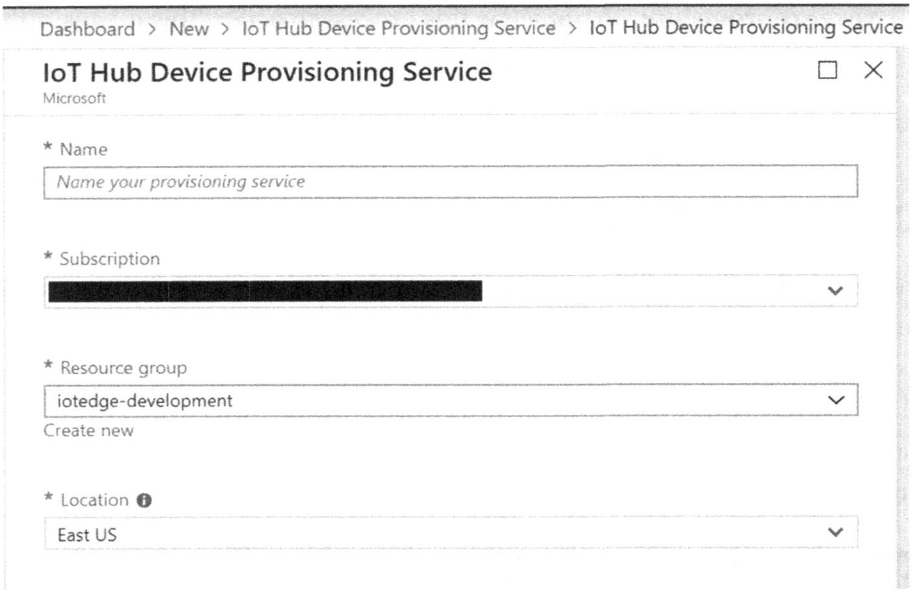

Dashboard > New > IoT Hub Device Provisioning Service > IoT Hub Device Provisioning Service

IoT Hub Device Provisioning Service
Microsoft

* Name

Name your provisioning service

* Subscription

* Resource group

iotedge-development

Create new

* Location ❶

East US

Figure 7-4. *Create a DPS instance*

Once the service has been provisioned, navigate to the service overview. The first action we need to perform is linking at least one IoT Hub. Click *Linked IoT Hubs* and then click the *Add* button at the top to add a new IoT Hub. The portal should prompt you to select the IoT Hub instance you want to link, as shown in Figure 7-5.

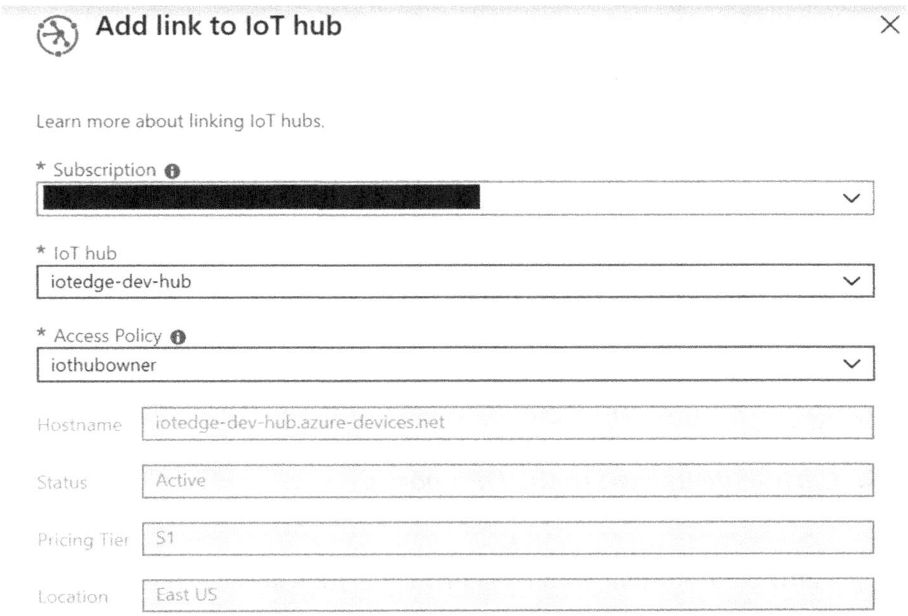

Figure 7-5. *Add a link to IoT Hub*

Once you have entered all the required information, click *Save* at the bottom and your DPS instance should now be linked to the IoT Hub instance you selected. Repeat these steps for any additional IoT Hub instances you need to link to the DPS. Once you have completed these steps, your DPS instance is ready to configure for device provisioning.

If you will be using certificates for device attestation, you need to explicitly upload the certificate files to the DPS. This is shown in Figure 7-6. Once you add certificates to the service, you will be able to select them in the enrollment setup.

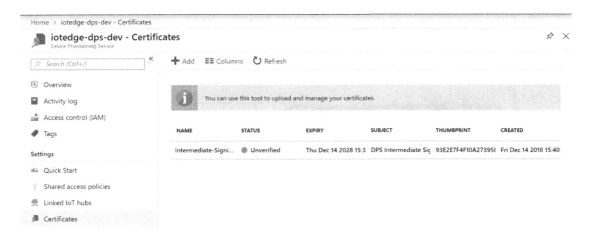

Figure 7-6. *Certificate upload in the DPS portal*

To set up a group enrollment with this certificate, look at the screen shown in Figure 7-7. This is an example of group enrollment, using a signing certificate.

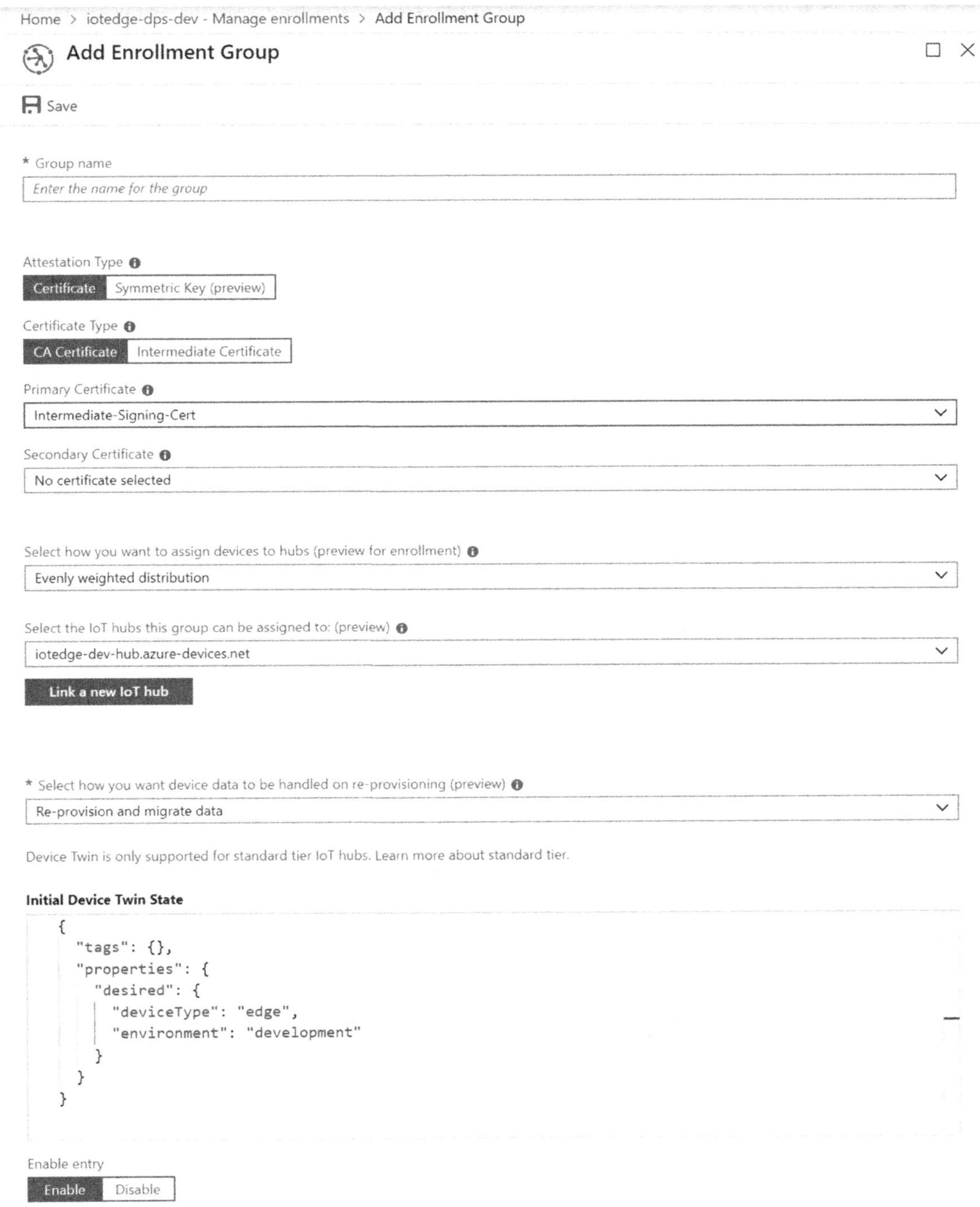

Home > iotedge-dps-dev - Manage enrollments > Add Enrollment Group

Add Enrollment Group   □ ✕

🖫 Save

* Group name

Enter the name for the group

Attestation Type ❶

| Certificate | Symmetric Key (preview) |

Certificate Type ❶

| CA Certificate | Intermediate Certificate |

Primary Certificate ❶

Intermediate-Signing-Cert   ⌄

Secondary Certificate ❶

No certificate selected   ⌄

Select how you want to assign devices to hubs (preview for enrollment) ❶

Evenly weighted distribution   ⌄

Select the IoT hubs this group can be assigned to: (preview) ❶

iotedge-dev-hub.azure-devices.net   ⌄

| Link a new IoT hub |

* Select how you want device data to be handled on re-provisioning (preview) ❶

Re-provision and migrate data   ⌄

Device Twin is only supported for standard tier IoT hubs. Learn more about standard tier.

Initial Device Twin State

```
{
  "tags": {},
  "properties": {
    "desired": {
      "deviceType": "edge",
      "environment": "development"
    }
  }
}
```

Enable entry

| Enable | Disable |

Figure 7-7. *Example DPS group enrollment using X.509 certificates*

In Figure 7-8, you can see an example of setting an individual enrollment with TPM attestation.

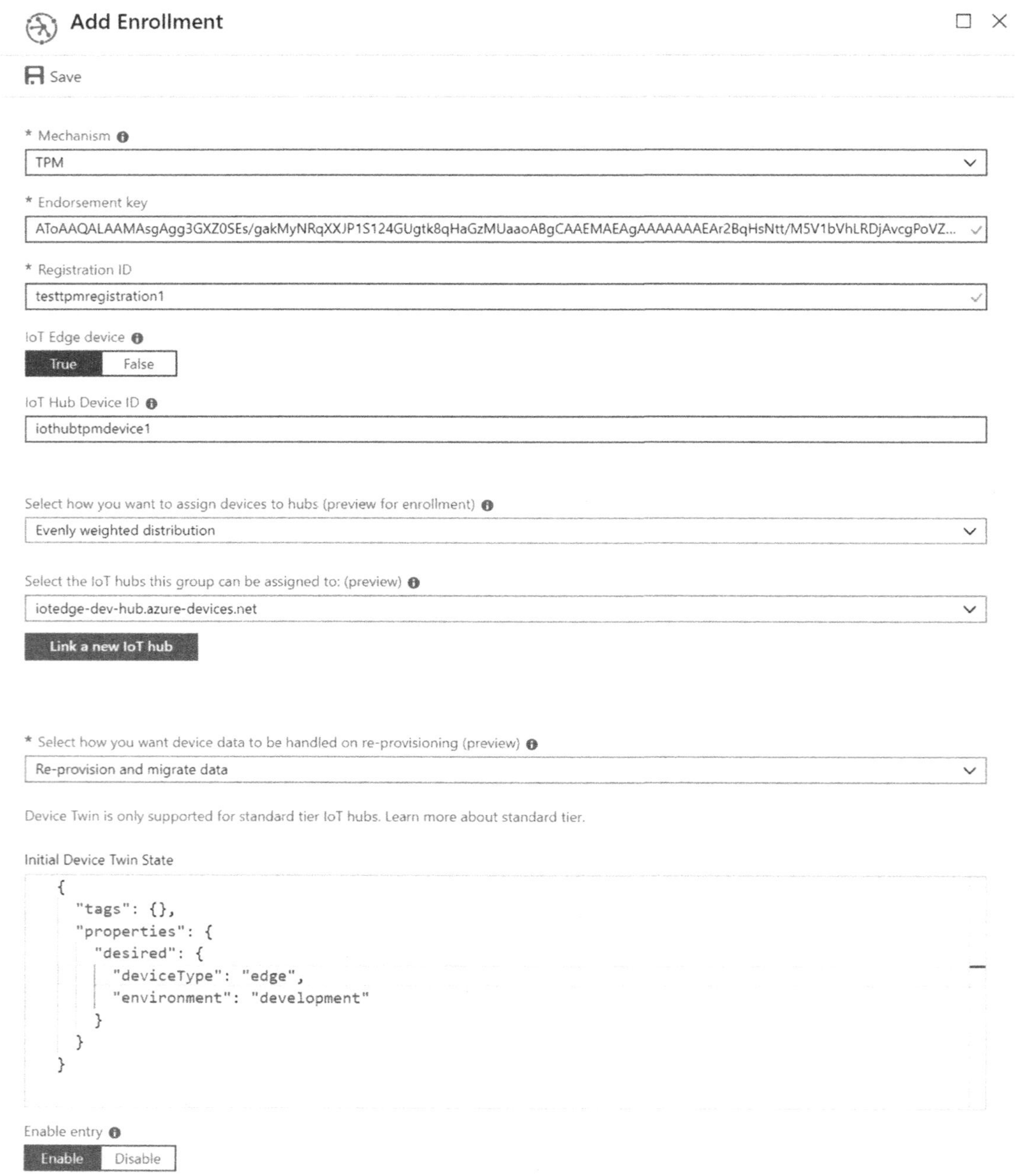

Figure 7-8. Example DPS individual enrollment using TPM

Configuring an IoT Edge Device

After we have created and configured your DPS instance, we need to configure our edge device to communicate with the DPS correctly. If you are running the edge runtime on a development machine that has a TPM, you will be able to use that TPM to test provisioning your development edge device. If you aren't sure if your machine has a TPM, you can run the Get-Tpm PowerShell cmdlet and look for the TpmPresent property.

If you do not have a TPM on your machine, you can create and configure a virtual machine with a virtual TPM, using Hyper-V. To do this, create the VM and on the VM settings screen, select the *Enable Trusted Platform Module* option, as shown in Figure 7-9.

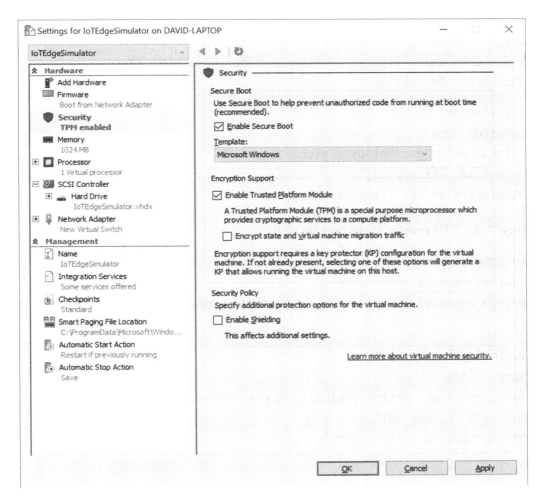

Figure 7-9. *Enable virtual TPM in Hyper-V*

Another option is to run a TPM simulator, using the code from GitHub repo `Azure-Samples/azure-iot-samples-csharp`. Once you download the repo, go to the `csharp\provisioning\Samples\device\TpmSample` subdirectory and run the command `dotnet run <IDScope>` to start the simulator. The value for the `IDScope` argument can be found in the Azure portal, on the overview screen for the DPS instance.

Once you have a TPM available, you should be to update the `config.yaml` file to use dps provisioning rather than `manual`. Listing 7-1 shows an example of the way your file should look before the changes and Listing 7-2 shows what the file should look like after the changes have been made.

Listing 7-1. Manual config.yaml configuration

```
provisioning:
  source: "manual"
  device_connection_string: "HostName=<name>;DeviceId=<ID>;
  SharedAccessKey=<key>"

# provisioning:
#   source: "dps"
#   global_endpoint: "https://global.azure-devices-provisioning.net"
#   scope_id: "{scope_id}"
#   registration_id: "{registration_id}"
```

Listing 7-2. DPS config.yaml configuration

```
# provisioning:
#   source: "manual"
#   device_connection_string: "HostName=<name>;DeviceId=<ID>;SharedAccessKey
=<key>"

provisioning:
  source: "dps"
  global_endpoint: "https://global.azure-devices-provisioning.net"
  scope_id: "{scope_id}"
  registration_id: "{registration_id}"
```

To provision the edge device using the DPS, you have to comment out the manual configuration settings shown in Listing 7-1 and populate the dps values shown in Listing 7-2. Here is a brief description of the four properties:

- source: Set this to *dps* to provision using the DPS rather manually.

- global_endpoint: The static, load balanced endpoint that all devices connect to.

- scope_id: A unique string value generated for each instance of the DPS. This can be found in the Azure portal DPS overview screen.

- registration_id: The device's unique registration ID, which is used when ownership of the TPM is established.

Summary

In this chapter we took a brief look at the Azure Device Provisioning Service (DPS) and how it can be used to automatically provision edge devices. We learned about DPS enrollments and allocation policies and security attestations for X.509 certificates and TPMs. We also discussed how to set up and configure the DPS using the Azure portal and the fully automated workflows that are available when the DPS is used in conjunction with the IoT Hub concept of deployments. Lastly, we looked specifically at what changes are required to switch your development edge devices from manually provisioned to automatically provisioned using the DPS. With this information in hand, you are ready to start managing your devices in the most efficient way.

## CHAPTER 8

Azure IoT Edge Security

Don't be misled by this chapter. You might be tempted to think that because this chapter is one of the last chapters in the book, it's an add-on topic to the Azure IoT Edge platform. That couldn't be further from the truth. In fact, many of the other chapters provide the context necessary to properly understand the way Azure IoT Edge is secured. Security is the core of Azure IoT Edge. All of the edge runtime components we have discussed previously are all managed by the edge security service. No code is installed or started on an edge device without first being initiated by the security service. But, to be truly secure, the edge device hardware must also be secure. It is not enough for the software to be secure. If the hardware can't enforce the requirements, then all the security baked into the edge runtime will still not yield a secure solution.

In this chapter, we will discuss not only some of the specifics about the security implemented in the edge runtime, but also how those security measures interact with various levels of security implemented by the IoT Edge hardware.

However, as you read this chapter, you must remember that securing your edge solutions is not an objective you achieve that is never revisited. Security is a continuing journey. What is secure this year, likely will not be secure 5 years from now. So, gaining an understanding of the right security approach for your solution is the first step, but you must evolve your approach going forward, which requires a more flexible design and architecture.

Assessing Security Risks

In order to effectively defend a solution or endpoint against security threats, the attack surfaces and threats must be correctly identified. A common practice used to uncover and capture the security threats is known as *threat modeling*. Modeling or analyzing security threats allows solution builders to collect as much information as possible when trying to understand how their solution might be compromised and informs their

© David Jensen 2019
D. Jensen, *Beginning Azure IoT Edge Computing*, https://doi.org/10.1007/978-1-4842-4536-1_8

designers to account for these attack vectors. When threat modeling is done during the design and development phases, security mitigations can be included as the system is designed rather retrofitted after the solution has been built and possibly deployed.

Note   If you are interested in a system designer that assesses threat models, Microsoft has created a utility that can be downloaded from here: `www.microsoft.com/en-us/download/details.aspx?id=49168`. It comes with a Getting Started guide and a User's Guide.

Microsoft has performed threat modeling for its reference IoT architecture.[1] One of the outputs of their process is the identification of four different threat zones in a typical IoT Architecture: (1) devices, (2) field gateways, (3) cloud gateways, and (4) services. Each of these zones requires nuanced security considerations that are different from the other zones. For example, in the device zone, protecting an IoT device from physical tampering is required, but is not required for the services running in a physically secure data center. As we think about each of these zones, IoT Edge devices span both the device zone and the field gateway zone. So, any threats identified for either of those zones should be considered to mitigate as many security risks on the front end of solution development.

IoT Edge-Specific Risks

There are two main nuances for the device and field gateway threat zones: physical access and commodity hardware. These nuances demand a closer look if we are to correctly think about our IoT Edge solution security.

One of the main security attack surfaces that is specific to an IoT Edge solution when compared to a typical cloud solution is the physical access. The devices in IoT Edge solutions are not deployed in a data center. And because these edge devices are usually very close to the origin of most of the data for IoT Edge solutions, when they are compromised, they affect everything that consumes their data. Therefore, they must be secured in such a way that allows us to trust the data they are producing.

---

[1]`http://aka.ms/iotrefarchitecture`.

A second security attack surface when dealing with IoT Edge solutions is the common nature of the hardware being deployed. More often than not, due to cost constraints, edge servers are commodity hardware. This means the technologies used to attack the edge device are commonplace and easily available, simply because of the hardware standards used in consumer-grade components. For this reason, attackers will usually have an advanced understanding of how to attack edge server hardware and might already have all the tools necessary to connect to and compromise an edge device.

A final factor involved in edge solutions is value of the asset. While IoT solutions share some of the same risks we just mentioned, they do not contain as much computing intellectual property as an IoT Edge device. And as more advanced analytics and custom enterprise modules, full of years of proprietary learning, get deployed to the edge servers, they will only become more and more valuable to, not only the owner of the asset, but also potential attackers. This makes IoT Edge deployments a unique scenario, where it is the perfectly accessible, high-value target. Figure 8-1 illustrates this point.

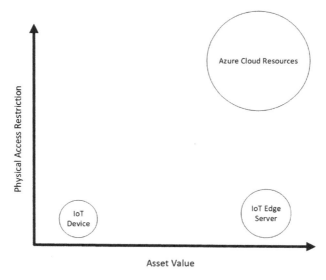

Figure 8-1. _Relation of access vs. asset value for IoT Edge components_

Figure 8-1 shows the uniqueness of IoT Edge components in the way they have the lowest access restriction paired with the higher asset value when compared with the other Azure resources and IoT devices. From this perspective, they are the most appealing low hanging fruit for would-be hackers.

Edge Security Attacks

Everything we've discussed so far is the *why* of edge security risks. We've only established why attackers will have a continued and increased interest in compromising an IoT Edge device. We have not discussed the specific security attacks, or *how* these attacks would attempt to exploit these devices. In order to properly defend against attacks, it's helpful to understand as much as possible about what methods and approaches attackers will use.

One of the main goals of nefarious individuals is to "spoof" malicious code as legitimate code to inject their own flavor of data into the system and/or read data out of the system. In order to appear as a valid data producer or consumer to other parties/components in the system, the infected code must somehow gain the trust of other data producers and consumers. This trust is gained by extracting and assuming a device's identity in the form of security cryptographic keys. These security keys must be protected in a way that this extraction and identity transference is never a possibility.

Another approach to compromising IoT Edge solutions is to tamper with the device, at either the hardware or the software level. Tampering can happen in many ways and is related to the spoofing example just mentioned, but tampering does not always include assuming the identity of a device. If an attacker can simply inject logic to either add to or remove data that is flowing through the system, their goal can usually be achieved. So, not only must the device identity be validated and repeatedly verified, the software running on the device must somehow be verified. This is usually done through code signing so that the code running can be authenticated against a trusted, known source – the signing authority.

A third approach of attack is to simply listen/monitor to the data flowing between the device and the cloud. Siphoning off the data stream to another data store can be done without any custom software if that path is not secured. Using simple network traffic monitoring tools, unsecured data streams can be captured and stored without the need to tamper with the device, extract the device identity or even inject malicious code. For this reason, all data traffic flowing between the cloud and the edge device must be encrypted and secured.

One of the last areas of concern is the data at rest on the device. If there is data stored in plain text on an edge device, anyone who is attempting to attack your systems needs only to physically access the storage media on the edge device and read the data out. As a result, the data at rest must also be encrypted to prevent hackers from accessing the data stored on these commodity hardware-based devices.

Given these attack approaches, how can these threats be addressed in a way that enables the same robust security present in the Azure cloud-only solutions? Is it possible for the cloud security capabilities on the edge to advance to the point of the cloud computing capabilities on the edge? The answer is *yes*.

Secure IoT Edge Hardware

Before we dive into the details of how the Azure IoT Edge runtime addresses the concerns and attack vectors we have mentioned, we need to briefly discuss one foundational topic – the hardware chosen for the edge server. As we have stated before, if the software is attempting to run securely and the hardware does not support it, the solution will not be secure. To support the edge runtime security, the edge device should have a hardware root of trust upon which to base the software trust. This is critical to the success of any IoT Edge deployment. In picking your hardware, you must understand what the components support and what they do not support. Let's take a quick look at what properties of hardware help determine if it's secure or not.

The devices used for edge deployments are usually not custom hardware. The hardware used in edge solutions is most commonly a preconfigured device with a limited set of options that can be modified. Therefore, it is important to verify that the device you chose supports the security scenario you need to implement.

The most common type of hardware security module is called a Trusted Platform Module (TPM).[2] TPM is really a set of security protocols created and maintained by Trusted Computing Group (TCG)[3] that have been implemented in a hardware component. One of the primary benefits of a TPM is the key protection they offer. Storing keys in a TPM prevent any malicious attempts to retrieve the keys. It is important to note that because TPM is a really a set of protocols, it can be implemented in hardware, firmware, or even software. The firmware and software options are more accurately "virtual" TPMs or VTPMs and are much less secure. So, when picking an edge device, verify it has a hardware TPM module. That is by far the most secure option.

However, if for some reason, you aren't able to select edge hardware that has a TPM, the edge runtime also supports custom Hardware Security Modules (HSMs), but you must verify that the hardware vendor also provides the HSM wrapper that complies to

---

[2]http://trustedcomputinggroup.org/work-groups/trusted-platform-module/.
[3]https://trustedcomputinggroup.org/.

the APIs the edge runtime requires. If a hardware vendor has implemented a custom HSM to support IoT Edge, the device will be listed in the IoT certified device catalog, located at: $https://catalog.azureiotsolutions.com/$. An example of this catalog is shown in Figure 8-2.

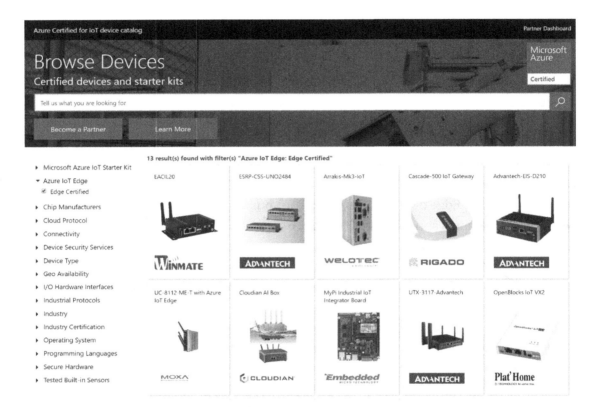

Figure 8-2. *Azure IoT Edge device catalog*

As long as you pick hardware from the Azure IoT Edge device catalog, you can be guaranteed that the hardware will support the requirements of the edge runtime. If you aren't able to use a device that is has been certified, make sure you understand how the vendor has implemented hardware security so that you can properly configure the edge runtime.

Now that we have reviewed the most common security attacks and how to select the right hardware to support the requirements of the edge runtime, let's look at how the edge runtime defends against the security threats by examining the IoT Edge Security Architecture.

IoT Edge Security Architecture

The security architecture for the Azure IoT runtime is designed to be flexible so it can evolve over time. And the core of the edge security architecture is the edge Security Manager service.

Security Manager

This service is responsible for bootstrapping the rest of the edge runtime and handles all of the security validation and verification checks at runtime. Figure 8-3 shows the components that make up the security service.

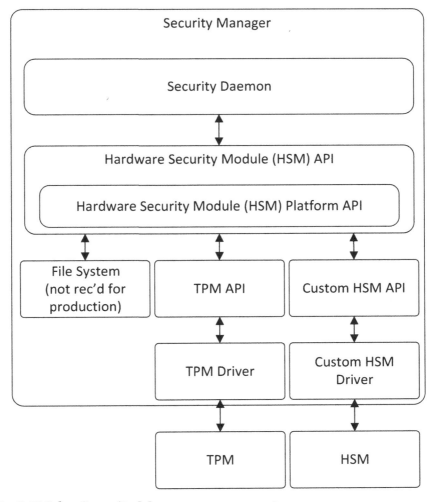

Figure 8-3. *IoT Edge Security Manager components*

Here is a brief description of each of these components.

- **Security Manager:** The general term used that refers to all of the security components, many of which are abstracted away from the user.

- **Security daemon:** The main orchestrating security service that runs on the edge device. This service is the primary worker that starts up the other edge runtime components like the edgeAgent and edgeHub modules, which in turn start up custom modules assigned to the device. The security daemon is also responsible for interacting with the available hardware modules (TPMs or other HSMs) for secure operations.

- **HSM API:** The exposed HSM API to the security daemon operations that require HSM interactions.

- **HSM platform API:** The platform abstraction layer that abstracts the actual hardware capabilities present on the device. This layer delegates the security operations to the hardware-specific driver. In Figure 8-3, only one of the underlying implementations would be used – either file system, TPM API, or custom HSM API – but not more than one. The Security Manager handles this delegation, based on the capabilities of the hardware.

- **File system:** A development-only virtual implementation of the hardware functionality. This is included with the Security Manager to help the initial startup process.

- **Hardware driver:** The platform and hardware-specific software wrapper of the hardware component installed on the edge device. This could be the TPM driver for the TPM hardware vendor or a custom driver for another HSM installed on the edge device.

- **TPM/Custom HSM:** The actual hardware security component installed on the device.

Security Daemon

The security daemon service that orchestrates most of the activity in the edge security runtime contains several internal APIs that work together in a secure set of exchanges to provide a secure environment that is resistant to attacks. Remember from the discussion on the types of attacks that stealing (spoofing) a device's identity and tampering, at either the hardware or the software level, are the two most common types of security attacks. The secure APIs in the security daemon directly combat these two types of attacks. In order to understand that, let's reexamine a diagram we looked at in Chapter 2, where we first introduced the Security Manager. Figure 8-4 shows the details of the security daemon service, identifying all of the internal APIs it uses.

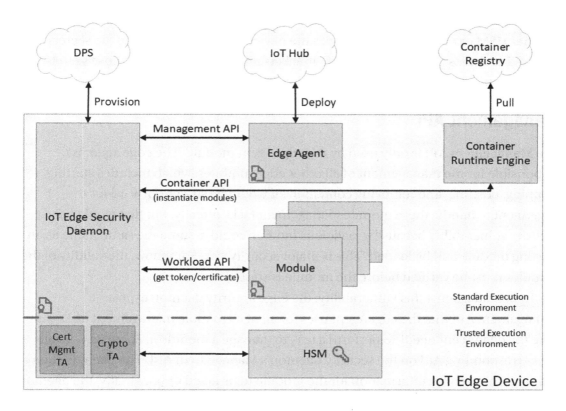

Figure 8-4. *IoT Edge security daemon architecture (Image from Microsoft blog post, "Azure IoT Edge Security Manager", July 29, 2018)*

The security daemon is intentionally separated into several components so that it can take advantage of hardware security functionality like trusted execution environments as well as verify the integrity of each of the software components during runtime operations. In the following sections, we will look in more detail at these components to better understand how they maintain a secure runtime environment.

Cloud Interface

The cloud interface is a generic interface that enables the security daemon to take advantage of services in the Azure cloud that might help it. Currently, this interface is used when the edge device uses the Device Provisioning Service (DPS) to bootstrap the device. Because this is a generic interface, other cloud services may be used in the future.

In order to access the DPS, the edge device must provide the unique ID of the TPM or other HSM or a certificate that proves the device's identity. By storing the secrets required to access the DPS in an HSM, attackers are unable to retrieve those secrets, and therefore, unable to assume the device's identity.

Management API

The Management API is only used by the edgeAgent module. The edge agent is responsible for the management of all other edge modules, which includes starting, stopping, creating, and removing containers. It would be straightforward for the edgeAgent to handle these module management tasks directly, but that would be a security vulnerability because a malicious module could assume the same name as an existing module and be loaded. This is major security risk. Somehow, the validity of the modules must be verified before the module is started.

To defend against this vulnerability, the edge security daemon exposes a Management API that the edgeAgent uses for all of its module management tasks. Any time the edgeAgent needs to perform a task to manage a module in some way, it calls the corresponding API on the security daemon's Management API. The daemon then validates the security information for the module to be acted upon. Finally, the daemon translates the edgeAgent's request into a command that is sent to either the container runtime using the Container API or to the active module itself using the Workload API. Module creation tasks use the Container API and all other module related tasks use the Workload API.

One last thing to note about the Management API is the way it limits access of the Management API to the edgeAgent module. Because the security daemon instantiates the edgeAgent module, it collects information about the edgeAgent at creation time and uses that information later to verify the edgeAgent identity and allow it access. No other module is allowed to invoke the Management APIs. In this way, it grants the additional permissions to the only module that requires them.

Workload API

The edge security daemon Workload API is responsible for securely interacting with the modules that have been created on the edge device. The Workload API handles issuing certificates or tokens to the edge modules as well as validating those certificates tokens on subsequent calls. All of the traffic between the modules and between a module and IoT Hub is encrypted using TLS, which means that some modules must present a server certificate and other modules must be able to trust that certificate. But, none of this is known at build or deployment time. The modules do not know what other modules they will have to trust when they are deployed to the edge device. This is where the Workload API comes in.

When the edgeHub module starts up, it registers itself with the security daemon as a valid server that will run on the edge device. The edge security daemon, is able to validate this using previously collected information about the module (collected when the module was created, but before it starts). Once that validation is done, a server certificate is generated and returned to the edgeHub. This server is responsible for creating the TLS sessions the other modules must use to send and receive messages. When other modules connect to the Workload API for identity validation, they receive all certificates they should trust, which they use to verify the TLS connection.

In these interactions the Workload API serves as the gatekeeper for any module interactions with other modules or the IoT Hub. Figure 8-5 shows a high-level view of these module interactions.

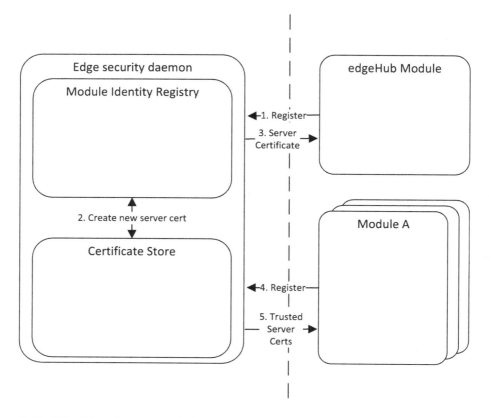

Figure 8-5. *Workload API module interactions*

Container API

The Container API provides an integration with the container runtime on the edge device. Currently, the Container API supports integrations with Docker and Moby. Moby is one of the container runtime components in the Docker family and the required container runtime for production scenarios. Docker should only be used on your edge device during development scenarios.

IoT Edge Certificates

In the chapter on the Device Provisioning Service, we briefly described the manufacturing requirements when provisioning certificates on edge devices. During that provisioning process, we discussed how the manufacturer would need to provision a device certificate to the edge device. This device certificate should be derived from a trusted CA in your organization (in this case, the trust is established based on signing certificate that has been uploaded to the IoT Hub). Once a device has been provisioned with a certificate that IoT Hub can validate, that edge device will be able to connect to the IoT Hub instance.

However, that is not the only purpose of the device certificate. The edge device itself uses that device certificate for establishing and validating internal trusted connections. When the edge runtime first starts, it generates a second device certificate called the "workload CA" certificate. This certificate is never actually used at runtime. It is created as an intermediate signing certificate so that other certs used on the device can be generated from it.

Note   The name "workload" should seem familiar to you. This is the certificate used to generate the certificate used to secure the Workload API interactions between modules and the edgeHub module.

The next certificate that's generated is a server certificate that is generated from the workload CA certificate. The server certificate is used by the edgeHub module as the server certificate during the initiation of the TLS connection that is created from all other modules that need to send or receive messages using the edgeHub message broker. Because the certificates are all generated from the original device certificate and that certificate is trusted by the edge runtime, then the modules are able to communicate over a trusted path, all based off the initial device certificate. Figure 8-6 illustrates the different certificates used on the device.

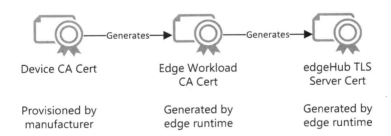

| Device CA Cert | Edge Workload CA Cert | edgeHub TLS Server Cert |
| Provisioned by manufacturer | Generated by edge runtime | Generated by edge runtime |

Figure 8-6. *Edge device-only certificates*

The server certificate (TLS) used by edgeHub will be given the common name (CA) that is used for the `hostname` property in the edge's `config.yaml` file. And in Figure 8-7, we see how the edge modules connect to the edge server in a secure way, using the device CA cert as the basis for the trust chain.

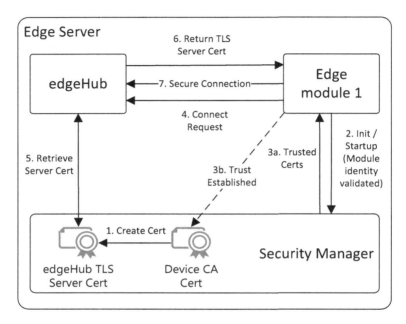

Figure 8-7. *Module trust workflow*

In Figure 8-7, we see a multistep process that takes place. Each step is important to understanding the use of certificates on the edge device. So, let's examine what's happening here, in just a little more detail.

1. The first step in establishing the secure connection is the creation of the device's server TLS certificate, which is signed by the Device CA root certificate. This device CA root certificate is provisioned by the manufacturer.

2. When the module starts up, it validates its identity with the Security Manager.

3. If the authentication is successful, a list of the trusted server certificates is returned to the module. This is usually only the device CA certificate. At this point (3b), the module has a trust relationship with the device CA certificate and any child certificates it creates.

4. The module then attempts to connect to the edgeHub message broker module to be able to send or receive message through the broker.

5. The edgeHub module retrieves the TLS server certificate from the Security Manager.

6. The TLS server certificate is then returned to the requesting module which is trusted, based on the prior trust established between the module and the device CA certificate.

7. The module successfully and securely connects to the edgeHub module.

Another scenario is when the edge server is configured as a gateway.

Note   This is only applicable to gateway scenarios where the child device can support a TCP/TLS stack and can be provisioned with an X.509 certificate. If the child device cannot support these requirements, then they will not be able to connect to the edge server with a connection built on the X.509 certificate chain of trust. The child devices most likely to support this scenario are in the transparent gateway pattern.

In this gateway scenario, the edge server acts a field gateway for the child devices connected to it. When there are child devices connected this way, those devices must trust the same root CA certificate of the edge device CA certificate and once they do, they connect to the edge server using a similar workflow as the module trust workflow shown in Figure 8-7. Figure 8-8 shows an example of the child device trust workflow.

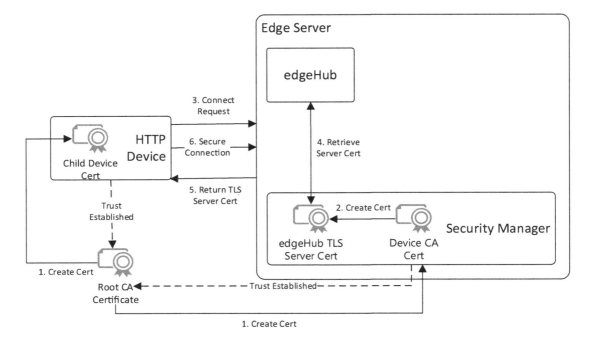

Figure 8-8. *Child device trust workflow*

Let's examine this child device trust workflow in a little more detail as well.

1. The root CA certificate is used to generate both a device CA cert
    and child device certificate. The child device cert(s) must be
    provisioned onto the child device.

2. The device CA cert generates the TLS server certificate just as we
    discussed before.

3. The child device attempts to connect to the edge server.

4. The edgeHub module retrieves the TLS server cert.

5. The edgeHub module supplies the TLS server cert to the child
    device, which it should trust based on the certificate that was
    provisioned earlier.

6. Once a trusted server certificate has be returned, the child device
    successfully and securely connects to the trusted edge gateway.

If you read the chapter on the Device Provisioning Service, you might remember that we discussed two different manufacturing scenarios. The first included using X.509 certificates as we are discussing here. The second scenario did not use certificates – it used the registration key from a TPM on the device. You might be wondering what happens when the device is registered with the IoT Hub using a TPM registration key rather than a certificate. I'm glad you asked.

When devices are manufactured with a TPM and are not provisioned with a certificate generated from a known CA, the edge runtime must compensate for this somehow, because it requires a certificate to support the TLS connections to other modules.

Note   Be aware that just because a device has a TPM it is not prevented from using certificates. The TPM provides secure storage of device secrets like certificates. TPMs do not exclude certificates. Certificates just aren't required when registering with the DPS if a TPM is present.

In this case, the edge runtime will actually generate a self-signed certificate at installation time and use that certificate as the root signing certificate for the TLS certificate. This scenario works in all cases except when a gateway is needed and child devices must trust the TLS server certificate. There is no (easy or recommended) way to provision the child devices with a certificate derived from the self-signed root CA certificate. So, if you foresee the gateway scenario in your future, you should make plans for the edge servers to be provisioned appropriately with the correct X.509 certificates.

IoT Edge Security Promises

As we discussed earlier, the emergence of intelligent edge computing has brought with it new security threats and attack surfaces. Edge servers support a wide range of business scenarios and, as a result, are very diverse in their hardware and security capabilities. An edge solution that counts the number of customers in a department store does not require the same amount of security and protection that a life support edge solution in a hospital requires. And because cost is directly tied to the security and hardware capabilities of the edge server, edge solution builders should not be expected to always purchase the most secure (expensive) option on the market. There are various levels of security required and there should be various levels of hardware available to match the need. This trend is becoming evident in the edge hardware that is available now. Hardware vendors are beginning to build hardware of various capabilities for different use cases.

One of the side effects of varying hardware and security processes is the effect on the solution developer. Historically, building apps that leverage secure hardware was not an easy task and was reserved for the seasoned security professional. The complexity increases considerably for a solution that needs to be customized for multiple hardware configurations at varying levels of security capability.

To help ease that difficulty, Microsoft designed the IoT Edge Security Manager to work with three levels of security capability or *security promises* (guarantees) while keeping the Security Manager API the same. The Security Manager API abstracts the underlying hardware implementation, which allows those details to remain hidden from you or me in any interactions with the Security Manager. These three promises are *standard promise*, *secure element promise*, and *secure enclave promise*. Here is a brief description of the capabilities of each promise:

- **Standard promise:** The standard promise maintains all of the attack countermeasures we've discussed so far in this chapter, but simply stores the secrets on the edge device's file system rather than in secure storage. This approach is meant to ease the startup tasks required to begin using the IoT Edge runtime. The standard promise scenario should be seen as a development- or test-only scenario and not a viable option for production solutions.

- **Secure element:** This promise contains all the capabilities of the standard promise, but secrets are stored in secure storage like a TPM or other HSM. This is baseline recommended for production IoT Edge solutions. This promise allows any certificates or other secrets required by the Security Manager to be stored in an HSM rather than the file system.

- **Secure enclave:** This promise is still emerging and is discussed in more detail in the section on trusted computing. It enables all the capabilities of the Secure Element promise, but additionally allows Trusted Applications (TA) to run code in a secure runtime environment that is analogous to the storage of secrets in an HSM, only for runtime execution, rather than data storage. This secure runtime prevents any outside access to the code running in its secure environment. This promise allows the Security Manager to not only store its secrets in secure storage, but it can also run the certificate management and cryptographic trusted applications (TAs) in a secure environment, enclave. This secure environment is sometimes referred to as a Trusted Execution Environment and can be seen in the bottom of the image in Figure 8-4.

Trusted Edge Computing

There is an emerging trend in technology to create secure runtime environments that shield data processing logic from outside tampering in much the same way a TPM shields and protects secrets from outside tampering. When designing and implementing a security architecture, a primary concern has always been protecting the data, at rest and in transport. There was much less emphasis placed on securing the runtime environment, mainly due to the physical deployment models that have existed up until now. When code runs in a secure facility, on secure hardware, the risk for tampering is greatly reduced. So, the money and energy for security have historically been placed on securing the transport of data into and out of these secure facilities, which brought about the ubiquity of SSL and TLS on the Web.

However, distributed computing patterns like blockchain and edge computing are creating new security attack surfaces by placing computing environments in unsecure or untrusted locations. With these computing patterns, one of your company's most protected assets (core business logic) is no longer locked away in a secure data center. It is deployed into unsecure and sometimes unknown environments. This creates new challenges to maintain the security required to protect that asset.

In an effort to address this challenge, hardware manufacturers are building more advanced capabilities into their security components like TPMs or other HSMs to enable more than just the storage of secrets. These new HSMs can allow small portions of code to run in a secure, protected space called a Trusted Execution Environment (TEE). Any code that runs in a TEE is not visible or accessible from outside the TEE, thereby eliminating a large percentage of the attack surface. Two of the leading hardware components that support these TEEs are the Intel SGX (for x86 and x64 processors) and ARM TrustZone® (for ARM processors).

But, securing code at the edge cannot be accomplished simply by running your existing code on a machine with the new HSM hardware. Code must be built for these secure environments and deployed into the trusted environment. Code that is built for a TEE must use different tools and SDKs and be packaged into a Trusted Application (TA). A Trusted Application is the deployment artifact that is deployed into the TEE. Two of the SDKs used to build TAs are OpenEnclave[4] and CoreTEE.[5]

OpenEnclave is a Microsoft-led open-source project that aims to create a common TEE API across hardware vendors so that Trusted Applications are as portable as possible. CoreTEE is a commercial implementation of the OP-TEE[6] open-source project. OP-TEE is an open-source TEE API for ARM-based processors and the security team at Sequitur Labs has enhanced that base functionality for their CoreTEE offering.

All of that background is to help you understand some of the internal features of the Edge Security Manager. The IoT Edge Security Manager was built with TEEs in mind. When you use an edge server that adheres to the "Secure Enclave" hardware promise, the Security Manager will take advantage of the TEE. To support this functionality, it includes an implementation of the Open Enclave SDK for Intel-based machines and an implementation of CoreTEE for ARM-based machines.

When the Security Manager detects that a TEE is present at installation time, it will also deploy two Trusted Applications to the TEE. The first TA is responsible for the management of certificates and the second TA handles the cryptographic routines that are needed.

You don't have to understand all the inner workings of the Security Manager and the nuances of TEE and TA development and deployment to be able to create IoT Edge solutions, but you should be aware of the TEE trend and what its goals are. Trusted computing has the potential to become a major focus over the next few years and understanding how it complements intelligent edge computing will be helpful.

Note   For more information on a cloud-based trusted computing offering, look at the Azure Confidential Computing service at `https://azure.microsoft.com/en-us/solutions/confidential-compute`.

---

[4]`https://openenclave.io`.
[5]`www.sequiturlabs.com/coretee/`.
[6]`https://github.com/OP-TEE/optee_os`.

Summary

In this chapter, we looked at how to identify and think about the security risks that are specific to IoT Edge solutions. We discussed why intelligent edge solutions are a prime target for attack and we looked into some ways attackers might exploit those vulnerabilities. Once we had a clearer understanding of these risks that are specific to IoT Edge solutions, we discussed what attributes of edge hardware make it secure and what a few of the options are when it comes to choosing hardware for your edge solution. We also took a detailed look at the internal APIs of the IoT Edge Security Manager and how it leverages the most secure hardware components available on the edge device, all the while maintaining a consistent API. Finally, we discussed an emerging trend called trusted computing that exists in some distributed computing solutions like blockchain or intelligent edge solutions. These pockets of trusted computing are made possible by some advances in secure hardware called Trusted Execution Environments (TEE). With this understanding, you should feel equipped to accurately assess the security of IoT Edge solutions and determine where improvements need to be made, if any.

CHAPTER 9

Azure DevOps for IoT Edge Solutions

Now that we have built a good foundational understanding of Azure IoT Edge solutions, understanding how to automate the build and deployment processes for those solutions is extremely helpful as you're getting ready to deploy your solutions to production. You may already be familiar with the Azure DevOps service, but if not, in this chapter you will see how to use Azure DevOps to build and deploy IoT Edge solutions. Azure DevOps is the latest evolution in Microsoft's hosted development team management environment. It enables teams to collaborate on project work, develop and track the project deliverables like code. and build scripts as well as track the release and deployment of the project artifacts. One of the reasons Azure DevOps is a great choice for managing your IoT Edge deployments is the integration it provides with Docker and the support it provides for containers in general. Additionally, there are tailored workflows for IoT Edge development that simplify much of the build and release process. Azure DevOps is a large topic. In this chapter, after we establish some of the basic concepts, we will focus our attention on the workflows and processes required to develop and deploy Azure IoT Edge solutions.

Signing into Azure DevOps

To get started with Azure DevOps, you need to sign in and create a project. You can access Azure DevOps by browsing to `http://devops.azure.com` in your browser. If you have never signed into Azure DevOps, you will see a welcome screen similar to Figure 9-1.

© David Jensen 2019
D. Jensen, *Beginning Azure IoT Edge Computing*, https://doi.org/10.1007/978-1-4842-4536-1_9

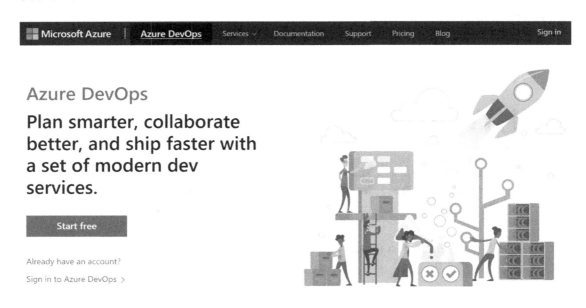

Figure 9-1. *Azure DevOps start screen*

Once you sign in, if you have not yet created any DevOps projects, you will be prompted to provide a name for the initial project. Another action that happens behind the scenes on your first login is the establishment of your organization. Organizations are the top-level concept in Azure DevOps, which means that an organization must exist prior to a project being created. If you sign into DevOps using a Work/Organizational account, that organization will be used as the initial organization in DevOps. But, if you use a personal Microsoft account, a default organization will be created for you.

Planning your DevOps structure is one of the most critical aspects of efficiently managing your organization and teams using the DevOps services. If your DevOps structure doesn't accurately reflect your actual organizational structure, you will struggle when working with the DevOps hierarchy you've created. The structure of your teams and repositories will feel more in line with your business needs if you take time up front to plan it correctly from the start. To help with the planning of your DevOps environment, let's review the basic concepts in Azure DevOps and what factors you should consider with deciding how to structure your environment.

Azure DevOps Basic Concepts

To effectively and correctly create your company's structure in Azure DevOps, you need to understand the levels of organization, what they logically represent and what capabilities are associated with each level. The diagram in Figure 9-2 shows the high-level organization structure in Azure DevOps with a brief description that follows. This overview information will help you plan out your DevOps organization.

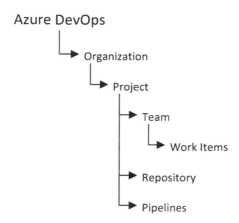

Figure 9-2. *Azure DevOps organization structure*

Organization

An organization in Azure DevOps is a logical grouping of projects. It is top of the structural model and should be viewed as a separate entity from any other DevOps organization, containing its own projects, teams, work items, code repositories, and build/release pipelines. The general guidance if you are just starting with Azure DevOps is to begin with one organization and add additional organizations later, only if needed. An organization can represent a company, a business unit, or a department. The number of organizations that is right for you depends on how many teams and projects make up each level of your organization.

Project

A project in Azure DevOps should be thought of as a security boundary. In a project, you may have multiple code repositories that separate the work streams or you may choose to have one code repository per project. The decision should focus on your team and how the code should be secured. If all code in the repositories will have the same permissions for the team members (user A will serve the same role across all repositories, etc.), then a single Project with multiple repositories makes sense. If, however, you need to secure some code differently than other code, separate projects, each with a dedicated repository is a better fit. Having a single project for multiple code work streams allows the team to share the iteration and area paths as well as the build and release definitions. These distinctions can help you determine the best option for your company.

Team

A group of users that work together to deliver the work captured in a work item backlog, using code repositories and pipelines to deliver the work and work item boards to manage the work. A team in Azure DevOps is a long-lasting concept and should not be tied to a single project.

Work Items

Work Items in Azure DevOps make up the backlog and the other scheduled work that is being tracked for an upcoming release. Work items are usually shown in a backlog or sprint board. Teams will use various work item boards to track the current state of the project work and report on project and sprint progress.

Repository

Project repositories are the version control system for the code and scripts created and managed by a project. These repositories come in two flavors: centralized and decentralized. Decentralized repositories are Git repos and there can be as many Git repositories as you need in your project. The centralized repositories are Team

Foundation Version Control (TFVC) repos (think back to TFS-style, centralized repositories), and in any given project, there can only be one TFVC project. Within that TFVC repo, you can create as many folders and branches as you need, but it all must exist within the single repo. When using Git repos, decisions must be made about how to organize the repos because there can be multiple Git repos in the project. The best option is to structure your repositories so that each repository is dedicated to a single, deployable product.

Pipelines

Azure Pipelines is a hosted environment in which you can create custom build and release workflows. There is a visual designer that enables an easy way to create and edit your Continuous Integration (CI), or build, workflows as well as Continuous Deployment (CD), or release, workflows. Build pipelines connect to a source repository and are typically configured to begin a new build process whenever some specified trigger happens (new push to the repo, etc.). Release pipelines use the output of a build pipeline as the input to its workflow. The build output is deployed to the target environment using the specified steps in the deployment/release pipeline. In Azure DevOps, there can be as many Pipelines as needed in the project.

   With the guidance above, you should be able to decide on an initial structure for your organization's DevOps projects, teams, and repositories. The structure of those will dictate how your work items and pipelines are setup. Once you have your initial structure in place you can begin to build and release code and continually evolve your DevOps environment as new projects and products are created.

Azure DevOps Configuration

Let's take a quick look at how to setup the initial environment in Azure DevOps so that you can begin to build and release your IoT Edge solutions. The screens we will look assume you have the appropriate permissions. To view the organization level information, you need to be a *Project Collection Admin*. To view the project level information, you need to be at least a *Project Admin* for the project.

The first area to look at is the settings for the organization. After you have logged into the portal, you can view the organization settings by first clicking the organization from the project overview page, which is shown in Figure 9-3.

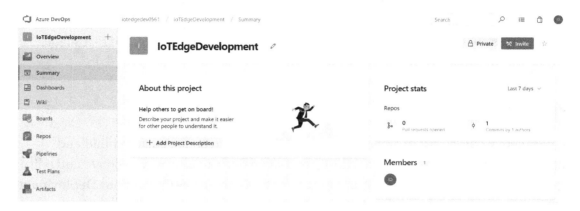

Figure 9-3. *Project overview page*

The organization can be found in the top "breadcrumb" section of this page. Click the name of your organization and you will see an option for *Organization settings* in the bottom left corner of the screen. Once you click that, you should see a screen similar to the screen in Figure 9-4.

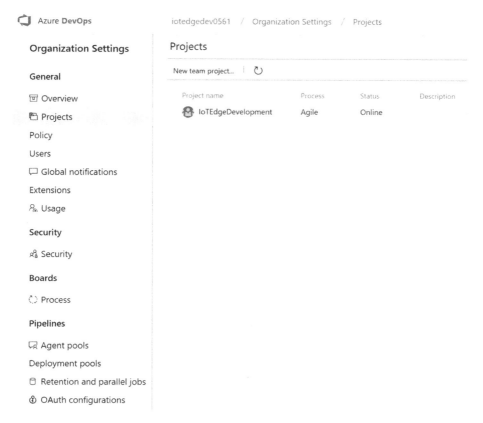

Figure 9-4. *Azure DevOps organization settings*

The most common settings organization admins need to inspect on this screen are the notification settings and the security permissions. If you have any experience with managing TFS security groups, the internal DevOps groups will look very familiar. As for the notification settings, the settings at the organization level are the global defaults for any projects created in that organization and can be modified at the project and the group and user levels.

Once you have verified the organization settings, navigate back to the project overview screen shown in Figure 9-3. In the bottom left corner, you will now see an option for *Project settings*. When you click that, you will see the Project Overview screen, as shown in Figure 9-5.

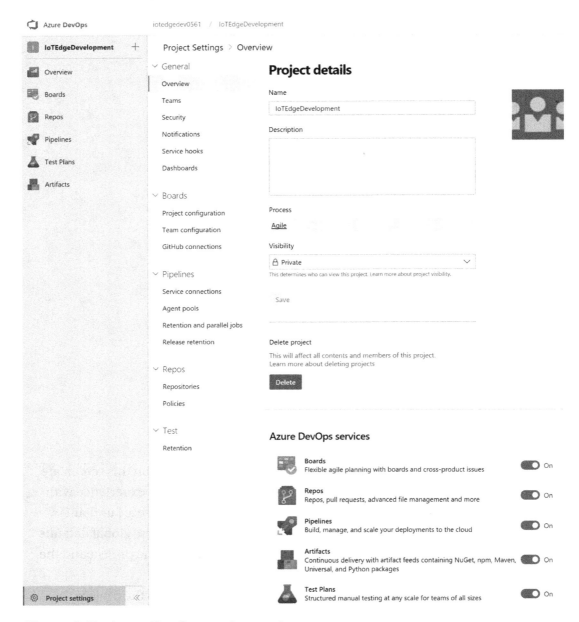

Figure 9-5. *Azure DevOps project settings*

This screen gives you the tools to manage the teams, work items, security permissions, and repositories. The most common settings to verify on the project setting page are:

- **Teams:** Verify the correct teams have been created and the members of each team have been correctly assigned.

- **Notifications:** Verify the project default settings for notifications are consistent with the notification strategy.

- **Dashboards:** Configure the permissions for creating, editing and deleting tam dashboards.

- **Boards:** Configure the specific information that drive the out-of-the-box boards for the project – iteration dates, whether to view epics, features, or user stories on the boards, etc.

- **Pipelines:** Manage the automation for building and deploying code, including creating a service account to external services that can be used during build and release automation (more on this later) and retention policies for build and release output.

- **Repos:** Create and manage the repositories needed in the project as well as the permissions associated with the repositories – this would be where a production branch is secured differently than a dev or test branch.

Once you have configured the organization and project correctly, another area for customization is the dashboards that your team will use to track the project. To create a dashboard (assuming you have the right permissions), click the *Dashboards* hub on the left side of the project screen. Click the button to add a new widget. You should then see a list of dashboard widgets that are available for you to add and resize, based on your team's preferences. An example of this is shown in Figure 9-6.

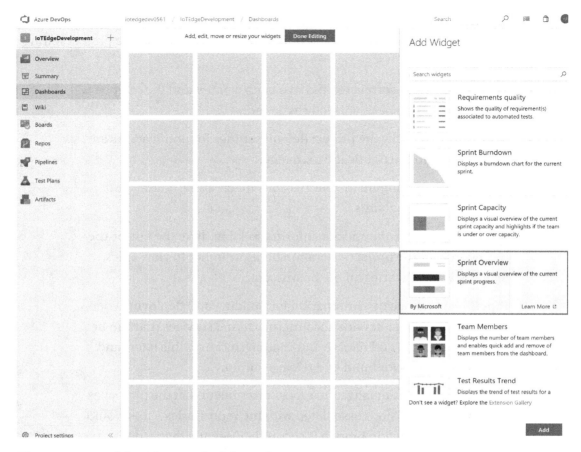

Figure 9-6. *Add widget to dashboard*

As you continue the process of configuring your DevOps project, another area that is imperative to set up is the repository section.

Note   This section assumes you are using Git repositories rather than a TFVC repository.

When you created your project, an initial/empty repository was created for you. But, chances are you will need to either rename that repository or create another repository. There is a shortcut to managing repositories from the repository hub in your project. Once you click the repos hub, you can manage repositories and switch between repositories using the pick list at the top of the screen. This is shown in Figure 9-7.

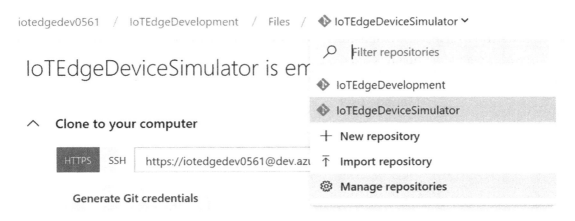

Figure 9-7. Repository management menu

The next area to consider setting up is the project artifacts section. When you initially click the *Artifacts* hub in the project, you might see a screen that looks like Figure 9-8.

Figure 9-8. Azure Artifacts initial screen

This indicates that your current user account does not have a license for the *Package Management* extension assigned. The *Package Management* extension provides five free user licenses. If you need more than that, there is a charge per user. To enable a license on the current user (if needed), click the *Go to Users hub* button and click your user account and click *Manage extensions* at the top of the screen. It should look similar to the screen shown in Figure 9-9.

Figure 9-9. Extension management for project users

When you click *Manage extensions*, you will see a screen as shown in Figure 9-10 that allows you to select the extensions you want to enable for the current user. Select *Package Management* and click *Save changes*.

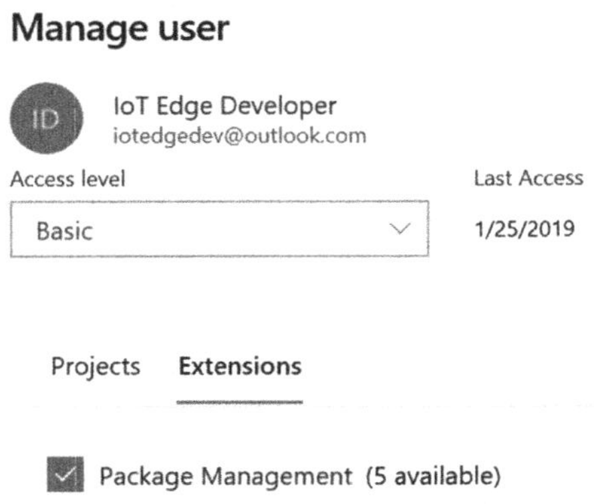

Manage user

ID   IoT Edge Developer
     iotedgedev@outlook.com

Access level   Last Access

Basic   ∨   1/25/2019

Projects   **Extensions**

☑ Package Management (5 available)

Figure 9-10. *Enable package management for user*

Once you have assigned a license to your user, when you click Artifacts, you will now be able to add a package feed to your project. A feed is a repository of reusable packages to enable efficient code sharing. Feeds can be extremely helpful within an organization to provide a common catalog of available packages. If you have used npm or nuget, Azure Artifacts provides a similar mechanism for organizations to publish their own packages through a version-controlled, internal interface. An example of a list of feeds in Azure Artifacts is shown in Figure 9-11.

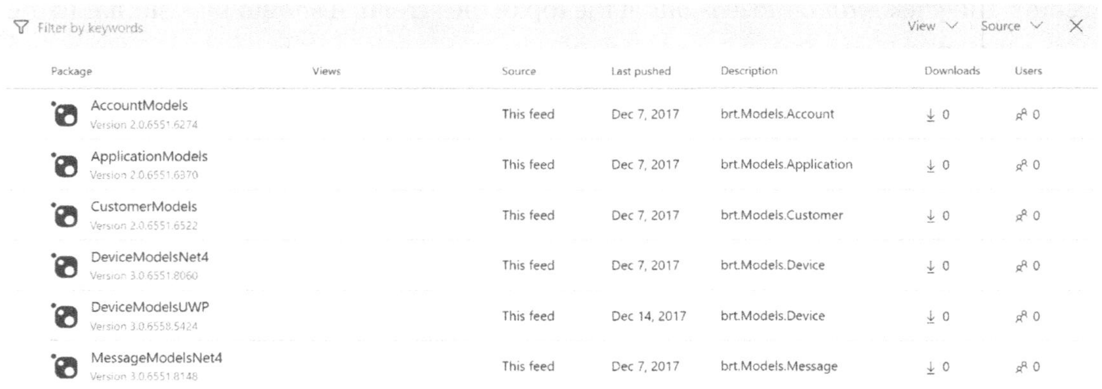

Package	Views	Source	Last pushed	Description	Downloads	Users
AccountModels Version 2.0.6551.6274		This feed	Dec 7, 2017	brt.Models.Account	↓ 0	⋒ 0
ApplicationModels Version 2.0.6551.6370		This feed	Dec 7, 2017	brt.Models.Application	↓ 0	⋒ 0
CustomerModels Version 2.0.6551.6522		This feed	Dec 7, 2017	brt.Models.Customer	↓ 0	⋒ 0
DeviceModelsNet4 Version 3.0.6551.8060		This feed	Dec 7, 2017	brt.Models.Device	↓ 0	⋒ 0
DeviceModelsUWP Version 3.0.6558.5424		This feed	Dec 14, 2017	brt.Models.Device	↓ 0	⋒ 0
MessageModelsNet4 Version 3.0.6551.8148		This feed	Dec 7, 2017	brt.Models.Message	↓ 0	⋒ 0

Figure 9-11. *List of feeds in Azure Artifacts*

Now that we have reviewed the initial setup and some of the configuration aspects of Azure DevOps, let's take a deeper dive into the automation capabilities that are available in a DevOps project. As an example workflow, we will now take a look at how to build and deploy our initial IoT Edge solution and the specific concerns that must be taken into account when building IoT Edge solutions.

Create an IoT Edge Build Pipeline

By this point, you should have signed into an Azure DevOps instance and created at least one project. As I stated earlier, if you do not have any projects in your account, upon your first sign-in you will be prompted to enter a project name and the project will be created for you. Once the project is created, we need to add our initial Edge solution to a repository in the DevOps instance. To do this, open up a command prompt to the root solution directory of the edge solution we built in Chapter 4.

Note   These steps assume you have Git installed on your development machine and have configured your user.name and user.email properties. If you do not have Git installed, you can install it from `https://git-scm.com/downloads`. If you need help configuring your user name and email, refer to the following help page: `https://git-scm.com/book/en/v2/Getting-Started-First-Time-Git-Setup`.

Once in that directory, run the following command: `git init .` as shown in Listing 9-1.

Listing 9-1. Local Git repository initialization

```
C:\Users\iotedgedev\edgesolution>git init .
Initialized empty Git repository in [...]/edgesolution/.git/

C:\Users\iotedgedev\edgesolution>
```

Next, you need to add the code to the tracked items in the local repository and check those files in. To do this, run the commands shown in Listing 9-2.

Listing 9-2. Add and check in files to Git repository

```
C:\Users\iotedgedev\edgesolution>git add .

C:\Users\iotedgedev\edgesolution>git commit -m "initial checkin"
[master (root-commit) c6cb12b] initial checkin
 12 files changed, 449 insertions(+)
 create mode 100644 .env.backup
 create mode 100644 .gitignore
 create mode 100644 .vscode/launch.json
 create mode 100644 deployment.template.json
 create mode 100644 modules/filtermodule/.gitignore
 create mode 100644 modules/filtermodule/Dockerfile.amd64
 create mode 100644 modules/filtermodule/Dockerfile.amd64.debug
 create mode 100644 modules/filtermodule/Dockerfile.arm32v7
 create mode 100644 modules/filtermodule/Dockerfile.windows-amd64
 create mode 100644 modules/filtermodule/Program.cs
 create mode 100644 modules/filtermodule/filtermodule.csproj
 create mode 100644 modules/filtermodule/module.json

C:\Users\iotedgedev\edgesolution>
```

Now, we need to get the address of the target repository. To view this information, click the Repos section of the project, as shown in Figure 9-12.

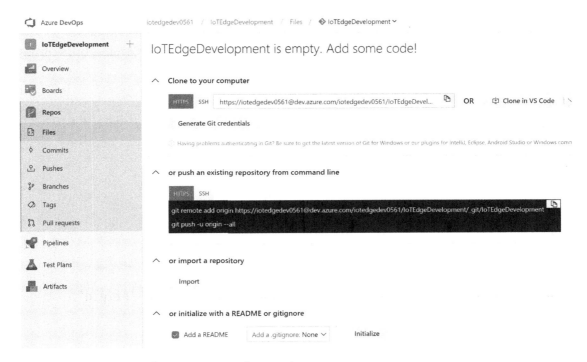

Figure 9-12. *Initial repository information*

Copy the command line that shows the addition of the remote repository and run that command in the local command window, as shown in Listing 9-3.

Listing 9-3. Add remote repository to local repository and push

```
C:\Users\iotedgedev\edgesolution>git remote add origin
https://<project>@dev.azure.com/[...]/IoTEdgeDevelopment

C:\Users\iotedgedev\edgesolution>git push -u origin –all
```

When you run the second command, which pushes the new files to the remote registry, you will be prompted to sign in to the Azure DevOps instance. When the prompt appears, enter your credentials. Once you sign in to the remote registry, you should see output similar to Listing 9-4.

Listing 9-4. Git remote push output

```
C:\Users\iotedgedev\edgesolution>git push -u origin --all
Enumerating objects: 17, done.
Counting objects: 100% (17/17), done.
Delta compression using up to 4 threads.
Compressing objects: 100% (15/15), done.
Writing objects: 100% (17/17), 5.54 KiB | 1.11 MiB/s, done.
Total 17 (delta 3), reused 0 (delta 0)
remote: Analyzing objects... (17/17) (5 ms)
remote: Storing packfile... done (186 ms)
remote: Storing index... done (91 ms)
To https://dev.azure.com/[...]/_git/IoTEdgeDevelopment
 * [new branch]      master -> master
Branch 'master' set up to track remote branch 'master' from 'origin'.

C:\Users\iotedgedev\edgesolution>
```

The build output should now show up in the Azure DevOps instance. In DevOps, click the *Builds* hub under the *Pipelines* section. Click the *New Pipeline* button, as shown in Figure 9-13.

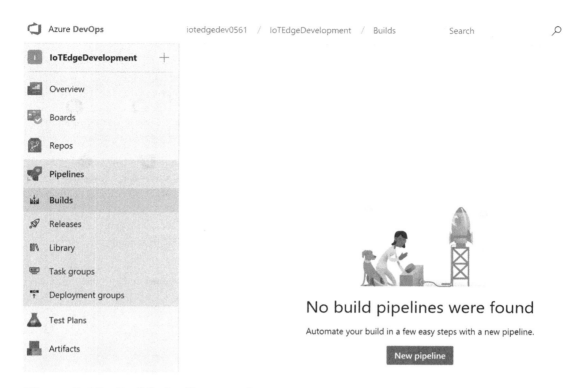

Figure 9-13. *Build pipeline creation*

When you select the New pipeline button, the default experience is the YAML editor. But, for our example, we will use the visual designer. So, select the option to use the visual designer. and then select the location of your newly populated Git repository. An example is shown in Figure 9-14.

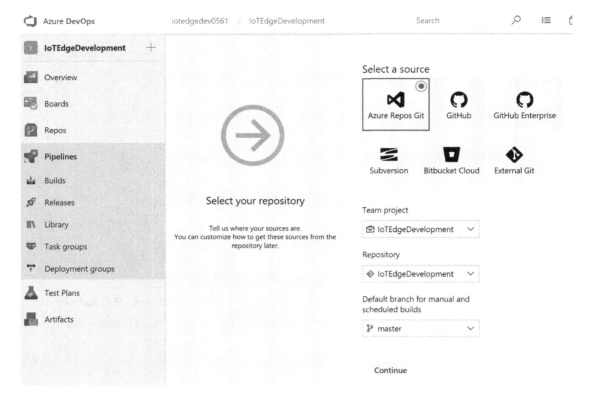

Figure 9-14. *Select Git repository in the visual designer*

On the next screen, select the option to start with an empty template. Starting with an empty template allows us to add just the tasks we need for the specialized task of building and deploying IoT Edge solutions. IoT Edge solutions require the hosted Linux build agent. So, you must change the build agent pool to *Hosted Ubuntu 1604*, as shown in Figure 9-15.

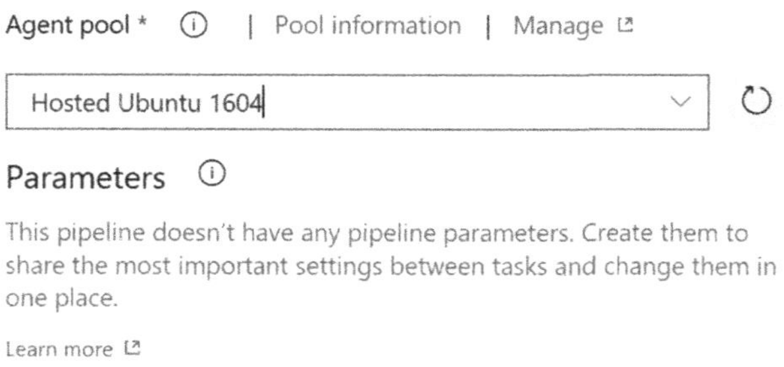

Figure 9-15. *IoT Edge build agent pool*

After updating the build agent, we can start adding the Edge build tasks. To add a task to the build pipeline, click the plus (+) sign next to the *Agent job 1* item in the task list. You will be presented with a list of task templates you can add to the pipeline. In the search box, type the word "edge." There is only one task that is already installed and does not have to be added from the marketplace. That is the task we will use and is shown in Figure 9-16.

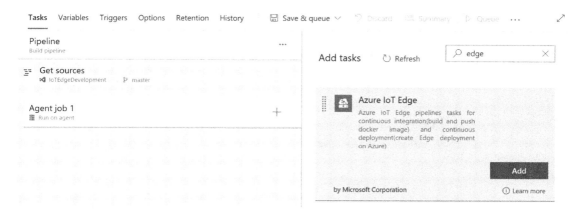

Figure 9-16. *Azure IoT Edge build pipeline task*

Once you add the IoT Edge build task, you have three options for the action parameter.

- **Build:** Uses the deployment.template.json file to build the solution. The only output from the step that is saved is the generated deployment.json file. It is published to a hosted Azure DevOps location that is part of the configuration for the task.

- **Push:** Pushes the build output to a container registry.

- **Deploy:** Deploys the deployment manifest generated from the deployment.template.json file to a set of devices defined in IoT Hub.

For this exercise, we need to build the solution first. So, select the Build action. Also, you must select the location in the repository for the `deployment.template.json` file and the build platform. The build task options should appear like the figure shown in Figure 9-17. You should notice that the output variable section has the reference name populated. This is so that other steps in the pipeline can reference the variable names from this step. Specifically, the `DEPLOYMENT_FILE_NAME` variable is used in the last step of this build pipeline so that a release pipeline has easy access to the generated deployment manifest when pushed to the IoT Edge devices.

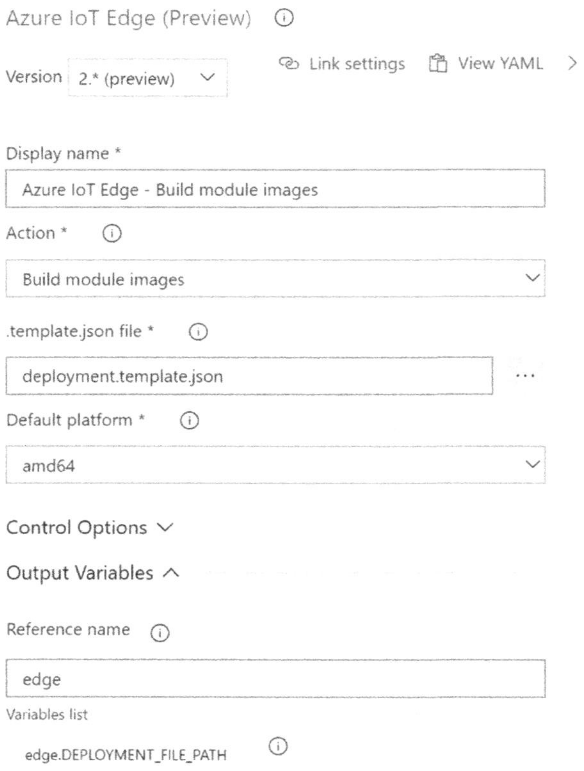

Figure 9-17. *Build task parameter values*

After configuring the build task, we need to add a task to push the output of the build task to a container registry. To do this, add another IoT Edge workflow task exactly like the build task you just added, but rather than selecting the build action, select the push action, as shown in Figure 9-18.

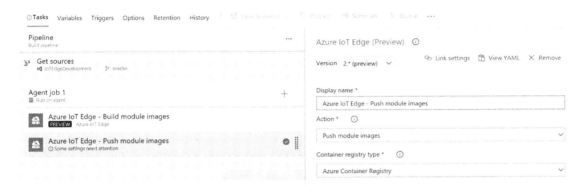

Figure 9-18. *IoT Edge push task added to build pipline*

Once you select the push action, you will see additional options specific to container registries. Because the publish action pushes the edge containers to a container registry, it will need access to the registry. The push task allows us to add container registry connection information, which is a delegated service connection the pipeline can leverage to gain the access permissions it needs.

Note   Service connections are not new in Azure DevOps. They have been around for a while. However, there are more out of the box services that Azure DevOps supports. The actual configuration of each service connection is different, but once you configure it, that service is available for any pipelines you or the team create. This can be a helpful way for DevOps admins to setup and configure the approved services that the development teams should be using, rather than development teams trying to manage that on their own.

If you do not have a service account you can leverage for this access, the easiest way to create it is to select the Azure subscription you'll be using from the subscription pick list and then press the Authorize button. This action creates a service link to you Azure subscription using a service principal in Azure AD. You can see a completed form in Figure 9-19.

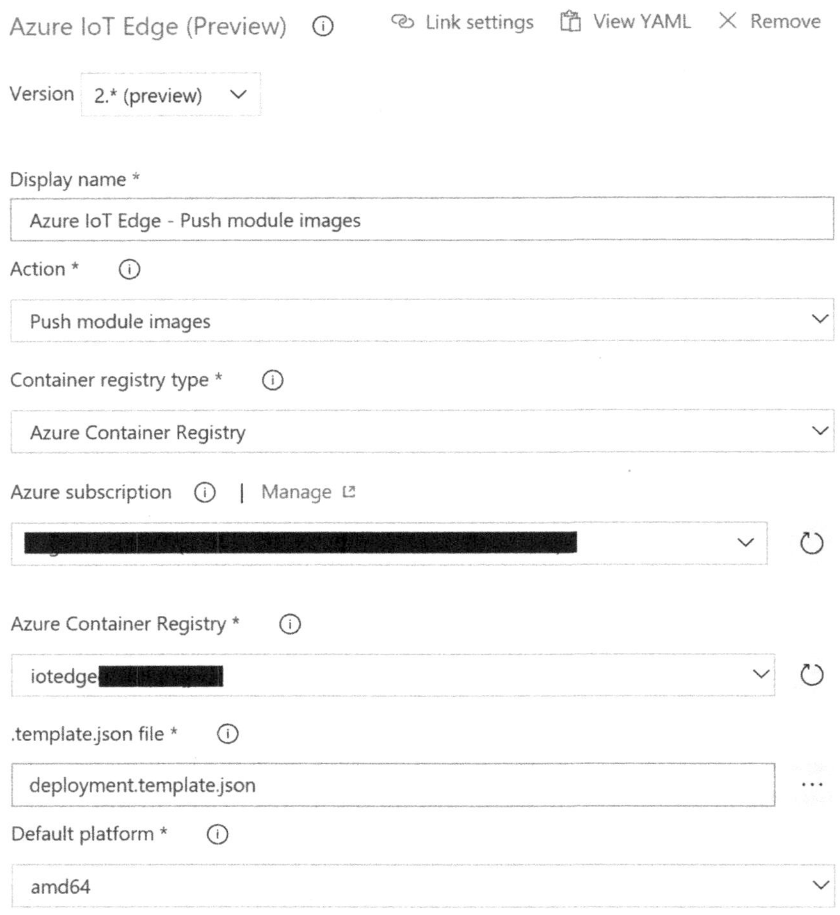

Azure IoT Edge (Preview)   ⓘ   ⚭ Link settings   📋 View YAML   ✕ Remove

Version   2.* (preview)   ∨

Display name *

    Azure IoT Edge - Push module images

Action *   ⓘ

    Push module images   ∨

Container registry type *   ⓘ

    Azure Container Registry   ∨

Azure subscription   ⓘ | Manage ↗

    ██   ∨   ↻

Azure Container Registry *   ⓘ

    iotedge████████████   ∨   ↻

.template.json file *   ⓘ

    deployment.template.json   ···

Default platform *   ⓘ

    amd64   ∨

Figure 9-19. *IoT Edge publish task*

Once you have selected the target Azure subscription and authorized the access, the list of container registries in the subscription will populate. Once that happens, simply select the registry you want to target. It is assumed that you have created at least one Azure Container Registry in your subscription. If you have not, you need to take care of that before you will be able to proceed.

Note   If you need to split your containers from a single edge solution into multiple registries, you must add another publish task that targets the second (or third, etc.) registry and use the Bypass module field in the advanced settings to add containers that should not be pushed to the second registry in that step.

Once you have entered all the registry information, you can add the final task in the Build pipeline, which is publishing the build output so that a release pipeline can consume it. This task is shown in Figure 9-20.

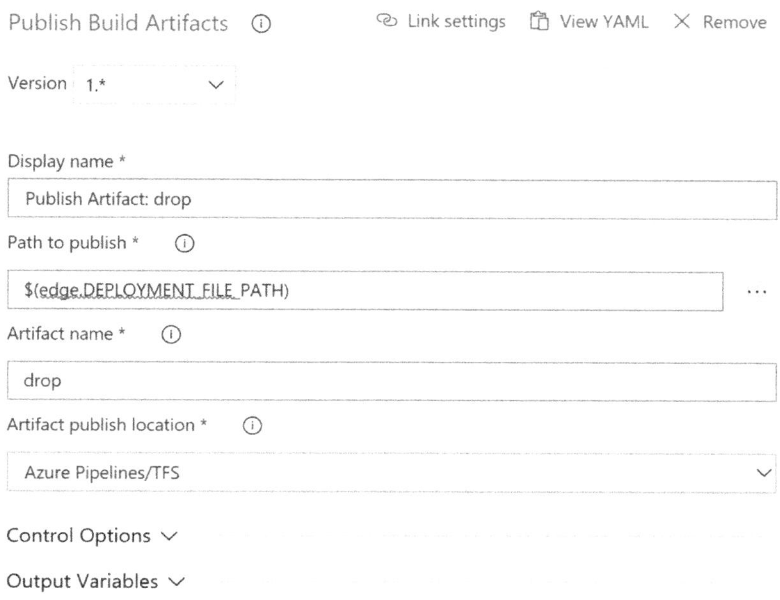

Figure 9-20. *Publish edge build artifacts*

Note that the *Path to publish* value should be entered exactly as it is shown. It references the output variable from the first step in this pipeline – the build step. The last step before saving the build pipeline is to click the *Triggers* tab and enable the Continuous Integration (CI) option and verify the CI trigger is set to monitor the correct branch in the repository. After that is complete, you can save and close the build pipeline task.

To trigger the build, you can trigger (queue) the build manually, or make a change to the source code and push the changes to the repository. When either of those events happen, the build pipeline will start. Once the build completes, you should see a summary screen that looks like Figure 9-21.

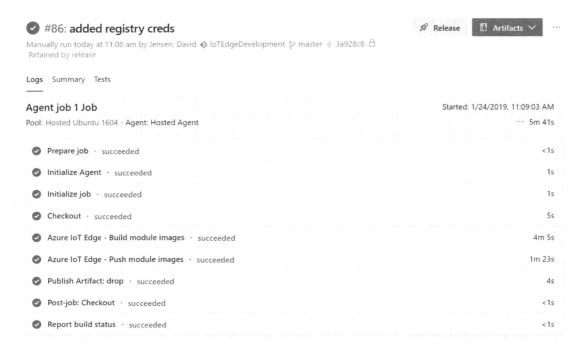

Figure 9-21. *Build pipeline summary output*

Create an IoT Edge Release Pipeline

We have just created a build pipeline that builds our solution containers and pushes them to our selected container registry and publishes the build output, which is just the generated deployment manifest file, to be consumed by a release pipeline. Release pipelines can begin with several different inputs, called artifacts. Here is a brief description of some of the artifacts supported by release pipelines:

- **Build:** Any build pipeline that publishes its output to Azure Pipelines/TFS can be consumed as an artifact.

- **Azure repository:** It is possible to deploy directly from an Azure Git repository. Take caution when using this option so that you don't lose traceability when skipping the intermediate step of build pipelines and retaining published build output.

- **Azure artifacts:** Azure Artifacts is a hosted package feed service and greatly simplifies the sharing and versioning of applications and services in an organization. It supports nuget, maven, and npm packages.

- **Azure containers/docker hub:** Any container repositories in either Azure Container Registry or DockerHub can be added as an artifact. This is helpful if you don't have control over a build process, but can monitor a container registry for updates.

This list is not exhaustive and the complete list is being updated all the time as more services are brought online. The important thing to note here is that there are many options that can be used as input artifacts. As a result, some planning must be done to determine when build output will be pushed to a container registry and when it will be pushed to a package feed like Azure Artifacts.

To get started with the release pipeline, select *Release* under the *Pipelines* hub and click the *New Pipeline* button and chose to start with an empty job. Once the designer displays, click the option to add an artifact. The screen shown in Figure 9-22 should appear.

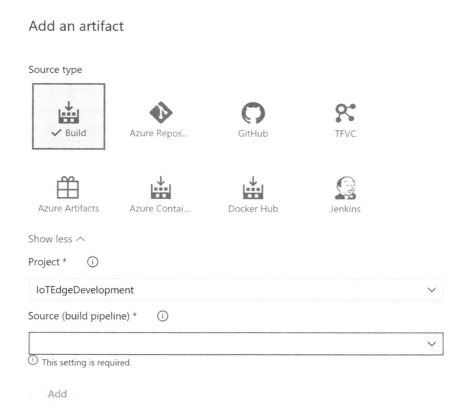

Figure 9-22. *Artifact type selection blade*

For our release pipeline, select the build artifact option that uses the published build output, which matches our build pipeline. You will be prompted to select the correct repository. Once you have added your artifacts, you need to enable the continuous deployment option for the pipeline, by clicking the continuous deployment icon and turning the trigger on, as shown in Figure 9-23.

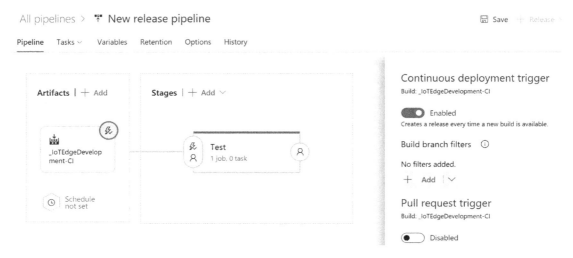

Figure 9-23. *Release pipeline continuous deployment options*

Next, we need to add a task to the stage we have created. Each stage has a workflow very similar to the build pipeline workflow. Release pipeline stages are the correct way to define different workflows for different deployment environments. In most organizations, there are stages for (at least) a development environment, a testing environment, and a production environment.

To edit the stage's workflow in our example, click the hyperlink for the stage that states how many tasks are included in the stage. The workflow editor screen will appear. Add an IoT Edge task to the release stage workflow just like you did in the build process, but this time select the *Deploy to IoT Edge devices* action. Once you select this option, additional fields will appear that allow you to target either a group of devices or a single device in the selected IoT Hub. If you target a single device, you must enter the device ID. If you target multiple devices, you must supply a name/value pair that represents a value in the device twin. Any device that matches the criteria you enter will be updated during the release process. Figures 9-24 and 9-25 show examples of the completed dialog, for a single device and multiple devices, respectively.

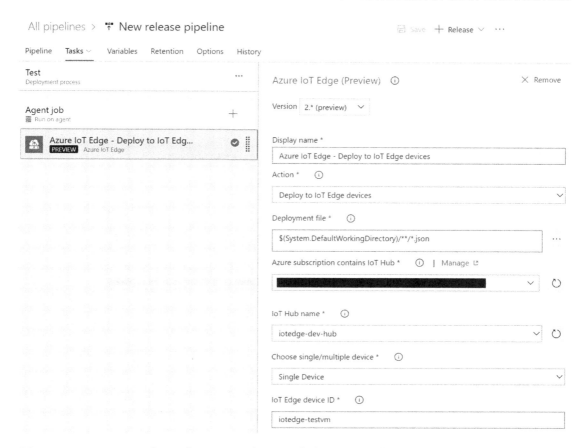

Figure 9-24. *IoT Edge release pipeline task for single device*

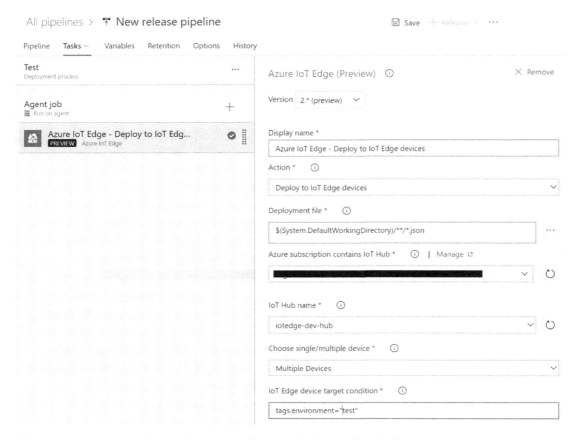

Figure 9-25. *IoT Edge release pipeline task for multiple devices*

Once we have entered this information and saved the release pipeline, make a small change to the code in the repository. The build pipeline should begin and once it completes our release pipeline should begin. This will validate our entire end-to-end process.

When we go back and look at the completed release pipeline summary, we can see the overall summary, as well as the detailed execution steps. Figure 9-26 shows the overall release status after our pipeline was triggered and completed.

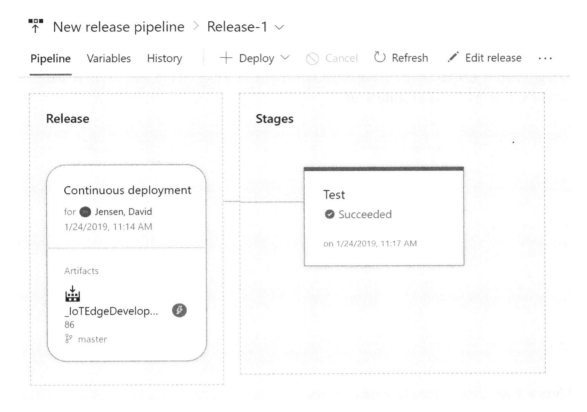

Figure 9-26. *Release pipeline summary screen*

When we click the completed stage card, we are able to see the detailed steps for that stage. Figure 9-27 shows the detailed steps for our *Test* stage.

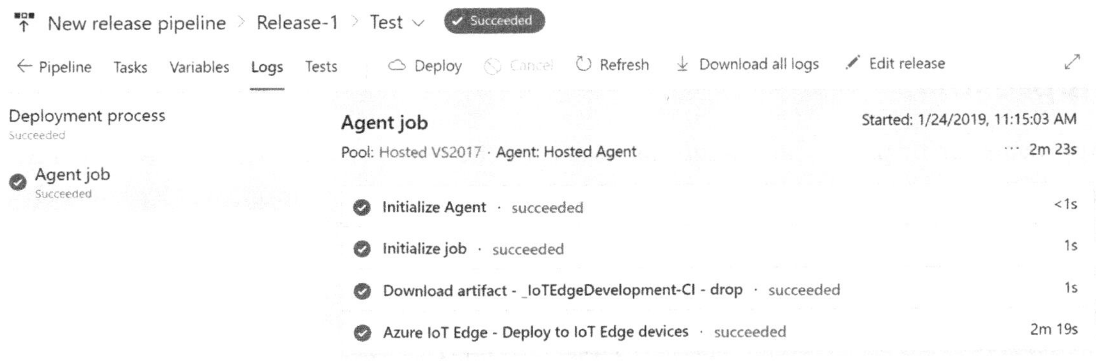

Figure 9-27. *Release pipeline stage detailed step output*

Another modification that should be made to our release pipeline is the addition of a production stage with an approval request before the stage executes. To add the production stage, you can hover over the Test stage and click the *clone* option. Cloning a stage creates an exact copy of the stage. Once you have cloned the stage, your release pipeline should look like Figure 9-28.

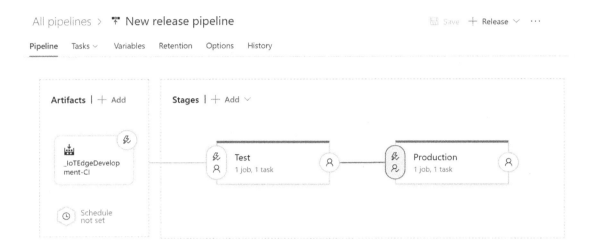

Figure 9-28. *Multistage release pipeline*

When you have multiple stages in your release pipeline, the stability of each environment is dependent on the quality of the code being deployed. So, if a release fails in one stage/environment, we don't want to propagate that to a second stage. To automatically control this, there are pre- and post-stage checks that can be performed. The two most common checks that are used are approvals and gates.

Approvals

Approvals can be pre- or post-stage approvals and the approval request can be sent to any number of approvers, but all approvers added to the request must approve it. If groups are added to the request, only one member of the group is needed to satisfy the group requirement. The release pipeline will wait until all the approvers have approved the change before moving on the next step. If the approvals are not received by the specified approval timeout, the release is canceled. Figure 9-29 shows the pending approval in the active pipeline and Figure 9-30 shows the approval pane in the detailed pipeline view.

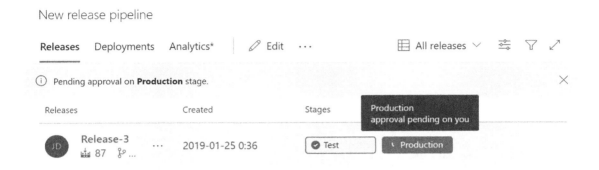

Figure 9-29. *Pending approval in active release pipeline*

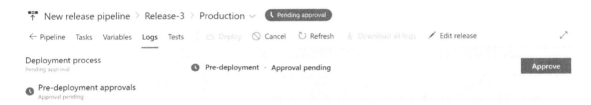

Figure 9-30. *Approval pane in active release pipeline*

Gates

Gates can also be either pre- or post-stage gates. Gates are an automated way of checking external sources for validation before proceeding to the next step in the pipeline. Gates can be custom logic in Azure Functions, a REST API call or work item query. Figure 9-31 shows the options available for a gate external validation check.

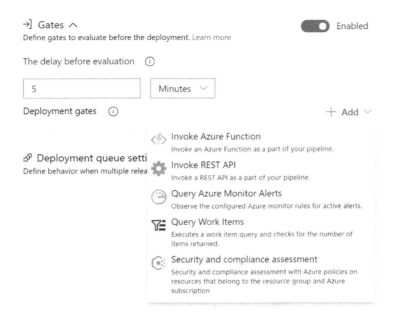

Figure 9-31. *Options for gate external integration points*

After the IoT Edge release pipeline tasks complete, you can see the new IoT Edge deployment in the IoT Hub portal. Figure 9-32 shows an example IoT deployment. Refer to our discussion on IoT deployments in an earlier chapter if you need a refresher on what IoT deployments are.

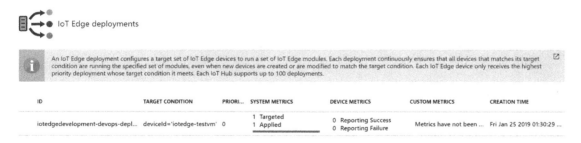

Figure 9-32. *IoT Edge deployment in the IoT Hub portal*

Summary

In this chapter, we have looked at some of the basic concepts and components that make up the Azure DevOps services. Next, we talked about the most relevant decisions points when planning the organizational structure in DevOps. Then, we walked through configuring and creating the basic DevOps services to enable a solid initial environment. Once all of that was complete, we moved on to creating a build pipeline that compiles a solution manifest, pushes the containers that are built to a container registry, and finally publishes the generated deployment manifest so that it can be pushed to a device in IoT Hub. We also discussed and built an automated release pipeline that is triggered by the build pipeline completed. The release pipeline pushes the deployment manifest to the IoT Hub and targets either a single device or a group of devices, based on the criteria in the Device Twin properties. All of these automation steps working together provide an end-to-end fully automated IoT Edge solution that can be customized and added onto as the company evolves going forward.

Index

A, B

Azure cognitive services
    cognitive services containers (*see* Cognitive services containers)
    knowledge API, 171
    landing page, 169
    language API, 170
    search API, 171–172
    speech API, 170
    vision API, 169–170

Azure container registry (ACR), 49

Azure DevOps
    configuration
        artifacts, 238
        dashboard, create, 235–236
        extension management, 238
        organization settings, 232–233
        project settings, 234–235
        repository management, 236–237
    IoT edge pipeline, creation
        agent pool, 244
        build hub, 242
        Git repository, 243
        Git repository initialization, 239–241
        initial edge solution, 239
        output, 250
        parameter, 245–246
        publish task, 248–249
        push task, 247

IoT edge release pipeline, creation
    approvals, 256
    artifacts, 250–252
    deployment options, 252
    gates, 257–258
    multistage, 256
    multiple device, 254
    output, 255
    single device, 253
  organization structure, 229
  pipelines, 231
  project, 230
  repositories, 230–231
  sign in, 227–228
  team, 230
  Work Items, 230

Azure IoT Edge
    device management blade, 19–20
    edge deployments, 45–47
    edge module adding, 24
    management blade, 22–23
    module management blade, 21
    security manager service, 43–45

Azure IoT Edge SDK, installation
    container runtime, 73–74
    Microsoft keys, 72–73
    powershell command, 75–76
    security service configuration, 76–78, 82
    security service install, 74–75

© David Jensen 2019
D. Jensen, *Beginning Azure IoT Edge Computing*, https://doi.org/10.1007/978-1-4842-4536-1

Printed in the United States
By Bookmasters